KEEP TALKING

David Dimbleby was chairman of the BBC's *Question Time* for 25 years. He has anchored election programmes and many other political programmes, and has been both a reporter for and presenter of *Panorama*. He is the commentator for a variety of State and other events. He has made film series for BBC television about the USA, South Africa, India and Zimbabwe as well as about the art, architecture and history of Britain. He lives in Sussex.

DAVID DIMBLEBY
KEEP TALKING
A BROADCASTING LIFE

H

HODDER

First published in Great Britain in 2022 by Hodder & Stoughton
An Hachette UK company

This paperback edition published in 2023

1

A CIP catalogue record for this title is available from the British Library

Paperback ISBN 9781399702430
eBook ISBN 9781399702447

Typeset in Plantin Light by Hewer Text UK Ltd, Edinburgh
Printed and bound in Great Britain by Clays Ltd, Elcograf S.p.A.

Hodder & Stoughton policy is to use papers that are natural, renewable
and recyclable products and made from wood grown in sustainable
forests. The logging and manufacturing processes are expected to
conform to the environmental regulations of the country of origin.

Hodder & Stoughton Ltd
Carmelite House
50 Victoria Embankment
London EC4Y 0DZ

www.hodder.co.uk

for Belinda

Contents

Contents

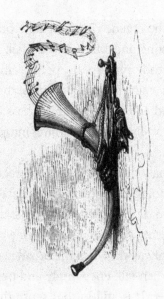

I

Not Fit to Run a Whelk Stall

I have been a broadcaster probably for longer than anyone on earth. I began when I was knee-high to a grasshopper, presenting my first radio programme at twelve years old. God knows what the audience made of it but I enjoyed it and I have enjoyed everything I have done since, whether holiday documentaries in my teens, or cutting my teeth on discussion programmes in my twenties, interviewing heads of state and powerful politicians, presenting election-night programmes, chairing *Question Time* for a quarter of a century, or guiding viewers through the arcane rituals of state occasions. Seventy years of broadcasting and I have loved it all. I am no intellectual. You do not study philosophy, politics and economics for three years at university, taught by some of the cleverest brains in the country, and end up with a third-class degree if you are an intellectual. I simply enjoy absorbing information and then communicating it.

Broadcasting has changed out of all recognition since I began. The technology is more sophisticated and the sheer quantity of radio and television available is on a scale unimaginable seventy years ago. But in one respect it has not changed: that it only works when the broadcaster can communicate effectively, can talk engagingly and persuasively to the listener and viewer. It is still in that sense the most intimate form of communication, almost a conversation. At any rate that is why I enjoy it and why, not surprisingly, I am grateful to the BBC for all the opportunities it has given me. Not just the obvious privileges but also the freedom to observe, close-up, how power works, how politics is conducted, how democracies thrive or wither. In return I have been a staunch defender of the BBC against all the attacks mounted by its enemies, whose number seems to grow year on year. It is not beyond reproach, it makes mistakes and struggles to provide something for everyone in a fracturing society. It has this curious and meaningless motto: 'Nation shall speak peace unto Nation'. 'Speak truth' would be better: an almost impossible aim, which nevertheless remains its intention.

A curious chain of events once led me to apply for the Director Generalship of the institution I have been involved in for all of this time. It was the mid-1980s – December

1986. Margaret Thatcher had appointed a new BBC Chairman, Duke Hussey, previously Chief Executive and Managing Director of *The Times* under Rupert Murdoch. Hussey's brother-in-law was William Waldegrave, the only politician I have ever counted as a friend. Because of this, Hussey invited me to dinner at his club in St James, Brooks's. I had been a member of it myself for a few years when I was living some distance from the centre of London in Putney. It had a useful toilet and a fine library where (those were the days) you could still smoke while you read. It was a bolthole in the middle of London and a classy club at that. My father had always been a bit in awe of aristocratic ways. He once came home from a stately home where he had been filming, disconcerted that a valet had unpacked his suitcase and put out clothes for him to wear. After three years at Christ Church Oxford (the first in the family to go to university), and membership of the Bullingdon Club to boot, I had no such qualms. In truth I rather enjoyed the sense of privilege that membership bestowed; the sense of acceptance into the world of a gilded class, which for a time I embraced, although I always felt like an outsider. However, when I sat down to dinner with Hussey I had long abandoned these pretensions, and my membership of the club. I met him because he knew nothing about broadcasting or the BBC and Waldegrave had told him I would give him the inside story of what was wrong with it. I cannot now remember what my litany of complaints consisted of. Everyone who works for the BBC can moan for hours about what is wrong. Few bother to talk about what is right. We were well into our lamb chops when Hussey leant forward and said, 'I'd like you to keep this to yourself. We are going to sack Alasdair Milne.'

Milne had, by general agreement, not been a particularly successful Director General and his rows with Thatcher over the BBC's treatment of the IRA had aroused her ire. Hussey had been appointed as Chairman in effect to remove him and, Thatcher hoped, make the BBC more compliant, an ambition incidentally that she failed to achieve. I thought it was surprisingly indiscreet of Hussey to tell me of his plan, but assumed it was because he trusted me to keep his secret. What followed was more astonishing. He leant forward again and asked conspiratorially, 'Would you like to become Director General?' I was so astonished by the suggestion that I could not reply. I should have said, 'Don't be ridiculous. I don't have the experience. I could never do it.' Instead I remained silent, thinking: Can this be true? Briefly, a vision of taking charge of the institution I loved crossed my mind. I saw myself putting right everything I thought was wrong, restoring it to glory. I could not bring myself to reply. After a pause, Hussey said, 'I take it from your silence, that you would.'

The seed of ambition had been planted and grew. When three weeks later Milne was taken to one side by Hussey just before a governors' meeting to be told he was being sacked, or that he could – to protect his pension – resign, he bowed to the inevitable and resigned. Applications for the role were requested and I applied. For the next few days, as I worked on a book and films about the United States, made plans for the general election expected in early summer of that year, and did the commentary on Harold Macmillan's memorial service in Westminster Abbey, I was focusing on the job for which I was now disconcertingly being tipped in the press as favourite. In truth, I had no clear idea how the BBC should be run, only an instinct that it had been going through difficult times and needed to restate its claim to impartiality and therefore regain the trust of the public who paid for it. I was summoned before the Board of Governors for my interview. Hussey chaired the meeting, and I explained my general approach without going into detail on the changes I would like to see. I probably had no very clear idea of these anyway. The Board listened politely. There were one or two sharp questions from the trade union governor (a role that Margaret Thatcher later abolished) and the philosopher Mary Warnock. Hussey thanked me and I left, without any sense of whether I had convinced the examiners that I was the man for the job.

The announcement was to be made two days later. I was told to stand by my phone and expect news by six o'clock. Six o'clock came and went. No news. I went to my son's school to watch him act in *Titus Andronicus*. I rang during the interval. Still no news. As the curtain fell on a stage strewn with dead bodies I tried again and finally Duke Hussey came on the line. 'I am sorry, but the Board have not chosen you but Michael Checkland.' I did not know Checkland. Few did. He was an accountant who ran the BBC's finances. Hussey went on to say that he had suggested I might become Checkland's deputy with responsibility for news and current affairs, but Checkland had rejected the offer. I do not remember being disappointed. I think in a way I was relieved. It would have meant the end of my career as a broadcaster. No more election programmes. No more trips to New York and

Washington. No more State Openings of Parliament. In retrospect it was a reckless ambition that would have led nowhere. Not that it was entirely extinguished. Subsequently, I twice applied for the chairmanship of the BBC. My views on how the BBC should be run received a warm reception, but with the caveat that I did not have sufficient experience of running a large organisation to warrant my becoming Chairman. Or to put it more crudely, I could not be trusted to run a whelk stall.

The two interviews I had for the chairmanship, two and a half years apart in 2001 and 2004, offered me the opportunity to think about and try to articulate my instincts about how the BBC could best adapt to survive. As part of the application process I was asked to set out my views on what I suppose would now be called my vision for the BBC. I said, 'The BBC belongs to the licence payer [and] therefore has a paramount duty to offer each of them something that justifies the levy. But it has another obligation springing from its privileged and protected position, which is to represent the common interests and loyalties of all the citizens of the UK and thus help bind society together ... Central to the strategy would be a shift away from the obsession with ratings as the dominant measure of success. The quality and originality of the programming and the reoccupation of the high ground in national life should play a more significant part.'

I suppose it was presumptuous to assume that I could navigate the BBC out of troubled waters. There were others far better placed to do this. But I felt, and have always felt, that I had an instinctive understanding of the BBC: of what it should do and how it could be made to work.

This is probably arrogant, but there must be a streak of arrogance in anyone who puts their face on the box and pontificates about the world around them, or for that matter decides to write a book about it.

This is not, however, an account of the BBC in its centenary year. It is instead an account of a broadcasting life, about the excitements and tribulations that life has afforded, the people I met, the lessons I learnt, and, yes, about the fun. It is the inside account of someone who loves the BBC, is steeped in it, is proud of it, is seen as part of it and yet, as a freelance whose applications to run the place were turned down three times, never considered himself fully inside it.

There is a book from the eighteenth century about a fictitious Baron Munchausen who tells tall tales. One story is of a journey by coach in freezing weather. It is so cold that as they travel over the mountains, the horn used by the postillion, to warn other coaches coming the other way, emits no sound. When at last the coach arrives at the inn, the postillion sits by the fire and puts his horn down beside him. The warmth thaws the frozen horn, and all the notes blown on the journey come flooding out. After seventy years in the business, here are some of my tunes.

2

Cradle to Grave

I was waiting for the taxi driver to write out a receipt when he looked up and said, 'My wife loves you on TV.' A flush of pleasure at being recognised. All that talking to the unblinking eye of the camera was not in vain after all.

'Yes, she loves you, especially when you are wearing those shorts.'

'Shorts?' I asked the driver. 'I never wear shorts.'

'You know. When you are talking to those gorillas.'

'Gorillas?'

'You are David Attenborough, aren't you?'

Heart sinks. Being mistaken for a different face from the box is salutary, a reminder that television is not the real world but a simulation of reality. Its apparent familiarity, a contrivance. But why Attenborough? It had happened once before when I was trying to buy a box of cigars.

'I am afraid we cannot give you any more until you have paid your outstanding account,' the assistant said, polite but firm.

'I haven't had a bill from you,' I protested.

'But Mr Attenborough, we have written to you several times.'

'I am not Mr Attenborough.'

I mentioned this to Attenborough much later. He, a non-smoker, was equally puzzled.

I like meeting people who have seen my programmes and want to talk about them or thank me for them – strangers who accost me on the street or in trains and want to know what I really think about the politicians I have interviewed, or to ask how I stay awake for all-night election programmes. They are always friendly. There must be others who do not like what I do or how I look or how I speak, but politeness holds them back from confrontation. Once, while I was walking in Soho, a man spat in my face as he walked past, but that is the only time I can remember a display of hostility and maybe it was nothing to do with *Question Time*.

Sometimes this public recognition can be embarrassingly inappropriate. On another occasion I was in the church of the Holy Sepulchre in Jerusalem, built over Christ's tomb. I was alone in a thoughtful, contemplative mood, in a quiet part of the church, when a voice disturbed me. 'Mr Dimbleby. What a surprise meeting you here. Would it be alright to ask for your autograph?' Not here, I thought. Surely not here. With a sense of shame at this incongruous merging of the sacred and the profane, I did what I was used to doing and signed.

My first brush with fame was on the pier at Hastings with my father, Richard. I was born in 1938, just before the Second World War, and for most of my early years my father was abroad, working as a war correspondent for the BBC in the Middle East, flying with Bomber Command over Germany and reporting from the D-Day landings and then across France as the allied forces advanced on Berlin. He had reported from the ruins of Hitler's bunker. Most memorably he had been with the British forces who had liberated the Belsen concentration camp in April 1945. From there he had broadcast the most vivid and horrifying descriptions of the scenes he saw, in a report that is still almost too distressing to listen to. All his reporting was on radio. There was no television during the war. What people knew of him was his voice – warm, authoritative, trustworthy. They had no idea what he looked like.

After the war, when he started working on television, all that changed. He became the best known broadcaster in the country and wherever he went he was recognised, fêted, the centre of attention. Around the same time, I was sent to boarding school near Hastings. I went there when I was eight years old and, as would most children of that age, suffered homesickness from being wrenched out of my family. The only brief respite we were allowed was a family visit one weekend a term, for the afternoon of Saturday and the morning and afternoon of Sunday. Lying in our dormitory beds, we would plan, for days before, every detail of what we would do when this 'half-term' came; and recount to each other what had happened on our return. Hastings was a frequent destination for these precious days, Eastbourne less so, though I remember a wet afternoon riding the lifts in the Grand Hotel at Eastbourne in a desultory mood, filling the time before the school curfew. Hastings had more to offer, not least Knickerbocker Glories. The Knickerbocker Glory was an unimaginable luxury in the 1940s when sweets were still rationed, its tall glass jar filled with layers of ice cream, jelly and fruit, then topped with whipped cream and a glacé cherry, all to be eaten with a long spoon specially designed to reach to the very bottom of the glass. I would drool over the thought of it for days before half-term and salivate on the memory for days after. Apart from the Knickerbocker Glories, my main other memory of these outings is of a scene in a Hastings car park. A group of women on their way back to their coach after a day trip to the sea surrounded my father, shouting 'Richard! Richard!' and waving their bras over their heads. Or so I thought. They were probably swimming costumes. I stood to one side embarrassed as my father, blushing slightly, signed autograph after autograph, until the last was done and we were free to go. It was the sense that they owned him that upset me: that because they had seen him on television they had rights over him, rights that were equal to mine. It was more than an intrusion. It seemed meretricious. If this was what being a famous broadcaster meant was it really a serious job at all or just an attempt to curry favour with the public? Chastened and ashamed, I talked to my headmaster, a man I liked and trusted, about the morality of working as a broadcaster against, for example, being a coal miner. Who was making the most valuable contribution to society? A juvenile exploration of ethics that seemed to have no impact on my own choice of career.

Mind you, I was doomed from birth. I was born in a flat in East Sheen in London. On the floor above lived John Logie Baird, the prolific Scottish inventor who had designed not only the first television transmission system, but also early versions of colour, 3D and even HD TV. One evening my mother had invited him down for cocoa and asked the famous man to kiss me goodnight. I can picture the fifty-year-old leaning over my cot and planting his kiss. The good fairy or maybe the bad?

I started television broadcasting at an absurdly young age. It was 1949 and I was eleven, though to skirt the regulations on theatrical performances I was described as being in my twelfth year. I remember nothing about the programme itself, except for the girl who appeared with me. She had long blonde hair and had just played Alice in Wonderland on the London stage. This precocious start was followed by an invitation, which my parents accepted on my behalf, to act as disc jockey for a special Boxing Day edition of a radio record request show called *Family Favourites*. It was broadcast live and there was no script, just a producer sitting next to me to help me choose the requests and read them out. Thrilling. Faced with a request for a Fats Waller song, 'My Very Good Friend the Milkman Said', I noticed that on the postcard, the sender had written in brackets, 'I am blind.' On impulse I blurted out, 'I am sorry you are blind, but I am afraid there is nothing we can do about it.' It is a remark that has haunted me ever since. I think I must have thought of the BBC as all-powerful, able to resolve any difficulty. It seemed to cause no offence though. I had more fan mail after my guest appearance on *Family Favourites* than for any broadcast since. I counted them. Over seventy cards, including one asking for a photograph of me 'in my shorts'. All, bar that one, were dutifully answered.

As I blundered through my adolescence and early adulthood my name and family connections gave me more chances to discover what working in television was like. In 1960, with legal constraints on the amount of currency that could be taken abroad recently eased, the British were starting to venture on foreign holidays. Our whole family made a short series of holiday films: guides to where to go, what to do there, and what it would cost. Together, my father, my mother, my three younger siblings and I made *Passport to Brittany*, *Passport to Norway*, *Passport to Portugal* and so on. My younger brother Jonathan and I made our own film, *No Passport*, in the Lake District. We toured the sites in my first car, an apple green Austin 7 tourer, built in 1929. I wish I still had it. It was the simplest of cars, no computer-controlled devices, no radio, no heater, and it could be started by hand. Its best torque was in reverse. So faced with the steep inclines in the Lakes we had to turn the car around and go up backwards. Perilous and probably illegal. One of the sites we visited was Kendal and a factory that produced not the famous mint cake but another Kendal speciality: snuff. We were filming a huge tub of this dark brown powder and, thinking it would make an amusing scene, I urged my twelve-year-old brother to put his head in the tub and sniff hard. He snorted the snuff, turned bright red, and succumbed to a paroxysm of sneezing, so acute that I thought for a moment he might collapse. To this day I think he believes it was a malicious (but wholly ineffective) attempt to prevent him from pursuing his own successful broadcasting career.

Nearly half a century later I came back to the Lakes, this time making a series about the effect that landscape painting had had on perceptions of the British countryside. *A Picture of Britain* was one of four television series – about painting, architecture, history and Britain's relationship with the sea – that I filmed during breaks from *Question Time*, all of them a welcome breath of fresh air from the overheated atmosphere of political debate. They were fun, like those earlier films. I was hoisted in a harness to the top of a church arch to examine a fresco of the Day of Judgement, vertigo just under control; caught frostbite doing a piece to camera in a blizzard on the slopes of Helvellyn; crash landed from a hot air balloon, ending up on my back in a cornfield with the cameraman and his camera on top of me; and rode a horse while pontificating to camera about Queen Elizabeth 1 and her royal tours. The saddle slipped and I was unceremoniously dumped in a ditch.

During one of the summer holidays from university I worked as a reporter at Anglia Television, the commercial station based in Norwich. The newly appointed Programme Director there was a friend of our family and had worked closely with my father at the BBC. Nepotism again. But nepotism only got me so far. When I was about to leave university I was offered an audition to be a presenter and interviewer in the current affairs department of the BBC.

Along with three other candidates I had to introduce a report on the refugee camps in Europe: displaced people still without a home in 1960, fifteen years after the end of the war. I watched the recording of the audition recently. It comes from another era. I speak with a clipped Oxford accent, am wearing an old-fashioned double-breasted suit and have a bouffant hairstyle. A passable performance but I don't think I would have given myself the job, and neither did they. That might have been the end of my life in television, which would have pleased my father. He hoped that the university education he had never had would lead me into what he thought of as a more serious profession: the law, or the diplomatic service.

It was not my father but someone else's father who led me down the slippery slope of a broadcasting career. I had fallen in love. In what might now seem an old-fashioned gesture I had asked my girlfriend's father for what used to be called 'her hand'. He, taking the first of many steps, ultimately successful, to prevent the marriage, insisted I must pay off my university debts before he would consent. I was £600 in the red (about £14,000 in today's money). The BBC paid £3 for a radio interview, £5 if it was broadcast on both medium wave and FM, and a further sum if the interview was used on television. I calculated that if I was lucky I could pay off the £600 in six months. So instead of heading for the Inner Temple or Whitehall I asked for another audition, this time at the BBC in Bristol, and was offered work as a freelance reporter.

Despite all the advantages of my background I did not take easily to broadcasting. My first major assignment from the newsroom was to report on a fire that had destroyed a primary school in Somerset. It was not clear how it had happened. It may have been the work of the local arsonist, though these were early days in what turned out to be a long career. A fireman by profession, he gave himself away because he was always first on the scene of a suspicious fire, an enthusiasm to admire his own work that led to his downfall. Armed with my tape recorder, which I had just learnt to operate, for the radio interview, and followed by a film crew for the television report, I headed for the charred ruins of the school and its distraught headmaster. But what to ask him? I knew even at this early stage of my career that 'How do you feel?' was not an acceptable question – too clichéd – although the answer to 'How do you feel?' is exactly what the audience would want to know. Instead I said, 'This must come as a great shock.'

'Yes.'

'I expect you will be needing the parents' support for rebuilding the school.'

'Yes.'

So it went on, each question eliciting only the answer 'Yes' – or, occasionally, 'No.' I had a suspicion this might not be quite the emotional interview the newsroom was expecting. The news editor listened to it, then said to me, 'You have to try to get people to say something, best of all something interesting, not just yes or no.'

I thought that might herald the end of a very brief broadcasting career, but BBC Bristol were forgiving and offered me more work. Within a year I had interviewed Noel Coward, Yehudi Menuhin, Elaine Stritch and Francis Chichester on the eve of another transatlantic voyage. Anyone famous passing through Bristol risked being hauled into our studio for an interview with me.

BBC Bristol also gave me a chance to read the local news. Newsreading is a harder job than it looks and not just because it demands the confident pronunciation of unfamiliar names. It also calls for a robot-like ability to keep going whatever happens – as I quickly discovered early in my brief newsreading career. I was announcing the death of the Mayor of Weston-super-Mare – a tongue twister in itself – when my chair started leaning to the left, slowly collapsing and leaving me clinging to the desk to remain in view of the camera. The position posed a dilemma: how to turn over to the next page of the script without letting go of the desk and disappearing from sight? I was saved by a quick-thinking colleague. The floor manager, armed with a pile of books, crawled towards me and gently slid them under the collapsing chair leg, allowing me to turn the page and reach the end of the bulletin, dignity intact.

I was only once tempted to go back down that alley. Towards the end of the 1970s, I was invited out to lunch by two senior BBC executives of the day, expensive lunches in those days being the preferred way of giving either good or bad news, promotion or the sack. On this occasion, along with the inevitable lamb chops, I was offered what my hosts thought would be an irresistible opportunity: to read the main evening news. 'You will be the face of BBC News,' they promised. 'Just like the American news anchors, giving authority to our bulletins.' I wondered what degree of control I would have over what was being broadcast. I did not want merely to simulate authority while in reality just reading scripts written by the sub-editors from the autocue. I told them this and asked for time to think it over. A few weeks later I was in New York and arranged to meet the main anchors of CBS, ABC and NBC to ask them about their influence over their respective networks' news bulletins. Each in turn explained how, to a greater or lesser degree, they were part of the editorial process. Back in London I asked whether the same influence over the shape of the bulletins and the stories to be given prominence would be on offer here. 'That is not the BBC's way of working,' I was told. 'The editor of the bulletin is in control, not you.' I turned the offer down. It was a relief. I think it would have been a cul-de-sac, and I would never have mastered the pronunciation of all those unfamiliar names.

In the 1960s the BBC was not yet stifled by the bureaucracy that hampers it today. Television was itself a relatively new medium and was searching for ways of attracting and holding the attention of the audience. In the days before computer-generated analysis of viewers' tastes and viewing figures, those commissioning programmes seemed to operate by instinct and hunch. Put forward a proposal today and it has to pass up through several layers of management before it can be agreed, each manager trying to guess whether the manager in the rank above will approve. I was a beneficiary of a more creative era and was able to present or chair an eclectic mix of programmes in my first few years working for the BBC. There was a science programme for children, *What's New?*, that had me illustrating scientific discoveries in a way that would not be allowed in our risk-averse culture today. I remember being persuaded to stand on a glass platform that was supposed to insulate me as thousands of volts of electricity were passed through my body. My trendy long hair stood on end, waving like ears of corn in a breeze as the electric current was turned on. What scientific point we were trying to make escapes me. Then there was the train driven by electric motors that accelerated at rocket speed. It was in the early stages of development at the old Gorton railway sheds in Manchester. To show how it worked I was strapped into a small trolley that hurtled down the railway track towards a brick wall at the end of the building. The health and safety instructions were, 'Do your seat belt up tightly and don't worry if it doesn't stop. It will hit a sandbank at the end of the track. Oh, and if it does hit the sandbank, release your seat belt and jump out quickly. Sometimes, we don't know why, it goes into reverse and hurtles back the way it came and there is no sandbank at that end.'

Another programme I was asked to chair was *Quest*, a thrusting title for a religious panel discussion with young people. I remember earnest discussions about whether sex before marriage was immoral, and whether homosexuality should be legalised (this was five years before the law was changed in the Sexual Offences Act 1967). Then there was *Top of the Form*, a radio programme that had been transferred to television as an experiment. It was a quiz show in which two school teams competed, each from their own school hall, and each with their own question master. For the question master it was an easy gig, as long as you could get the answers right yourself of course and pronounce names correctly. Early in the series I raised an eyebrow at my team from a girls' grammar school for not knowing where the annual festival celebrating Wagner's operas was held. 'It is of course Beirut,' I chided them. We had to do an embarrassing retake extricating Wagner from what was then still one of the most beautiful seaports in the Mediterranean as I tried again: 'It is of course Bayreuth.' Any thoughts I may have had of one day rising to the dizzy heights of chairing *Mastermind* or *University Challenge* died that evening.

There was one other programme in my portfolio. *Any Questions* had long been staple fare on Radio 4. It was organised and produced, as it still is, by the BBC in Bristol. In the summer of 1962 Bristol persuaded the BBC in London to try the programme on television, with me as Chairman. *It's My Opinion* was not a success. There was no chemistry between panel and audience. I sat with my back to the audience facing the panel who were seated on a stage above me looking like the board of directors at their AGM. We plodded through a few questions submitted on cards without any of the lively debate and angry exchanges that later came to define *Question Time*. It only lasted one season.

Looking back on these early years when I had so many invitations to take part in new programmes it would be easy to conclude that nepotism was at play again. I think that would be wrong. My father was certainly at the peak of his illustrious career, but he had no power within the BBC to promote his son. My mother confided in me years after his death that he had confessed to being slightly apprehensive about my choice, thinking two Dimblebys might prove one too many. My father only once gave me advice, when I was chairing *Quest*. He told me not to wriggle in my chair and move my feet about. I think producers were just curious to see whether I had inherited an ability to broadcast. Perhaps inherit is the wrong word. I do not think there is some configuration of the brain that makes children so often follow in their parents' footsteps. It is rather that seeing a parent confidently performing a tricky task – whether it is tightrope walking or mountain climbing or brain surgery or perhaps broadcasting – can make a child think, 'If they can do it why can't I?' I watched my father talking to millions of people while seeming to be speaking informally only to one, and perhaps in doing so I developed the belief that I could do it too. As I watched him I instinctively grasped how to use the camera, how to speak as though it was a person not the camera I was talking to, and how to avoid sounding stilted, or appearing nervous. These contrivances of broadcasting, the simulation of intimacy, came to feel natural to me, rather than contrived. I was not aping my father's style, contrary to what the Sunday newspaper *The People* thought. No sooner had I begun regular broadcasting than the paper went on the attack. Under the headline 'Oh Mr D. Can't you fix a job in the city for that carbon copy son of yours?' it reported that viewers in the West Country were horrified that I had chosen their channel to groom myself to take over from my father. I had, it said, a 'familiarly plump figure' and a 'sonorously pompous manner'. 'One Dimbleby is as much as Britain can take', was its conclusion. The following week, after what its author described as a cascade of letters about his article, he had to admit, somewhat chastened, that the pro-Dimbleby comments outnumbered the antis.

Fame, or rather being well known from appearing on the box, is seductive but can be unsettling. For many years, working on a variety of programmes, I lived in relative obscurity. It was when I moved to more popular strands, presenting general election programmes, doing a brief stint on *Nationwide* in the early 1980s and particularly chairing *Question Time*, that my face started to become more recognised. I was not famous in the way pop stars are famous. I was not mobbed in the streets. Crowds of autograph hunters did not lie in wait outside the studio doors. This was different. I would notice people recognising me, and smiling as they walked past, or stopping to ask for a selfie.

I suppose it would have been odd were it otherwise. The aim of my kind of television is to come into the viewer's home as a welcome guest: informal, friendly, putting the viewer at ease so that they feel comfortable with my presence. The viewers are inviting broadcasters into their private space and it is no surprise that they feel they know them. I see it as a natural consequence of my work and in a way a mark of success. Actors are sometimes heard complaining about public intrusion on their private lives, but they are actors, by definition portraying a different personality on stage or screen from the people they actually are. With a broadcaster it is different. We are trying to be who we are, not seeking fame but accepting it if it comes. I have never resented it, but it has a price. I lost my privacy in public places, and became self-conscious, feeling I was always being watched, always noticing that I had been noticed, or wondering whether I was about to be noticed. Even walking in the countryside I would feel a small tremor of tension as other walkers approached. Would they smile and say good morning and walk by? Would they turn around when they had passed to stare at me? Or would they stop, surprised, and say, 'What are you doing here?', then ask for a selfie. These meetings were benign but it meant I was always on parade, never able to relax. And it must be disconcerting for friends and particularly for the family never to know when a private moment will be disrupted by an unexpected intrusion.

And yet, now that I have stopped appearing regularly, the gradual decline in recognition and the adjustment to greater anonymity is also disconcerting. I used to relish the freedom of walking the streets of New York or Paris knowing no one would know me there. Maybe the same will one day be true of the streets of London, but my spirits still lift when someone stops me to tell me how much I am missed or, better still, 'I have watched *Question Time* since I was at school and it got me interested in politics, taught me all I know.' But it is will-o'-the-wisp. My wife was sitting next to a distinguished psychiatrist recently who asked her who she was married to.

'David Dimbleby,' she replied.

'What does he do?'

'He works on television.'

'Never heard of him. Oh, hold on. Is he that person who points at people?'

'Yes,' she said, 'I suppose he is.'

Fame. Will-o'-the-wisp.

THE DIMBLEBY CIRCUS

3

The Struggle for Independence

If I were a politician I would pick daily fights with the BBC. I would attack its bloated bureaucracy, complain that hardworking people had to pay for it, whether they used it or not, and accuse it of bias against whatever side I was on. Independent radio and television, and newspapers, I would either ignore, if they were not important, or schmooze if they were, because I would have no stick to wield, so would need to use carrots instead. But the BBC, whose role, funding and very existence is determined by the government of the day

– that is, by politicians – would be the perfect target. And so it is that from early morning until late at night, week in week out, the BBC's political reporters and editors are subject to a barrage of complaint about every question they ask and every opinion they offer. Complain to the *Daily Mail* or the *Guardian*, the *Mirror* or the *Sun*, and it makes no waves. Complain to the BBC and it is headline news. The press can be relied on to encourage and exaggerate any grumble about the BBC because it serves their purpose, aggrandising the printed word against the spoken, and undermining what they see as the unfair competition offered by the BBC, feather-bedded by its licence fee and apparently arrogant and unresponsive in its self-defence. Except that is not true. The BBC goes to extreme lengths to ensure its political coverage is fair, and to examine the most serious complaints against its journalistic conduct, even reaching for judges to examine the case and pronounce their verdict. Lord Dyson, a former Supreme Court judge, was brought in twenty-five years after Martin Bashir's interview with Princess Diana ('There were three in this marriage') to examine how the interview had been obtained. He condemned the BBC for failing to conduct a proper enquiry into the deceit. Impossible to imagine the *Daily Mail* examining its behaviour with such diligence or any of Rupert Murdoch's newspapers even now making a serious attempt to come clean about phone hacking. But the BBC is different. It has higher standards than the written press, and being funded and therefore owned by the public it has a duty to maintain those standards. It must be the only institution in Britain that inculcates in its members the cleansing power of self-flagellation.

I may be seen as a safe pair of hands, entrusted to narrate state occasions, and to anchor flagship programmes such as *Question Time* and election-night broadcasts, but I have managed to rub my fair share of people up the wrong way. Fifty years ago, in the early 1970s, I was embroiled in a row that was at the time the biggest bust-up with a political party the BBC had ever provoked. It was recently described by the *Daily Telegraph* as 'the most controversial moment in the BBC's history'. For the way it rocked the organisation internally and for its long-term impact on the BBC's relationships with politicians, it ranked alongside arguments with Margaret Thatcher's government in the 1980s over coverage of the Falklands and the IRA, or with Tony Blair's government in the 2000s about 'sexing up' the intelligence on Saddam Hussein's weapons of mass destruction. Compared with the tensions between the 'mainstream media' and Jeremy Corbyn when he was Leader of the Opposition, or the charges levelled at former Prime Minister David Cameron about how he tried to make money for himself after leaving office, its intensity seems slightly comic, yet it scarred the relationship between the BBC and the Labour Party.

Everyone was surprised when Labour was defeated in June 1970, after six years in government. Harold Wilson and his cohort of formidable ministers were suddenly removed from office and replaced by Edward Heath and a similarly formidable cohort – politicians in those days being a cut above what we have to put up with now. I had spent election night in Harold Wilson's constituency, Huyton, just outside Liverpool, interviewing him there late in the evening, driving back to London with his convoy overnight, and interviewing him again in the morning at Downing Street, when he in effect conceded defeat. When I came out of No. 10 the removal vans were already at work loading the private effects of Roy Jenkins from No. 11 under the curious gaze of the crowd. I was struck then by the overwhelming effect of defeat on those who had so confidently been expecting victory.

Some days later, I lay in the bath thinking about Labour's fate and how this unexpected humiliation would affect the big beasts of Wilson's government: Denis Healey, who had been Wilson's Secretary of State for Defence; Roy Jenkins, Home Secretary and then Chancellor; Anthony Crosland, who had held five different positions in those six years, including three in the Cabinet; Barbara Castle, who had been Secretary of State for Employment and Productivity, and First Secretary of State; and others. Today there would be no interest in the impact of defeat on any government, so unimpressive have our political leaders become, but on both sides of the House of Commons in the 1970s there were still distinguished figures, politicians of intellect and experience. It struck me that talking to them about their defeat would be revealing. My intention was to give a sympathetic portrayal of lost status, of wounds being licked, of people who had felt themselves invincible, now vanquished. On one side of paper I wrote a proposal headed *Yesterday's Men*, which I sent to my boss at the BBC, John Grist, Head of Current Affairs. He agreed with what I was suggesting and we got to work.

It began so innocently. Angela Pope, my director-producer, had a lively sense of mischief but not an atom of malice in her approach to the film. She and I wanted to reveal the human side of the people who until recently had wielded power over us. The proposal promised interviews and background material shot with the senior members of the last government, 'as well as their wives, friends, secretaries etc. where these can be revealing'. It said we would explore what it was like to lose high office suddenly and unexpectedly. How had 'these men' (I seemed to have temporarily forgotten about the two women, Barbara Castle and Shirley Williams, who had been in the Cabinet) coped with the sudden change in their lifestyles and the demands made on them? How were they responding to the absence of hard work and heavy responsibility, to which they must have become used? Was the material loss a hardship? (Christopher Mayhew, who had been a junior Defence Minister until 1966, had said that the worst thing about resigning from the government was losing his chauffeur-driven car.) How were they making up their income?

On the political level, the film would consider the job of being in opposition. How hampered were they by lack of information? How did they think Labour could be effective in opposing the new Conservative government led by Ted Heath? Did the electorate take any notice of the opposition? The appeal of *Yesterday's Men*, the proposal concluded, would lie in seeing how people whose faces had become so well known were reacting to their enforced retreat from the limelight.

We made a slow start. At first the politicians seemed reluctant to take part. I told John Grist that maybe we should abandon the idea. He told us to keep going because – and this is ironic in view of what happened later – he was concerned that the BBC would be seen as anti-Labour if we gave up. His view was that the relationship between the BBC and politicians was so delicate that if you made a proposal and then dropped it, it would be seen as a hostile act. So we went the rounds once more and this time they were more amenable. One after the other they gave us long interviews about the impact of defeat, both political and personal. Roy Jenkins allowed us to film him playing tennis, a perfect image for political battle. He was an engaging, nervous man. When we came to interview him at eleven o'clock in the morning he took me to one side as the camera crew were setting up their gear and asked, mixing a Martini, 'Do you think it's too early for a drink?' Tony Crosland was endearingly frank, saying, 'Oh I think yes, great humiliation. It was very unexpected, certainly to me, and I don't believe anybody who says they expected it' and 'You suddenly realised you hadn't got an office to go to on Monday morning . . . You actually hadn't got any work to do on Monday morning.' James Callaghan, later himself Prime Minister from 1976 to 1979, tried to dodge an awkward question by turning away from me as he answered it, saying, 'I am talking to your producer so that you won't be able to use this.' So, of course, we did. An initial meeting with Harold Wilson himself, now Leader of the Opposition, in his room in the House of Commons, went smoothly enough. The notes I made straight afterwards recorded, caustically, that

Wilson with his sidekick Joe Haines [Haines had been Wilson's Press Secretary] *as ever deferring, flattering, bowing and scraping beside him, looked beaten still. That is to say he no longer exuded that exhilaration which power gave him. He sat*

in an armchair, with his pipe, the lizard eyes flicking back-
wards and forward, narrowing when we talked about leader-
ship challenges, 'frank' when we talked personal details.

However, he was happy to talk to me about the challenges, and
the compensations, of being in opposition. He was, he said,
finding opposition more exciting than being in government,
because they could speculate on what was going on in Cabinet,
what decisions were being taken, what rows and splits were
happening. He had not given much thought to long-term
policy planning and did not think four years was a long time to
wait for the next election. He thought the Labour Party had
come through the election very well and was now a party interested in power rather than one that felt opposition to be its
natural state. He complained about how few staff he had, and
how little research support. He didn't seem too worried about
plots against him, saying that the last time they had plotted in
May 1969 he had been really weak, but they had not been able
to produce anyone to take over, and he thought it was the same
now. When I suggested that Callaghan was being put forward,
he said, 'Roy Jenkins' friends won't like that.'

Wilson continued to be helpful. We filmed him on the golf
course and later in church in the Scillies. He sang, 'Oh God
Our Help in Ages Past' and read the lesson, 'To everything
there is a season and a time to every purpose under the
heaven . . . A time to get and a time to lose. A time to keep
and a time to cast away.' He must have known that we could
make mild mischief with this. When we came to interview
him with the cameras rolling, however, his benign acquiescence in our project faded. The interview was planned to

take place in his room in the House of Commons. He arrived late, and Angela and I speculated afterwards that maybe he had lingered too long at lunch. Whatever the cause, his behaviour, that afternoon, was entirely out of character. Wilson was a skilled interviewee. He knew how to deflect a question by studiously lighting his pipe and blowing out a cloud of smoke. For some reason on this particular afternoon there was no twinkle in the eye and no smokescreen. Wilson had been getting some criticism from people in his own party for disappearing from sight to write his memoirs. Jealous colleagues were complaining that he was being paid a huge sum for this, raking in the money instead of attacking the Tories. I decided it was a question that had to be put. This is the transcript, complete with ums and ers. None of it was broadcast in the end.

Me: *Many of your colleagues have, em, have said – told us that they're suffering, financially, from being in Opposition, but you're said to have earned something between £100,000 and £250,000 by writing this book. Has that been a consolation to you over this year?*

The word 'consolation' was a deliberate tease, to which I thought he would respond in kind.

Harold Wilson: *I wouldn't believe any of the stories you read in the press about that. My press handling over a long period of time has been one of rumour – if they got the facts, they twisted them – so we can dismiss that from the case right away. I got a fair – I think a fair – um, compensation for what I wrote, but I*

wouldn't er, accept any of those views. I get [cough] I get a
salary as Leader of the Opposition.

Sensing I was onto something I had another go, but still thinking this was a question he could easily swat aside.

Me: *You couldn't set our minds at rest on the vexed question of*
what the Sunday Times *did actually pay for the book?*
Harold Wilson: *No, I don't think it's a matter of interest to*
the BBC or to anybody else.
Me: *But by …*
Harold Wilson: *If you're interested in these things you'd better*
find out how people buy yachts. Do you ask that question? Did
you ask him how he was able to pay for a yacht?

It was obvious he was referring to the new Prime Minister, Ted Heath. His financial backers in the Conservative Party had introduced him to sailing and helped fund a yacht in an attempt to give a more rounded image to an otherwise rather serious and plodding politician. By equating gossip about his earnings from the book with what he clearly saw as Heath's impropriety in accepting money for a yacht, Wilson only made things worse.

Me: *I haven't interviewed …*
Harold Wilson: *Have you asked him that question?*
Me: *I haven't interviewed him.*
Harold Wilson: *Well, has the BBC ever asked that*
question?
Me: *I don't know.*

Harold Wilson: *Well, what's it got to do with you then?*
Me: *I imagine …*
Harold Wilson: *Well, why do you ask this question when … I mean … why, why if people can afford to buy £25,000 yachts, do the BBC not regard that as a matter for public interest? Why do you come snooping with these questions here?*

He could perfectly well have said, 'How silly, if you tell me how much you're being paid for this interview, I'll tell you what I get paid.' And I would have just laughed, and it would have gone away. But no, we had touched a raw nerve, and I knew we just had to stick in there. I kept trying to ask my question, and Wilson kept protesting.

Harold Wilson: *You're just repeating press gossip, you've not put this question to Mr. Heath. When you've got an answer from him, come and put that question to me.*

And then:

Harold Wilson: *Is this question being recorded?*
Me: *Well it is because we're running film.*
Harold Wilson: *Well, will you cut it out or not? – Right we'll stop now.*

At this point it struck me that this interview was not going very well. In fact I had never known a politician to behave like this.

Harold Wilson: *No, I'm sorry I'm <u>really</u> not having this, the press, the press may take this view – they wouldn't put this*

question to Heath – they put it to me; if the BBC put this ques-
tion to me, without putting it to Heath, the interview's off – and
the whole programme's off. I think it's a ridiculous question to
put. Yes, and I mean it: cut off. I don't want to read in, in The
Times *diary or Miscellany, that I asked for it to be cut out.*

The more he blustered the more determined I was that we
should carry on.

Me: *Are we still running? Can I ask you this then, which I*
mean I-I-I, let me put this question – I mean, if you find this
question offensive . . .
Harold Wilson: *Go on, ask if your curiosity can be satisfied*
– I think it's disgraceful. Never had such a question or inter-
viewer in my life before.
Me: *I . . .*
Joe Haines [Wilson's Press Secretary]: *Well, let's stop it*
now and talk about it, shall we?
Me: *No, well, let's keep going I think, don't you?*
Harold Wilson: *No, I think we'll have a new piece of film in*
and start all over again. But if this film is used or if this is
leaked, then there's going to be a hell of a row.

We were mystified by the fury of Wilson's response, bewildered by his demands that the filming stop and that what we
had shot should not be shown. Afterwards, in the corridor,
his Press Secretary Joe Haines cornered Angela and shouted
at her that she would never work in television again unless she
removed the whole section from the film. It was an extraordinary reaction to a question that the old Harold Wilson

would have brushed aside. With hindsight I think the reason for Wilson's anger may have been that we had touched on a legal but potentially embarrassing tax 'dodge'.

An immediate complaint was made to the BBC. Without talking either to Angela or to me the Chief Assistant to the Director General, John Crawley, assured Wilson and Haines that most of the section about his memoirs would be deleted. Angela and I were both outraged. I wrote to John to complain.

> *I gather that it was agreed by everyone who read the transcript that nothing in the questions could have given the least offence. Mr. Wilson, however, as the record shows, behaved in an offensive and bullying manner. He threatened me, he rang the Director-General while we were still filming to complain, and his Press Secretary in the best blackmailing manner told the producer that if the incident leaked, Mr. Wilson would stop the film going out, and 'You wouldn't like that, would you? That wouldn't be good for you, would it?'*

> *It is evident that Mr. Wilson grossly over-reacted. The truth, I believe, is that we touched on a particularly raw nerve, and he saw the best way of getting out of it was to make a scene.*

> *The least that I would have expected from you is that, knowing all this, your instinct would have been to protect the people working for you in this extremely delicate area. Instead, with no attempt at consultation, you agreed with Joe Haines what would and would not appear in the film. Game and set, it would seem, to Mr. Wilson.*

At the eleventh hour, the day before transmission, Wilson instructed his lawyer, Lord Goodman, to seek an injunction to stop the film from going out. The BBC's Chairman, Lord Hill, incidentally a Wilson appointee, decided that the BBC governors should watch the film and decide whether it should be shown, and if so whether further cuts should be made. It was the first time in the BBC's history that the governors had decided in advance of a programme's being shown whether and in what form to permit it. A terrible mistake. The job of governors of the BBC was to stand apart from editorial decisions, not to choose to make them themselves. Once they had watched *Yesterday's Men* and allowed it to be broadcast, they were in no position to arbitrate on subsequent complaints.

The governors insisted on removing the reference to Wilson's earnings. Angela and I were outraged and responded with the totally futile gesture of having our names taken off the credits.

The governors' cut of the film went out almost a year to the day after the 1970 election. In the days that followed the broadcast, Harold Wilson, Richard Crossman and James Callaghan were among those who joined in a howl of complaint against the BBC. I suspected that some of these complaints were trumped up, probably out of loyalty to Wilson. Crossman wrote a vitriolic attack in the *New Statesman*, where he was editor, accusing us first of persuading politicians to take part by deliberate fraud and then of editing their interviews to give a false impression – an even greater fraud. The word fraud raised my hackles and I was tempted to sue him for defamation. A few days later I was told by a reliable political correspondent that Crossman had watched the film with a group of Labour MPs and had 'enormously enjoyed it'. Roy Jenkins for his part not only failed to make a complaint but went out of his way to take me aside at a public event a few days later and say he had no objection to the film. That's politics for you.

The BBC subsequently held an enquiry into how the programme had been made. A senior executive was despatched to examine all the film we had shot, to list all the questions I had asked each interviewee, and to time how long their answers had been, and how much of the replies was included in the film. His report exonerated us of the charge of unfair interviewing. We were reprimanded only for the music and the title. Both were, admittedly, mischievous and for obvious though arguably improper reasons had not been disclosed in advance to our interviewees. The title *Yesterday's Men* was itself the slogan that the Labour Party had used on its poster campaign against the Tories during the 1970 election that it had just lost; and the music, commissioned from The Scaffold, the satirical Liverpool pop group behind the 1968 hit *Lily the Pink*, included lyrics like 'They're yesterday's men and it's no fun at all/Getting sacked and put out to graze'. Mischievous, but hardly a hanging offence.

The BBC promised Wilson that the film would not be shown again in his lifetime, an offer that I never understood. It wasn't until 2013 that it was finally repeated, as part of 'Harold Wilson Night', an evening of programmes marking fifty years since his election as Labour leader. Against that, the BBC's report ended with the Board of Governors firmly restating the rules of political coverage.

The basic principle is impartiality … Deference is not required but courtesy is … Politics is a minefield. There is inevitably a

divergence between the aims of politicians and the aims of jour-
nalists ... The politician may want to expose his view of the
truth, whereas the journalist wants to expose all the truth as he
knows it ... each needs the other, and ground rules have been
developed on which trust and understanding rest ... This inci-
dent has impaired that relationship and the BBC greatly
regrets that this should be so ... We shall however do nothing
that could put at risk the independence of the BBC. Broadcast
journalism has special obligations, but it cannot surrender to
any individual or party or government its right of independent
editorial judgement.

When the governors' report was published my first reaction
was not to be relieved, but to cavil at their rebuke about the
music and the title. While we had not told interviewees that
the film would be called *Yesterday's Men*, we had not tried to
bamboozle them with some other title such as *Her Majesty's
Opposition*. If you give an interview to a newspaper, you have
no control over the headline they choose, mischievous or not.
Inappropriate, the Governors said, for the BBC. The following day I complained to John Grist about these details. He
simply said, 'Don't worry about that. Look at the newspapers.' He was right: it was the overall exoneration of the film
that made the headlines. I still have a framed copy of the
front-page splash in the *Daily Express* hanging in my office:
'CARRY ON DIMBLEBY'.

Yesterday's Men was a *cause célèbre*. Some of my colleagues
thought it had damaged relationships between broadcasters
and politicians. I thought that was far-fetched. Normal political interviewing soon carried on regardless and I like to think

the long-term effect of the film was to make reporters less squeamish about trying to show the human side of politics – not just asking the obvious questions but taking the trouble to explore the character and background of those seeking power. Although I was never allowed to interview Wilson again – his closest political confidante Marcia Williams complained that up until then they had always thought of me as a 'friend' – the controversy did me no long-term harm. If anything it boosted my career, raising my profile as someone willing to challenge the conventional way of reporting politics.

If the governors' enquiry had found against me it could have been curtains. The BBC can be ruthless in its despatch of reporters who fall foul of its edicts. In the wake of the affair I wrote an article about the governors and why I thought they were inadequate protectors of the BBC's reputation. Before publication I showed it to the BBC, as my contract required. The Director of Programmes at the time, taking a break from filming gorillas, was David Attenborough, whose ability to enforce difficult decisions with great charm had landed him with the nickname 'the baby-faced killer'. He summoned me to see him and told me that unless I removed one particular passage from my critique I would never again be able to work in politics at the BBC, although he said a place might be found for me in children's television – a threat for which to his credit he has since frequently apologised. I cannot remember whether I obeyed. I think I must have done because I never appeared on *Blue Peter*.

There were other dangerous skirmishes with the BBC that nearly did for me.

My worst public dressing-down was for remarks I made on

the occasion of President Nixon's 1969 visit to Britain. I had decided to poke a little fun at the pomp surrounding the event, thinking in a jaundiced way that it was overdone, and had offered a commentary that was a little less bland than the usual. The event itself played into my hands. Nixon arrived outside 10 Downing Street in his armour-plated limousine with the flags of Britain and the United States flying from the wings of the car. I noticed that the Union Flag had been hoisted upside down with the narrow rather than the broad white stripe at the top. I knew because of my years in the Sea Cadets that the Union Jack hoisted upside down was a naval signal of distress. So with Harold Wilson's Britain in the throes of a perennial financial crisis I thought it apposite – instead of simply intoning 'here comes the presidential car, and out steps the President' – to point this out. Next, Prime Minister Wilson and President Nixon went inside No. 10 and paused on a Turkish carpet, whose inscription I had researched. Woven into it were the words 'I have no refuge in the world other than thy threshold, my head has no protection other than this porchway'. Given Britain was as ever in need of American support, I also mentioned this, adding, 'which might perhaps be a more appropriate message for Mr Wilson when he's at the White House than for Mr Nixon when he's at Number 10'.

But my real offence was to say, as the two leaders disappeared into the Cabinet Room for discussions, that we would be kept in ignorance of what transpired and would only be offered a version of it by 'expensively hired press secretaries whose job is to disguise the truth'. All hell broke loose. The Director General of the BBC, Hugh Carleton Greene, authorised an apology for my 'unfortunate and inappropriate' remarks, which ran on every news bulletin the following day. My immediate boss rebuked me: 'Quite frankly, it did not hit the right note for this occasion. Whatever you felt about it, it was still the arrival of the President of the United States and "bizarre" is not the word I would choose for this event.' Wilson's then Press Secretary, Trevor Lloyd-Hughes, threatened to sue over my description of his job.

I thought I had spoken nothing but truth, a truth that my experience of Press Secretaries in the years that followed amply demonstrated. What is more, I knew what I was talking about. The first Press Secretary ever appointed to Downing Street was under Prime Minister Lloyd George. The announcement of this new role was criticised in the papers, which questioned whether there was a need for the Prime Minister to have a spokesman standing between him and the press, acting as an interpreter of policy. Far better to hear from the Prime Minister directly. That first Press Secretary as it happened was my grandfather, Frederick Dimbleby.

I was roundly rebuked for what I had said. I later discovered that the BBC's internal view, recorded in its weekly programme meeting, was that 'he was trying to get his father out of his system' and 'it was reasonable to change the style of commentary' but I had gone too far. The Director General, at a meeting of the BBC's Advisory Council, said that the incident had not affected the BBC's view of me as a reporter but that I 'should not be used for the time being in the role of commentator on State occasions'.

I thought that after the furore I would be removed from commentating on the day of Nixon's departure. Instead I was simply told by my producer to 'be careful what you send up'. I am afraid that I ignored him. I thought it would be feeble to back down after all the complaints and instead went for broke, delivering a tongue-in-cheek description of Nixon's departure as, in the words of a famous song by Eartha Kitt, 'the day that the circus left town'. My poor producer. At the time he let it go – what else could he do?

One other skirmish that could have put paid to my career was not with the BBC but with the National Union of Journalists, who succeeded in keeping me off air for a year. It was the 1980s: trade unions were still a powerful force in the country, and the NUJ was a powerful force within the BBC. Since my father's death in 1965 I had, alongside my work for the BBC, been running our small local newspaper group in Richmond. By 1980 I was the sole owner of the *Richmond and Twickenham Times*, the *Brentford and Chiswick Times* and the *Thames Valley Times*. It was an old-fashioned business, its employees divided into four separate trade unions, each with their own rules and working practices, and each able to bring production to a halt if they withdrew their labour. As well as newspapers we printed magazines and brochures and so on, but in the early 1980s a slump in the print industry meant our commercial printing shop had no work. The business was draining cash and I had to take action or risk going into debt. I suggested to the print union, the National Graphical Association, that in return for negotiating substantial redundancy payments two of our printing staff should leave the company. There was no work for them, and no prospect of any. They were sitting in the carpark playing cards all day. The NGA, who represented printers for the entire newspaper industry in London, from Fleet Street giants like *The Times* and the *Daily Telegraph* to our cottage industry in Richmond, refused the offer. After several weeks of fruitless negotiation we made the two redundant, offering them the statutory payment. The NGA's response was to call all our printers out on strike. In those days no votes were taken on strike action. The printers were simply ordered out and threatened with losing their union card if they disobeyed.

For several weeks none of our papers was printed. On the verge of bankruptcy I discovered a non-unionised printer in Nottingham who would do the work for us. We were back on the streets. At this point the NUJ joined the fray. They had discovered an age-old dispute with a newspaper related to our new Nottingham printer and decided to rekindle it and call all our journalists out on strike. Next, the NUJ at the BBC decided to join in, by walking out of any studio I walked into. I was a pariah. All of the NUJ actions were illegal. Secondary picketing – where unions target organisations that are not directly involved in the primary dispute, but which can be used to ramp up pressure – had just been made unlawful by the Thatcher government, and this was secondary picketing of the most egregious kind. I took the NUJ to the High Court and won my case. The NUJ appealed and the Appeal Court found in my favour. The NUJ then took their case to the House of Lords, the precursor to today's Supreme Court. The House of Lords found in my favour.

It could have become one of those never-ending disputes that dogged industrial relations in those days, but for the fact that it was not just me going broke but the printers' union too, leaching money in strike pay to their members in Richmond, who were still out on strike. About eighteen months after this had all started, the leader of the London branch of the print union asked for a meeting. We met in a room in one of those anonymous hotels near Heathrow Airport. He proposed a settlement. He accepted that we could no longer afford to reopen our print works and said he would call the strike off if I paid everyone affected an agreed sum for redundancy based on the years they had worked for us. I said I agreed in principle but had no cash left in the bank because of the strike. To my astonishment, he made me an offer: 'How about we lend you the money. And you can pay us back as your business picks up.' Which is what we did. Finally the NUJ officials at the BBC, whose illegal action against me had been tolerated by BBC management, decided to end their boycott and I went back to work.

The *Yesterday's Men* affair made headlines, but while it involved a ferocious attack on the BBC, that attack was different in kind from those that came later from the Thatcher and Blair governments, to say nothing of Johnson's. The Labour Party was not in office at the time and had no way of influencing the next licensing round by which the BBC's revenue is fixed for the year, or years, ahead. Nor, in truth, was it an attack mounted by the Labour Party as a whole, but rather by an aggrieved Harold Wilson. And his complaint was no more than that I had asked him an embarrassing question about his earnings from his memoirs.

I was a close witness to, and sometimes participant in, some of the battles between the BBC and the government in the years that followed. Every political leader would like to get the BBC on their side, though it's easier said than done. Three particular battles stand out for me. Two were with Thatcher's Conservative government, when it accused the BBC of a lack of patriotism, even amounting to treason, over its reporting on the IRA during the conflict in Northern Ireland, and its coverage of the Falklands War. The fight with Blair's Labour government on the other hand was over the BBC appearing to accuse the government itself of treachery by lying to the public and parliament about the reasons for the war in Iraq.

The main plot points are well known. On 11 September 2001, terrorists had flown planes into their targets in New York and Washington killing nearly three thousand people. From that moment on Tony Blair as Prime Minister had sworn to support the US President, George W. Bush, in whatever action he decided to take in retaliation. The first target was Afghanistan, which had harboured the terrorists thought to be responsible. Next the US focused on Iraq, whose President, Saddam Hussein, had long been thought of as a danger to peace in the Middle East.

This last row had until recently always seemed to be a most unfair attack on the BBC, and a moment when the BBC first spoke the truth, then ultimately failed to hold its nerve. My view has changed. I have come to realise that one journalist made one error, one slip of the tongue. Then he stood by his error and the BBC wrongly stood by him.

In Britain, opposition to war with Iraq was proving intractable. Blair's own Labour MPs were wavering. Blair and his Director of Communications and Strategy, Alastair Campbell, decided to take the unprecedented step of releasing secret intelligence on Saddam Hussein, which they hoped would convince opponents of the rightness of their cause. But intelligence is, as

I subsequently discovered from talking to American intelligence officers, often patchy, tentative and unprovable. Some sources of information on Iraq at this time were later revealed to be fraudsters, inventing stories for the compensation they would receive from the CIA. Others were Iraqi politicians on the make, feeding stories about Hussein's regime, which they hoped might lead the US to unseat him and put them in his place.

On 3 September 2002 Blair instructed the Joint Intelligence Committee, the country's top intelligence assessment body, to put together all the information it had on the threat Saddam Hussein posed to Britain and the West, intending to use it to win over hearts and minds in Britain to the necessity of war alongside the United States. This is where the trouble began. The dossier the intelligence services produced was in 10 Downing Street's view too cautious in some of its judgements to be persuasive when it was published, as planned, with an introduction by the Prime Minister. Campbell asked John Scarlett, the Chairman of the Joint Intelligence Committee, to provide more detail and information. Over several drafts it appeared that some of the language was toughened up to make it clearer, more vivid, more persuasive or as Lord Hutton concedes 'sexing it up'. Hutton in his subsequent enquiry accepts that for it to be 'sexed up' in this way was legitimate.

A series of meetings took place, involving senior officials from the Cabinet Office, the Foreign Office, Number 10 and the intelligence services, chaired by Campbell, and the dossier was published three weeks later on 24 September 2002. In its revised form it included the claim that some weapons of mass destruction would be ready for use within forty-five minutes of an order from Saddam Hussein. This information, from just one intelligence source, had come in late but had been seized on as evidence for the urgent need to remove Saddam. The eye-catching forty-five-minute claim, which it later emerged applied to battlefield weapons not long-range missiles, led to lurid headlines such as the *London Standard*'s '45 Minutes From Attack', the *Sun*'s 'Brits 45 mins from doom' and the *Daily Star*'s 'Mad Saddam ready to attack: 45 minutes from a chemical war'. The *Sun* suggested that British forces in Cyprus would be a target Saddam could reach.

Not everyone in the intelligence service had been happy with the revised dossier. Some felt their cautious analysis had been hyped for political purposes. Andrew Gilligan, the defence and diplomatic correspondent for BBC Radio 4's *Today* programme, had regular contact with a source in the intelligence community, and heard about this unease. In May 2003 he prepared a news report based on the information from his source, checked it with his editor, and broadcast it. But at 6.07 a.m., on 29 May 2003, Andrew Gilligan departed from his pre-agreed script, telling John Humphrys on the BBC's *Today* programme, 'What we've been told by one of the senior officials in charge of drawing up that dossier was that, actually, the government probably knew that that 45-minute figure was wrong, even before it decided to put it in.' He went on to say, 'Downing Street, our source says, a week before publication, ordered it to be "sexed up", to be made more exciting, and ordered more facts to be, to be discovered.'

By the time of the *Today* report, the invasion of Iraq was over. No weapons of mass destruction had yet been found and the arguments that had been used for going to war were coming under intense scrutiny. Gilligan's suggestion that

Blair had taken Britain into war on a lie was toxic. This was a moment of profound crisis. Alastair Campbell's response was a spate of increasingly furious attacks on the BBC for lying, ultimately focusing on the comment at 6.07 a.m. that the government had added the claim about forty-five minutes probably knowing it was wrong. Gilligan stood by his news report, saying that this was what his source had told him. What followed was tragic. David Kelly, a biological weapons expert who had worked as a weapons inspector for the UN, told the Ministry of Defence that he might be one source of the story. The government decided to out him, I assume thinking that if they could pin the responsibility on him and then discredit him, the allegation that 10 Downing Street had added the now notorious 45-minute claim would be seen to be false. The MOD said they would not name the source, but that if the right name was suggested to them they would confirm it, and by this shameful ruse Kelly's name became public. Kelly was then forced to appear before two parliamentary committees where, under aggressive questioning, he denied having been the source of Gilligan's 6.07 a.m. allegation. Two days later his body was found by a wood near his home.

The government called in a judge, Lord Hutton, to discover the truth of the events around David Kelly's death. Only then did Gilligan admit that Kelly did not tell him that 10 Downing Street had put the 45-minute claim in the dossier 'knowing it to be untrue'. He admitted that he, Gilligan, should not therefore have used those words, 'knowing it to be untrue', in his 6.07 broadcast. When Lord Hutton published his report in January 2004 he exonerated the government of the charge of 'sexing up' the intelligence dossier and strongly criticised Andrew Gilligan, the corporation's management processes and standards of journalism, and the BBC.

Within a day, the BBC Chairman Gavyn Davies and the Director General Greg Dyke had both resigned. Andrew Gilligan resigned too. The new acting Chairman, Richard Ryder, made a toe-curlingly craven televised statement: 'I have no hesitation in apologising unreservedly for our errors'. It was too much for many BBC staff, who protested at Dyke's departure and saw Lord Hutton's report as a whitewash, an establishment stitch-up. I thought the same at the time, and until very recently. I thought it was a bad day for the BBC, which had been quite properly revealing uncomfortable truths, and was now cowed and toadying to the government of the day. The public too were unimpressed. Hutton had investigated only the narrow point that the government had put claims in the intelligence document knowing them to be untrue. It took two further enquiries by Lord Butler and Sir John Chilcot for the more important truth to be revealed: that the intelligence about Saddam and his possession of weapons of mass destruction was not just wrong, but presented in an exaggerated form, giving it a weight it could not bear, and which should not have been used as a justification for the invasion of Iraq.

But getting the intelligence wrong is one thing. Deliberately lying your way into war is another. I can understand now Alastair Campbell's fury, and I understand the BBC's culpability and why heads had to roll. What still puzzles me is, how did the BBC allow itself to get in this mess?

Andrew Gilligan's confession to Lord Hutton came too late. Too late of course for David Kelly and too late for the

BBC, which had decided in May 2003 to back Gilligan to the hilt. The intelligence dossier *had*, in vulgar language, been 'sexed up'. Campbell and Blair had wanted the intelligence services to be clearer in their judgements, particularly on the threat posed by Saddam's weapons of mass destruction and the fear that they could be launched in forty-five minutes. Campbell, though, had agreed in writing with John Scarlett, the Chairman of the Joint Intelligence Committee, that nothing would be published unless Scarlett – representing the intelligence community – was 100 per cent in agreement with the wording. That was a crucial element that had been omitted from Gilligan's report. If Gilligan's report had said the government and the intelligence services both played a part in 'sexing up' the document, it would have been the truth. But 'sexing up' aside, it was in the ad-libbed, untrue allegation that the government had deliberately, knowingly, falsified the intelligence to make the case for war – not just made it clearer or more vivid, but falsified it – that the BBC came unstuck.

Had Gilligan said when first challenged that this allegation was untrue, and stood by his main claim that some in the intelligence community were unhappy at intelligence being 'sexed up' for public consumption, events might have taken a different turn. Had someone at the BBC asked to see Gilligan's notes and really got into the detail of the claims in his broadcast in an analytic way – Where did you get this from? Why did you say that? How do you justify it? – again, things might have taken a different turn. Instead the BBC paid the price – not for the original mistake, but for having failed to discover the truth and issue a swift apology.

So Hutton was right in just this one respect: that Gilligan had no evidence for the claim that the government had knowingly made false claims about WMD. But Hutton made no criticism of the sexing up of the dossier, nor of the way the Ministry of Defence, after confirming Kelly's name, had failed to protect him. Everyone, according to Hutton, was innocent except the BBC. No wonder his hefty 700-page report was, one senior judge told me, used in her house as a doorstop: 'all it was fit for'.

Handling a hostile government, as the current Director General Tim Davie quickly discovered, requires a feline ability to do enough to ward off the blows that rain down on your head but not so much as to undermine the BBC's independence. It is always a difficult judgement. Critics are quick to attack the BBC for caving in to government pressure or, to put it more subtly, tending to lean towards government rather than away from it. The public does not know what pressures are being applied behind the scenes, nor for that matter do most broadcasters or producers. It is in the nature of huge organisations like the BBC with long complex management chains that a nudge from the top can become an elbow in the ribs by the time it gets to the bottom.

It is rare that government pressure is exposed so blatantly as it was in Margaret Thatcher's day. It began in the early years of her premiership when she sent a British task force to recover the Falkland Islands from Argentinian occupation. The BBC infuriated her by reporting on news from both sides of the conflict in an attempt to analyse the progress of the war accurately and dispassionately. Where the *Sun* was urging the country to stand with 'our boys', Peter Snow on

Newsnight talked of 'the British' and, in trying to assess the truth of British claims about the progress of the war, said, 'we cannot demonstrate that the British have lied to us so far'. Snow was attacked in the House of Commons. His reporting, it was said, was 'almost treasonable'. Thatcher said it was upsetting to see both sides in the conflict treated as though they were equals and the *Sun* weighed in. 'Dare call it treason. There are traitors in our midst.' In his attempt to remain impartial, Snow's saying that the British had not 'lied to us so far' was provocative. But nobody seemed to have noticed that the spokesman for the Minister of Defence giving daily accounts of the progress of the war never referred to 'our forces' but always to 'British forces'.

This was the first run-in Thatcher had with the BBC under the Director Generalship of Alasdair Milne. There were others to come. The BBC accused the Conservative Party of having extreme right-wingers in its midst and had to pay damages and apologise. There was a battle over the BBC's coverage of an American bombing raid on Libya, which reported heavy civilian casualties. Then there was the *Real Lives* affair. During the worst years of the Troubles in Northern Ireland, shortly after the IRA had blown up the Grand Hotel in Brighton killing five of Thatcher's colleagues, the BBC, in an effort to explain the background to the hatred between Protestant and Catholic, between Unionists and Republicans in Northern Ireland, decided to make a film about the family life of two leading protagonists in the Troubles. One was a Unionist paramilitary, the other was Martin McGuinness, later Deputy First Minister for Northern Ireland but at the time a known member of the

IRA. The film showed the two of them at home, enjoying family life and talking about their upbringing. Margaret Thatcher got wind of the project from a newspaper reporter and said that she would deplore anything that gave 'the oxygen of publicity' to the IRA. Her faithful Home Secretary, Leon Brittan, wrote to the Chairman of the BBC and – while in a brief sentence acknowledging that any decision was for the BBC to make, not him – launched into a diatribe against the programme, which he had not seen, urging the BBC not to transmit it. Some of the governors agreed with the Home Secretary. The Chairman suggested that it would be best if the governors were to watch the film and decide whether it should be broadcast.

Institutional memory on this occasion suffered a temporary lapse. When the governors had watched my film *Yesterday's Men* before transmission and edited out the parts they thought were unfair to the former Prime Minister, Harold Wilson, it was generally agreed that they had blundered. By allowing themselves to take an executive decision they had abdicated their power to adjudicate on the programme subsequently. Fourteen years on, forgetting this lesson, the governors watched *Real Lives* and decided it should not be shown. This time the news and current affairs staff of the BBC, seeing the balance of power between government and the BBC so blatantly tipped in the government's favour, went on strike, refusing to write news bulletins. The governors' decision also alarmed broadcasters working for the BBC World Service abroad, who asked simply how they could explain to their listeners that the BBC was not a state broadcaster, under political control, if editorial decisions were seen to be so blatantly taken under government pressure. The foolish governors, with some exceptions, saw the error of their ways and agreed that with a few minor cosmetic alterations the programme could be shown. When it was there was no public outcry.

By now Thatcher was determined to bring the BBC to heel, egged on by her husband Denis who claimed the 'pinko BBC' were 'a nest of long-haired Trots and wooftahs'. She took the first opportunity to appoint a new Chairman, Marmaduke Hussey, and he promptly sacked Milne, who, in Thatcher's view, had failed to control the BBC. Hence my dinner at St James's with Hussey and my failed application to run the place myself.

Politicians never give up. The BBC is no longer run by governors but by a Board of Trustees, which does the same job and is as much prey to political influence as the old governors were. It is chaired by Richard Sharp, who was an adviser to Boris Johnson during his time as London Mayor and who has donated more than £400,000 to the Conservative Party; and among its members is Robbie Gibb, a former BBC producer of political programmes, brother of a Conservative MP, and former Director of Communications at No. 10 Downing Street. Not necessarily any harm in that. The Boards have always contained political appointees who, in theory, leave their politics behind when they are doing the job of protecting the BBC. But Gibb appears to have attempted to intervene in a BBC appointment to the news division. He was reported to have told the Director of News and Current Affairs, Fran Unsworth, that she should not make a particular appointment – of Jess Brammar, someone I happened to have known years earlier as a clever, young producer on *Question Time* – as the government's 'fragile trust in the BBC will be shattered'. The apparent grounds for objecting to the appointment were the downfall of so many: her tweets. She was pilloried by the *Daily Telegraph* for 'a series of now-deleted Left-wing tweets in which she railed against Boris Johnson, Brexit and Britain's imperial past'. Fortunately for the BBC, the intervention came to nothing, but not before a long and insidious campaign had been carried out against her, orchestrated by the BBC's old enemies in the right-wing press. The lesson for the BBC's trustees is to keep out of executive decisions, but in these febrile times that is probably too much to hope.

Occasionally a government understands that the BBC can be not just a thorn in their side, or a fearsome adversary, but an indispensable tool and powerful ally. Even the BBC's staunchest critics turn to it in times of need because, as Boris Johnson's government discovered during the Covid-19 pandemic, the BBC can deliver reliable, trusted information with unparalleled effectiveness during a crisis. In 2020, at the start of the Covid pandemic, the government needed the BBC to get its message across that everyone, except, as we discovered later, people who worked at Downing Street, had to obey strict rules restricting social contact. Night after night the message was driven home by the Prime Minister, Boris Johnson, flanked by medical experts and backed by the Union Flag. 'You must stay at home … You should not be meeting friends … You should not be meeting family members who do not live in your home.' A country in fear watched every twist and turn of the spread of infection illustrated by barely comprehensible graphs. BBC audiences for the nightly news rose from its usually modest level to 15 million, outstripping its rivals.

But no sooner was the worst of the crisis over than, back on form, the newly appointed Secretary of State for Digital, Culture, Media and Sports, Boris Johnson's attack dog, betraying a lifetime loathing of the BBC, was saying the licence fee must come to an end. Though with no idea how to replace it.

The relationship between politicians and the BBC will always be fractious. How could it be otherwise? The BBC seeks the truth and the truth often makes politicians uncomfortable. Politicians seek a favourable hearing for their arguments, and pressure from the powerful to bend one way or another makes the BBC uncomfortable.

My instinct – going back all the way to *Yesterday's Men* – is that standing up to political pressure should be the BBC's default, visceral reaction. And usually it is. Hence its reputation for arrogance. But the correct instinct is to push back. The challenge then is, beyond the initial instinct, to be able to distinguish the occasions when the BBC is in the wrong, and should accept censure, from the occasions when it is right and should continue publicly to resist political pressure. The problem is that many disputes tend to be neither the one nor the other but fall somewhere in between, leaving the BBC having to judge between its enemies without and its defensive staff within. Trapped between Scylla and Charybdis.

4

'Not the answers, you fool. The questions'

Political interviewing risks terminal decline, victim of its evolution.

It all began so well back in 1958, over sixty years ago, when Harold Macmillan was leading a Conservative government. On his return from a tour of the Commonwealth he became the first Prime Minister to submit to a full-length live television interview, for the BBC programme *Press Conference* by a group of three prominent journalists, one each from the

Observer, the *Economist* and the *New Statesman*. *Press Conference* set the rules of engagement between politicians and broadcasters that still apply today. Politicians would appear by invitation, not as of right. A political balance would be observed. Questions would never be revealed in advance. And interviewers would be expected to follow up questions if they did not think they had been given a satisfactory answer. Nonetheless, three interviewers makes life easy for the interviewee, who can play one off against the other. Probably for that reason, this is not a format that has survived. Macmillan emerged unscathed. It was a different story though a couple of days later when he was questioned by Robin Day for ITN, the new independent TV news company run by ITV.

Day had trained as a barrister. His lifelong ambition was to win a seat in parliament, an ambition in which he failed. Instead he emerged as Britain's first serious political interviewer, the model against which all others would be tested. His style was flamboyant – wearing the same blue white-spotted bow tie he successfully created an image for himself long before strutting their stuff on Instagram became normal behaviour for broadcasters. He was puffed up, always seeking to dominate a conversation, to be the centre of attention, never humble. His confidence meant he approached the Macmillan interview as though he was on equal terms with the Prime Minister. He asks in what sense Britain having independent nuclear weapons can be considered a deterrent, whether it is acceptable to use unemployment to control inflation and whether reports that he was planning to sack his Foreign Secretary Selwyn Lloyd were true. None of these questions would be thought outlandish today but back then in the late 1950s the rigorous tone with which they were put was a daring, ground-breaking departure from a more deferential convention. Macmillan's habitual political posture was to affect an air of supreme self-confidence, a theatrical pose of autocratic disdain and aloofness: curious coming from someone who claimed to be of crofter stock.

Robin Day: *How do you feel, Prime Minister, about criticism which has been made in the last few days in Conservative newspapers particularly, of Mr Selwyn Lloyd, the Foreign Secretary?*

Harold Macmillan: *Well I think Mr Selwyn Lloyd is a very good Foreign Secretary and he's done his work extremely well. If I didn't think so I would have made a change. But I do not intend to make a change simply as a result of pressure. I don't believe that that is wise, and it's not in accordance with my idea of loyalty.*

Robin Day: *Is it correct, as reported in one paper, that he would like in fact to give up the job of Foreign Secretary?*

Harold Macmillan: *Not at all, except in the sense that everybody would like to give up these appalling burdens which we try and carry.*

Robin Day: *Would you like to give up yours?*

Harold Macmillan: *In a sense yes. Because they are very heavy burdens ... but we've gone into this game, we try to do our best, and it's both in a sense our pleasure and certainly I hope our duty.*

By today's standards it does not seem particularly provocative, but asking a Prime Minister whether he wanted to give up his job was akin to *lèse-majesté* in the 1950s when those in authority were treated with a respect that would be unthinkable now. It is noticeable that Day was careful to ask whether Macmillan wanted to step down not as a standalone question but as a supplementary to Macmillan's remark that 'everybody would like to give up these appalling burdens'. He said it with a slight smile as if to imply, 'I don't really expect you to answer this.' As for not sacking people under pressure because it was not 'in accordance with my idea of loyalty', Macmillan sacked a third of his Cabinet in what became known as his Night of the Long Knives four years later, his close ally Selwyn Lloyd, by then Chancellor of the Exchequer, among them.

When he was into his nineties, I sat at Macmillan's feet at a soirée given by Paul Channon, the MP son of the indiscreet diarist Chips Channon. Trying to think of something to say to the old man, I asked him about political interviewing and in particular what it was like to be interviewed by Day. He thought for a moment and then, aloof and patrician as ever, murmured, 'Never gave me any trouble.'

The newspapers, however, were taken aback at what had happened that night. The *Daily Express* wrote that it had been 'the most vigorous cross examination a Prime Minister has been subjected to in public'. The *Observer* said the Prime Minister should now be interviewed by the press on the same terms, everything on the record, calling the television interview a 'subtle instrument for conveying or concealing his thoughts'. The *Manchester Guardian*, as the *Guardian* was then called, commented that 'once an individual has consented to be questioned in front of television cameras he has deliberately exposed himself to a process which some prime ministers of the past – perhaps all – would have dismissed as impertinent. It will be fascinating to discover if any politician has the strength of mind to resist the temptations of television.'

Until Robin Day's interview a journalist's access to politicians was principally through the Lobby system, a conspiracy between an elite corps of political correspondents and politicians. Membership of the Lobby was secret and like membership of the Freemasons had to be denied. Everything said there was unattributable, off the record. Anyone who broke the rules was expelled. This cosy arrangement suited both parties. The politicians could float ideas, discuss policy, signal disagreements in government without fear of being revealed as the source. The journalists had the benefit of insider knowledge denied to their peers. It is not surprising that it was a closely protected privilege. Elements of it survive. The irritating phrase 'my sources tell me . . .' is still used by reporters to suggest they know something that no one else does, something they have been told off the record. This something may be true, it may be false, it may be designed to mislead. Who is to know? No wonder the distinguished journalist Louis Heren revealed that whenever he was told something 'in confidence' he asked himself, 'Why is this lying bastard lying to me?'

Robin Day's 1958 interview with Macmillan set a new precedent. Live TV interviews usurped the power of the Lobby and changed the way we judged our politicians. The Press Secretaries could do their best to make sure their clients were presented in a good light but it was no longer simply a matter of securing favourable press coverage, a flattering profile or a clever analysis of policy. For the first time we could see our leaders in the flesh, analyse their gestures, note nervousness or hesitation, spot the bully, and with the interviewer's help smoke out evasion and contradiction. There was no guarantee that the policies promised would be carried out or even resemble what was propounded, but at least the words were on the record. The traditional defence of words 'being taken out of context' was no longer available.

Robin Day's interviewing technique derived from his training as a barrister. It was legalistic, forensic. He never gave the impression of being particularly interested in political policies or their outcomes for their own sake. He preferred the excitement of a duel, cross-examining MPs against what they had said in parliament. He prepared himself with the dedication of a fencing master working out when to parry and when to lunge. Each morning a copy of the parliamentary record, *Hansard,* was delivered to his house. He would read the verbatim account of the previous day's debates, spotting good arguments and noting inconsistencies, and then use what he found to hone his interviews.

From the mid-1970s year after year I sat beside Robin in the BBC commentary box at party conferences. We used to broadcast all day long, from end to end or 'gavel to gavel'. These were strange affairs, a holiday by the seaside for political geeks. Each autumn we would traipse to Blackpool or Bournemouth or Brighton, the regular three Bs, and occasionally further afield. The Liberals being less numerous though no less loquacious usually took us to smaller towns – maybe Llandudno or Eastbourne. In our box in the gallery

Robin and I would while away the time while a Labour delegate passionately argued for a word to be removed from a
subparagraph of a subsection of a motion about to go to the
vote; or, if it was the Tories, a representative from the Shires
delivered their annual rant about the death penalty or fox
hunting. I suspect the Liberals may have talked about climate
change – a topic in which few were particularly interested in
those days.

To keep us alert, as the platform speeches weighed down
our eyelids, Robin would tell me the latest gossip and discuss
his own prospects at some length. Should he accept a knighthood? I thought not. Should he become a director of British
Airways? 'Probably not,' I said. I never knew whether the
British Airways offer was serious, but the knighthood was
and he took it. My puritanical view that journalists should
never accept honours that have to be approved by the incumbent of Downing Street fell on very deaf ears. He was cross a
few years later when Margaret Thatcher called him 'Mr Day'
throughout an interview rather than 'Sir Robin'. In her
memoirs she rebukes herself for the mistake. It was odd that
she made it, since it was she who had approved his honour in
the first place.

The torpor of these party conferences was occasionally
broken by unexpected drama. The party leader's speech
would have us looking for signs of a change in policy and
trying to gauge their popularity by the length of the applause
at the end, sometimes measuring it with a stopwatch. There
were other excitements. Denis Healey in 1977 being called to
speak not as a senior member of the Cabinet but, in the self-
consciously democratic Labour Party and at the insistence of

the hostile National Executive Committee, as just another delegate. Britain's Chancellor of the Exchequer stood at the delegates' lectern below the stage, shouting to be heard above the baying of party members. Being Healey he made the best of it. 'I prefer on the whole,' he said, 'the dust and sweat of the arena where the gladiators slog it out together, to the rather rarefied atmosphere where the Imperial Caesars look down from the chair.' That same year there was the sixteen-year-old William Hague telling the Tories that rolling back socialism was more important to him than it was to most of those in the hall (middle-aged or elderly) because 'you will not be here in thirty or forty years'. And unforgettable was the startling appearance in 1978 of a lugubrious Jeremy Thorpe, the Liberals' former leader, unexpectedly taking his place on the platform having been charged a few weeks earlier with conspiracy to murder his former lover Norman Scott.

After a few years of this gavel-to-gavel coverage the BBC decided that it was not enough just to do its duty by the political class. It must make a greater effort to attract viewers. In future the coverage of the conference in the hall would be interspersed with interviews with the main protagonists. One morning Robin left the box to interview the Home Secretary of the day. I watched on the bank of monitors in front of me in the gallery. When it was done he came back, squeezed in beside me, lit his cigar, turned to me and asked, 'What did you think of that then?' 'I didn't think he said anything very new,' I replied. 'Not the answers, you fool. The questions.'

He was right. The questions are everything.

Questions: not just the wording of a question, but the choice of areas of questioning, are two of the most powerful weapons an interviewer has, with the subjects raised as important as the precise questions. The third weapon, not to be underestimated but overused by some interviewers, is the look of puzzlement, incredulity or affected boredom at the answers being given.

The questions frame the political debate for the viewer. Out of a wide range of possible topics, which matter most? Which do the public care about? The questions asked, and the form in which they are put, can reveal the weaknesses of a government's position, and for that matter of the alternatives proposed by the opposition. (And it is the job of interviewers to seek out weaknesses, not extol successes, though politicians would love it to be the other way round.) It is what Robin Day meant when he called me a fool: the questions are as powerful as the answers.

The preparation for a big interview can take several days, beginning with question areas and only later working out the precise questions to ask.

My first experience of a live prime ministerial interview was over fifty years ago, when I was in my early thirties. It was January 1969. The Labour Prime Minister, Harold Wilson, was at the peak of his power. No one anticipated that his first spell in Number 10 was about to come to an end with his unexpected defeat in June 1970. The Monday evening interview was to be three-handed, though as that first interview with Harold Macmillan had demonstrated this is never a good formula. Robin Day was to be the Chairman. Robert MacNeil, the distinguished Canadian broadcaster who went on to present the daily *MacNeil/Lehrer* show on US television and had just joined *Panorama*, was the second interviewer, and I was the third, the innocent at the table. We met, together with an editor and a researcher, on the Sunday morning before the interview in Robin's house on the edge of Notting Hill. We discussed what issues we should raise and what questions might pin down the notoriously tricky Wilson. On the agenda were relations with the new US President, Richard Nixon, Britain's relationship with the Soviet Union, Wilson's refusal to take part in the Vietnam War, the national debt, and reform of trade union law. 'Anything else?' Robin asked. 'How about: is this government putting through too much legislation? Why don't you ask him that David?'

I made a note and drafted what I thought would be a suitable question. The following evening as the interview was coming to a close I took my chance and asked:

Isn't there at the same time, Prime Minister, a great danger and a general feeling in the country that there are too many laws and regulations being passed by your government, and a feeling of what the Duke of Edinburgh called, having 'practically to have a licence to breathe' – if you remember – that in fact there is too much law-making going on?

I cannot imagine why I dragged the Duke into the question. Maybe I was hoping to sting the Prime Minister into rebuking the Royal Family for interfering in politics. Whatever the motive it was to no avail. Wilson, brushing away the question as casually as the ash that had fallen from his pipe, replied in effect: 'Funny you should ask that. People are always asking me to introduce *more* laws, not least Her Majesty's Opposition.' Collapse of question. Useless. I did not speak again until the programme came to a close. It was a good lesson though. New to the game I had failed to remember that as an interviewer, you need to think through where a question is going, what the likely response will be, and what supplementary questions you have to hand. Ideally, you game it with your colleagues. When we had sat round in Robin's sitting room I failed to insist we use this technique to test the question. Had we done so I would have quickly spotted the obvious reply and found a different way of framing it. I have always wondered whether a mischievous Robin had offered the question to me as a trap, knowing the likely outcome. Maybe an unworthy thought, but then I was the upstart and he was nothing if not competitive.

Gaming an interview is the key to having any chance of prising even a half-true reply from your prey. And it is fun, playing different roles, and trying out different wordings and constructions for the same question. What will they answer if I ask this? How about if I put it like that? Where will they go if I ask the other?

There are many different ways of interviewing. Some, like Robin Day, act as though they are the prosecuting counsel in a trial – or as the epitaph on his tombstone in a Dorset churchyard has it, 'The Grand Inquisitor'. Others prefer a more cerebral, analytic approach. The best exponent of this technique was the former Labour MP Brian Walden, who used to present a weekend political interview show during the Thatcher years. Holed up in the Savoy Hotel on the eve of his interviews he would chart on a piece of paper the course he planned to take, with arrows joining one question to another. If the answer to question A is no, go to question B. If yes go to C. Armed with this cryptic diagram he would subject his interviewee to a merciless interrogation. Walden had no qualms about it. He once said: 'I know I understand politicians but ... I detest ambiguity. It's always my instinct to ask people exactly what they mean.' Walden became an admirer of Thatcher and what he described as her 'Victorian values' – a phrase she herself adopted. He even, according to one of Thatcher's biographers, wrote her speech for a rally in the 1983 election. None of this cramped his interviewing techniques. He was merciless in his cross-examination, in one famous interview saying to her, 'You come over as someone who one of your backbenchers said is "slightly off her trolley": authoritarian, domineering, refusing to listen to anybody else – why?' 'If anyone is coming over as domineering in this interview it's you,' she replied. A bit limp. 'Off her trolley' was the phrase that stuck.

In her memoirs Thatcher wrote that Day was the most aggressive interviewer but Walden the most probing. But there are as many interviewing techniques as there are interviewers. Jeremy Paxman, eyebrows raised in incredulity, would batter his interviewee with aggressive questions, whether they were powerful figures in government or lowly and inexperienced ministers sent as cannon fodder to feed the remorseless demands of nightly news programmes. The late David Frost, by contrast, built his reputation by adopting a quite different style: always genial towards his guests unless they were scoundrels. His questions seemed soft in style, coaxing rather than accusatory. Politicians flocked to his Sunday morning sofa for their *Breakfast with Frost*. They knew they could make headlines for Monday's papers, one of the targets of the Sunday political shows.

I was irritated when the BBC picked up Frost's sofa show from TV-am in the early 1990s. I told anyone who would listen that the BBC would never again persuade senior politicians to come to *Panorama* – which I was presenting at the time – if they were offered the easier option of talking to Frost. I argued that persuading a politician to do a tough interview was like herding livestock into a pen: the only technique that worked was to shut off all other possible escape routes so that the animal had no choice. If there were easier options being offered, who wouldn't take them? Sure enough our supply of politicians to *Panorama* began to dry up. But when charged with taking the soft option, politicians would always say, 'Ah, that David Frost. Dangerous interviewer. Lulls you into saying what you don't mean to.'

My own first political interview, long before the humiliating Harold Wilson incident, was with Edward Heath, later himself to become Prime Minister but at that time Harold Macmillan's appointed negotiator for Britain's entry into the Common Market. I had been engaged to present a short summer replacement programme for *Panorama* called *Outlook Europe*. I remember that series as the only time I have dried up on air. I just forgot what I meant to say. It was long before the invention of the autocue. As a presenter you either learnt your lines by heart or wrote prompts on a card stuck to the camera just below the lens. Unfortunately my camera had moved away just too far for me to read my card. I began a fatally constructed sentence: 'On the one hand the Prime Minister may choose . . . and on the other hand . . .' At which point I forgot what was on the other hand, stopped talking, gasped for a moment like a goldfish in a bowl, and then somehow recovered. But the most daunting challenge of the series was the final programme when I was to interview Ted Heath. His negotiations with Europe centred on arrangements that would allow us to continue importing cheap food from Canada and New Zealand – a relationship that ironically we are now seeking to restore after Brexit. Lamb imports from New Zealand were on Heath's agenda, as was Canadian wheat, which was said to be harder and better suited to making British bread than the softer wheat that the French use for their delicious baguettes. I had tried to absorb the detail of these arcane subjects but was still nervous about the interview. I adopted a technique that I had read about somewhere. If you are nervous of a person in authority do not be cowed. Think of them naked and you will realise they are just another human being like you. The interview itself passed off well enough, the aftermath less so. The night after the programme I had a disturbing dream in which Ted Heath appeared before me naked, as I had tried to imagine him. I will spare you the details of that encounter but it warned me against ever again using this particular technique for calming my nerves.

All political interviewing is of its nature confrontational. That does not mean it has to be aggressive. But all parties have to accept the truth that a good interviewer will always want to be revealing information that the interviewee wants to hide. Doing the job properly means focusing on precisely the issues and questions the interviewee wants to avoid: the decisions that are most difficult, the objections that are hardest to refute. If it were not so it would be pointless.

At the same time, political interviewing has to give politicians the opportunity to explain. Democratic politics fails if politicians cannot explain what they are trying to achieve in language the voters can understand. It follows that political interviews must be conducted in the same way – in simple language and based on whatever policies the politician has claimed as his or her own.

There have been attempts to make interviews more rigorous and more informative by turning them into a kind of seminar, designed to teach the ignorant viewers what they did not know or understand. It was an approach favoured by John Birt, who in 1987 became the BBC's Deputy Director General with responsibility for political broadcasting. He believed that television had what he called a bias against understanding, and that by highlighting or dramatising conflict it was failing to explain the complexities of the decisions politicians had to take. In other words, we needed less confrontation.

This led to a spate of interviews that were both boring and often over the heads of the viewer. However worthy the attempt to explain, for example, monetary policy and its different definitions of money supply, M_0, M_1 and M_3, the effort is futile if the viewer is left wondering which motorway is being discussed and why. I fell foul of this new doctrine when, during a general election, I had to interview my friend William Waldegrave, then Secretary of State for Health. He and I had often privately discussed the topics I was going to raise, and the only way I could keep a straight face as we went through what we knew so well was by adopting an unusually severe tone. John Birt, now promoted to Director General, watched the interview and decided that it was against the new order he was trying to impose. He rebuked me. I argued my point but he was, I was starting to discover, intransigent.

Birt's criticism did nothing to change my view of how political interviews should be conducted. Political interviews will always have an element of confrontation. My credo is very simple: the public has a right to know and any question is justified if it serves that end. The job is to probe, test and if necessary express scepticism about a politician's intentions. The knowledge that I was in a sense trying to hold power to account on behalf of the viewer gave me the legitimacy and the cover to ask even the most awkward or difficult questions.

Steeled by the knowledge that I was there to find out what viewers had the right to know, and armed with the most carefully prepared questions, these gladiatorial confrontations with some of the world's most powerful and charismatic politicians were always exhilarating and often unpredictable. Shortly after Margaret Thatcher was chosen as leader of the Conservative Party in 1975 I went to meet her in her room in the House of Commons for an informal discussion of her policies. She was always a flatterer of men, asking me before we started on the affairs of the country where I had bought my tie and saying she wanted to buy something similar for her husband Denis. We then talked about the ideas she and her adviser and close political friend, the right-wing MP Keith Joseph, had been propounding: using control of the money supply to prevent inflation – our discussion including the motorway definitions I mentioned earlier. It is an arcane topic and like all economic theory unprovable. This did not prevent Mrs Thatcher from pronouncing on it with her usual certainty. Our informal meeting laid the ground for a full-blown interview a few months later when she flew to Washington to make her number with senior American politicians including the Republican President, Gerald Ford. She was an object of intense curiosity across the Atlantic: the first woman who might become our Prime Minister, and a politician with firm views about restoring the British economy by nurturing individual enterprise, a message the Republican Party enjoyed hearing. She was accompanied by her public relations consigliere, Gordon Reece. I remember him as an affable man, unless he was crossed, short with heavy horn-rimmed spectacles, usually smoking a cigar. His job was to advise Thatcher on everything that affected her public image: her clothes, her voice – which he thought too high-pitched and strident – and how to conduct television interviews. These are not, he told her, the place for lectures. You must try to make yourself sound informal, friendly. As part of his brief he was also pernickety about the setting for an interview, insisting on soft lighting and elegant flower arrangements. On the visit to Washington he had agreed that Thatcher would give us an interview for *Panorama* and had decided that the best venue in Washington would be the park directly in front of the White House, using this symbol of power as the backdrop. The only place to sit for an interview in the park was on one of the benches firmly anchored beside the tarmac paths. We asked Thatcher to sit at one end of a bench and I sat at the other, both of us at a slightly awkward angle with our knees turned inwards so that we could face each other. We were about to start the interview when Reece asked to look through the lens at the shot we were taking. He decided Thatcher did not look sufficiently commanding sitting, as she was, sideways on to the White House. She had to sit four square in front of it. This meant I could not sit beside her but had to find a way of facing her directly. I tried perching on one of the boxes that contained the camera equipment, but it was too low. Casting around slightly desperately, I noticed a rubbish bin a little further down the path with a heavy plastic lining. Hoping to avoid the gaze of the officious park attendants who had already been asking us what we were up to, I removed the plastic container, turned it upside down on the path in front of Thatcher and sat down. Perfect. Everyone was satisfied. The eyelines (meaning the angle at which she had to look at me, and vice versa) were exactly right and Thatcher had the flattering backdrop Reece had prescribed. But as we started the interview I felt the plastic container slowly subsiding under my weight and then collapsing. We stopped the interview. Reece looked at his watch and said Mrs Thatcher was now running behind schedule. Drastic action was needed. I realised there was now only one way to get the interview done in the way we had agreed. I knelt down on the footpath in front of Thatcher. We checked the eyelines again. It was perfect. The interview began. At this moment a passing British tourist noticed us and took a photograph of the scene: Margaret resplendent on her bench with the BBC on its knees before her: an image that would surely not have displeased her. I always believed that Downing Street was sent a copy of the photo and kept it as a hostage to fortune. That at least is what I told Thatcher once she had become Prime Minister, and she never denied it.

Twenty years on, in the general election of 1997, Tony Blair unseated the Conservative Prime Minister John Major and brought Labour to power after eighteen years in opposition with a landslide majority not seen in over sixty years. Blair's New Labour, as he had rebranded the party, won a majority of 179 seats. The Tories, mired in accusations of sleazy and corrupt behaviour by some of its MPs and torn apart by arguments over Europe, were swept aside. These were heady times for Labour. As Blair said on the morning of his victory, 'A new dawn has broken has it not?'

In the run-up to polling day I had the job of interviewing Blair live on *Panorama*. It was a difficult assignment. Here was a man leading a party that was way ahead in the polls. He had convinced a majority of the country that Labour under his leadership was offering something they could feel safe with, that there would be no radical upheavals. His Chancellor, Gordon Brown, had even promised to stick to the spending plans already outlined by the Tories for the next two years. New Labour would claim the centre ground: not radical, not heading for higher taxes and more spending, just reassuringly centrist policies but with new fresh faces in charge.

So what questions should we put? What would voters want to know about Blair and New Labour before they cast their votes?

We decided that the only possible course was to test the claim that Labour really was a different party from the one that had lost the last three elections under Michael Foot and then Neil Kinnock. Was Blair genuinely proposing a change of direction or was this just a clever rebranding exercise? The best way to do this, we felt, was to question Blair about his own apparent personal conversion. How could this be the same Blair as the Blair who had supported unilateral nuclear disarmament and opposed reform of trade union law? He was now a multilateralist and a supporter of the trade union reforms that Thatcher had introduced. Had he been hypocritical back then or had he had a genuine change of heart? Was this new Blair for real or was he an opportunist hoodwinking the British public?

For several days my producer and researchers scoured old editions of *Hansard* to track down what Blair had said on the record that was at odds with what he was saying now. On the eve of the interview, reading through the transcript from 1983 of the standing committee examining Thatcher's proposals to restrain the power of the trade unions, they came up with what in interviewer's jargon was a killer quote: something that Blair had said, that went to the heart of what we were trying to test. This is the key section of the subsequent interview. After covering various aspects of his policy I asked why he was proposing to leave Thatcher's anti-trade union laws on the statute book. He delivered his carefully constructed explanation. I waited until he had finished and then, bringing the select committee proceedings out from under my pile of papers, said:

Me: *And you were the person as a barrister who dealt with trade union affairs who sat on a Select Committee and opposed root and branch every detail of the Conservative Government's attempts to reform, to even make the most modest reforms in trade union law.*

Tony Blair: *David, those were in the days when people thought that the best way to look at collective bargaining arrangements between employer and employee was not to have a legal*

framework. We changed that and let me say something to you.
I'm proud of the changes that the Labour Party has made.
Me: *No but hang on. I'm asking you about what happened*
before. You may be proud of what you've done now. That
implies you're ashamed of what happened before.
Tony Blair: *I'm not ashamed of it at all.*
Me: *Well was your instinct right for instance when you talked*
about the Tories as 'people with hobnail boots waiting to tram-
ple over the rights of trade unionists'? I mean was that some-
thing you defend saying now? Did you mean to say it?

Blair looked startled at the line of questioning.

Tony Blair: *Look at that time people thought for perfectly*
understandable reasons that the best way to have an industrial
relations framework was to get the law out of it. That changed.
Indeed I was one of those people that changed that position of
the Labour Party . . . I'm afraid that this is sort of Conservative
propaganda that I was some sort of extreme left-winger that
suddenly trimmed after I became Labour leader.

We went backwards and forwards a bit more. Had he said it
or not?

Tony Blair: *I mean David, we can sit here arguing about*
what happened in the 1970s and early 1980s.
Me: *Well it's quite important because you were there.*

Always the professional politician, Blair had kept his cool
throughout.

Outside the studio, on the other hand, his Press Secretary and closest adviser Alastair Campbell was erupting in fury (not an uncommon occurrence), I suppose because I was questioning whether the image he had so carefully projected was to be believed. Had it been a recorded interview I suspect he would have found a way of preventing its transmission, but this was being broadcast live. There was nothing he could do except swear a good deal and tell anyone who would listen that I would never be allowed near Blair again – a promise that he kept for several years.

Campbell decided to make the best of it by having party officials phoning round all the key newspapers to make sure they appreciated what a tough interview it had been. The *Telegraph* duly described it as Blair's 'roughest ride so far . . . it was almost as though the two had had a row before the beginning of the programme and we had walked in on something'. The *Mirror* said that TV viewers 'saw red' over the line of questioning and the *Independent* reported that the BBC was swamped with calls from Labour Party supporters complaining about it. Several pieces also referenced my headmasterly style, short haircut and half-moon glasses: 'There were no smiles, there was no warmth, as he battered away from behind his half-moons,' said *The Times*.

The BBC, however, stood by me. The interview, tough though it may have seemed, had been agreed by *Panorama*'s editor and by the Head of Current Affairs. It was the right interview to do. It left it to the voters to judge the issues and three weeks later the voters gave Blair the thumbs-up.

There was, however, an unsettling change of mood at the BBC when the scale of Blair's victory became clear. I first noticed it during the election results programme, which I was anchoring. On the morning of his victory, Blair decided to emulate Thatcher's triumphant walk up Downing Street to the door of Number 10 after her first victory in 1979. In 1979, Downing Street had been open to the public. Anyone could stroll up the street and take a photo outside the famous door. The crowd that had cheered for Margaret Thatcher nearly twenty years earlier had not been selected by the party but were a random collection of supporters, members of the public and tourists. In the years since then the predations of the IRA had led to much tighter security. Imposing wrought-iron gates had been erected to close the street off to the public. Passes were now needed to get through. On television, however, the scene looked like a replica of Thatcher's triumph, a spontaneous burst of public enthusiasm for the newly elected Blair. I had been told by a reporter at the scene that in reality this was no such thing. The welcoming crowd was mainly composed of Labour Party supporters who had been issued with passes to allow them in. A minor but significant difference I thought. I pointed it out in commentary and the voice of my editor came through my earpiece: 'Steady on David. This is a great moment.'

Worse was to follow. In the days after the election there was serious discussion about whether the tone of our political interviewing should change to reflect the change of mood in the country. If even the *Sun* had endorsed Blair, it was argued, perhaps there was a national consensus around the new administration and the BBC should reflect it. The editor of *Newsnight* wrote to his team: 'The model of five years of Tory coverage must be thrown away. The template of split, disunity, Europe and chaos may one day apply, but it doesn't yet and we mustn't behave as if it does. Labour has a huge mandate and our job should not be to quarrel with the purpose of policy but to question its implementation.' It was an unsettling argument, fortunately soon abandoned in favour of our proper stance that all administrations, however popular or unpopular, are treated the same.

The use of the quotation from committee proceedings many years earlier was, I suppose, an ambush. Blair could not have been expecting it. But it was not simply for the sake of a gratuitous 'gotcha'. An ambush in the form of an unexpected question can be an effective way of disrupting an interview, bringing a touch of reality to what might otherwise be a parade of stock answers. The element of surprise can help to reveal something that otherwise might remain hidden.

In 1977 on the eve of a general election in India I was sent to Delhi to interview the Prime Minister, Indira Gandhi. For many years India had been under pressure from various United Nations bodies to try to reduce its birth rate. As part of the response, sterilisation camps had been set up to offer vasectomies to young men, with financial inducements if they agreed. In 1975, faced with mounting problems of famine and political insecurity, Mrs Gandhi had declared a state of emergency. During this period of rule by decree, known simply as the Emergency and now widely considered the darkest period in post-1947 Indian history, she had decided, with the enthusiastic support of her son Sanjay, to enforce the sterilisation policy with vigour. In theory sterilisation remained voluntary and was compensated with a cash payment. In reality ministers of the various states were instructed to pursue sterilisation quotas and devised ingeni-ous ways of meeting the targets. Their methods varied from threatening head teachers that they would lose their jobs unless they could prove a proportion of their teachers had been sterilised to denying trading licences to poorer workers such as rickshaw drivers, market stall holders, and washer-men. These excesses had made Mrs Gandhi very unpopular and she looked certain to lose the election, although she vehe-mently denied that anything improper was happening. Before interviewing her I had been to her own constituency in Uttar Pradesh to report on the mood of the voters. There I had met a washerman or dhobi man, who told me the terrible story of what had happened to him:

Me: *Ram T is a washerman with two sons and a daughter. When a team of officials from the birth control campaign came to his village to fill their quota of candidates for sterilisation he ran away.*

Interpreter for Ram T: *He hid in a field of beans nearby for two days but thought that he couldn't stay because he was threatened that if he didn't get sterilised he might be beaten up.*

Me: *And was he promised anything?*

Interpreter: *He says he was promised land if he got sterilised.*

Me: *He was promised land. Can you ask if he was given any land?*

Interpreter: *No.*

Me: *Did he get anything?*

Interpreter: *He says that he was promised that his house that was washed into the monsoon last time would be repaired. That was not done.*

A few days later I was in Delhi for my interview with the Prime Minister. Here is part of the exchange:

Me: *Can we look at one or two particular aspects of the Emergency and its consequences. Do you now accept that there was fairly widespread coercion and indeed some force used in the implementation of family planning?*

Indira Gandhi: *No there wasn't. There are isolated cases but the stories that are now being circulated or started are not true.*

Me: *I have met villagers for instance who told me that whenever anybody from authority came near, they ran and hid in the fields for two or three days because they were frightened they were going to be forcibly sterilised.*

Indira Gandhi: *No this was the atmosphere that some of the people created; therefore they hid even when somebody had nothing at all to do with any health programme, they went for something else.*

Me: *Isn't it a failure of your planning that they did react like that? Isn't that a consequence of the Emergency, that they were so frightened?*

Indira Gandhi: *No that has nothing to do with the Emergency. That is if any time you create, you know, a Hitler type of pressurised publicity, well some of it sticks.*

Me: *Can I just ask, do you yourself approve for instance of the salaries of government employees being stopped unless they are sterilised, if they qualify for sterilisation?*

Indira Gandhi: *No we had told them that this should not be done.*

Me: *Why did it happen then?*

Indira Gandhi: *It is very difficult to say. You see the people wanted to create an atmosphere – they wrongly thought that* *this was how they could motivate people. Our policy has not been only sterilisation. The point is that people should realise that smaller families make for better families, that parents can look after their children; it's not just the negative aspect of controlling the population. It's the positive aspect that every child has certain rights. He has a right to better health, he has a right to food, he has a right to education, and both the family and the state should be able to give it to him.*

Mrs Gandhi was duly defeated and subsequently apologised for the excesses of the Emergency.

An unexpected question threw another interviewee off-guard twenty-five years later in 2003. I was sent to Washington to interview the US Secretary of Defence, Donald Rumsfeld, on the eve of the US-led invasion of Iraq. Ironically, my editor suspected that the interview had been granted to me rather than any of the others clamouring for it because they knew me as a commentator on state occasions and therefore some-one who might offer an easy ride. I raised the issue of previous US support for Saddam Hussein and Rumsfeld's own involvement and suggested it was at odds with the bellicosity the administration was now showing.

Me: *America took [Iraq] off the list of terror states twenty years ago.*
Donald Rumsfeld: *I don't know that. I accept—*
Me: *When you – when you – sorry. When you visited Iraq and negotiated with Saddam Hussein, when America wanted Saddam Hussein for its own purposes, America took Iraq off the list of terrorist states and, indeed, supplied it with the*

*wherewithal to make the chemical weapons they're now trying
to remove.*

Donald Rumsfeld: *I've read that type of thing, but I don't
know where you get your information, and I don't believe it's
correct. They may have been taken off. I was a private business-
man. I was asked for a few months to assist after the 241
Marines were killed in Beirut, Lebanon. And I did meet with
Saddam Hussein. I did not give him or sell him or bring him
any chemical weapons or any biological weapons, as some of the
European press likes to print. It's just factually not true.*

*Now, whether or not the United States at some point, when I
was not part of the government, decided to take him off a terrorist list, you may be right. In fact, I—*

Me: *Are you saying you don't know, you didn't know when
you went there whether he was on the list of terror states or not?
You were trying to reopen—*

Donald Rumsfeld: *I believe he was.*

Me: *– a relationship between the United States and Iraq.*

Donald Rumsfeld: *That's right. And I believe he was on the
list of terrorist states when I went there.*

We went backwards and forwards for a bit on Mr Rumsfeld's
personal involvement. And then:

Me: *But what I'm suggesting is that the United States in the
world outside, over and over again people say, well, now they're
trying to get rid of the weapons, as Jesse Jackson put it when he
was at Hyde Park Corner a week ago, for which the United
States has the receipts. I mean, that's the problem, that you
created this monster, evil, as you know—*

Donald Rumsfeld: *You who?*

Me: *You, the United States, not you personally.*

Donald Rumsfeld: *Well, first of all, you're wrong. If you look at the record of the European countries, and the other technologically advanced countries of the world and the relationships with Iraq, I think you'll find that the United States ranks relatively low in terms of trading with Iraq and assisting Iraq with respect to weapons. I think that's correct. I don't have the data, but I think you'll find that's the case.*

Mr Rumsfeld was not pleased. He left the interview with a curt goodbye. His Press Secretary came across to me afterwards and complained. 'That's not the way we conduct interviews over here.' Later she told my producer, 'I will lose my job over this.' (I don't think she did: she is now on the Board of the Rumsfeld Foundation.) The irritation was understandable. Although my questions were unremarkable for a BBC interview, indeed were the way we expect interviews to be, the US practice at the time was different. The division of political power between the President, the two houses of Congress and the Supreme Court means that political decisions are not determined by an all-powerful executive, as in Britain, but by agreement from all these branches of government. Perhaps as a result, interviews tended to be more about process than the rights and wrongs of policy. 'How will this idea play on the Hill?' was a more common question than the direct 'Why are you proposing this?' My blunt approach was not appreciated.

Even the suavest of interviewees can be disconcerted by the unexpected question. In 2004 the publishers of the recent memoirs of former US President, Bill Clinton, invited interviews to publicise the book. My BBC producer and I decided that Bill Clinton talking about his presidency was too good an opportunity to miss. I read the book and discussed possible questions in the usual way. There was one issue I was determined to tackle. Had Clinton lied about his relationship with his young intern, Monica Lewinsky? He had said publicly, 'I did not have sexual relations with that woman.' Lewinsky had since testified under oath that she had had oral sex with him – and he had acknowledged that they had had inappropriate intimate contact. So had Clinton lied and, if so, would he admit it? I could not think of a way to put this that would not just lead to further obfuscation and decided that the only course was to be absolutely blunt: Did oral sex not count as sexual relations? The interview had been going well up to this point, but when I put the question all hell broke loose. Clinton complained that I was part of a right-wing conspiracy to bring him down, while in the background his PR adviser was calling New York to ask his publisher to withdraw permission for this interview to be broadcast.

Despite his outburst, and unlike Rumsfeld, Clinton did not storm out after the interview. He stayed for another half an hour discussing the prospects for the Democratic Party in the upcoming mid-term elections.

It is rare, but it can happen, that a politician ambushes themselves. It happened to me once in another interview with Thatcher. She was always the most assured performer, well prepared and immaculately turned out, ready for the battle ahead. On the eve of the 1987 general election, the BBC had arranged to interview Thatcher, and the leaders of the Labour Party and of the SDP–Liberal Alliance. All three interviews were to be shown on the *Nine O'Clock News*.

Earlier in the day I was sent to Westminster to do the Thatcher interview, focusing on the campaign and whether she thought she had been getting her message across successfully. I asked her whether she would have gained more support if she had shown some sympathy for the unemployed and underprivileged in society – this at a time when the pain of industrial decline in Britain was being widely felt. She replied by citing Britain's unemployment as being no worse than in most of the rest of Europe. I pursued the point, asking whether answering with statistics might make people think she accepted high unemployment, and suggesting that she never said she cared about people being out of work. There followed a long exchange about how a society was best cared for. She then said:

Margaret Thatcher: *If people just drool and drivel that they care I turn round and say, 'Right. I also look to see what you actually do.'*
Me: *Why do you use the words: 'drool and drivel that they care'? Is that what you think saying that you care about people's plight amounts to?*
Margaret Thatcher: *No I don't.* [pause] *I am sorry I used those words. But I think some people talk a great deal about caring, but the policies which they pursue – and I am sorry I used those words – the policies which they pursue do not amount to what they say.*

As my final question I asked her what lessons she had learnt during the campaign. Her answer: 'Perhaps you have taught me one – that it is not enough actually to do things that result in caring, you also have to talk about it.' It was a startling admission. Her political stance at the time was that the measures she had been taking to revive the economy were necessary and admitting to the pain it caused was an indulgence that would benefit no one. I rang the newsroom, told them what she had said, and asked them to use that section of the interview immediately, in the lunchtime and evening bulletins. It was certainly newsworthy. But the deal struck with the three main political parties was that these interviews would all be run together later in the evening and taking one section out of Thatcher's interview and running it separately would break the agreement. So the words 'drool and drivel' were not heard until too late to have any influence on the outcome of the election. Had they been broadcast earlier they would certainly have been seized on by her opponents with relish.

It was out of character for Thatcher to make a slip like this. Of all the politicians I have interviewed she was probably the most assiduous in preparing for these encounters, which she says in private letters she found 'rather an ordeal'. She understood the perils but was determined that her voice and her arguments should be heard: she was a conviction politician who believed she could convince. The approach extended beyond the interview itself. I remember one encounter at Number 10 for a *Panorama* interview that was to be broadcast live. It began with her complaining about the number of technicians and camera crew we had brought with us. She worked round the room counting them: 'one, two three …

thirteen.' I explained that this was because we could not allow a live broadcast with the Prime Minister to go off air because of a technical fault. We had therefore doubled up on people and equipment. 'We only do it for you and the Queen,' I said, hoping to mollify her. Not a bit. 'We had NBC here this morning and there were only two of them.'

During the interview she unexpectedly announced a full-scale review of the National Health Service, to the consternation of her political staff who were listening in the back of the room and who had heard nothing of the proposal. When she had left the room they asked my producer what she had actually said, puzzled by what it meant. It seems her impatience with the inefficiencies of the NHS had led her to announce a plan for reform without having discussed it in Cabinet or with her own staff. Maybe it was impetuous, her exasperation at the difficulty of getting things done being well known. Six months later her newly appointed Secretary of State for Health, Ken Clarke, was equally confused. Writing years later he said, 'the Prime Minister had firmly committed herself to a radical reform of the NHS in a television interview on *Panorama* ... without giving the slightest indication – and probably with no clear idea – of what these reforms might involve'.

Her bombshell duly dropped, Thatcher invited me up to her study after the interview for a glass of whisky and returned to the fray, jabbing at pages of statistics that compared hospital waiting times in Liverpool with those of other hospitals in the South. Sensing that if I took no action there might be no escape from this lecture I interrupted to ask if I could phone my wife to see how the interview had gone. 'Yes of course,' she said, adding cryptically, 'Aren't we both lucky to have one?'

In a perfect world a political interview would resemble a Socratic dialogue, the technique of eliciting truth by question and answer. The politician would set out his aims and then cooperate with the interviewer in exploring the three Cs: the confusions, complications and consequences of the policy. Socrates described this process as midwifery, a technique that gives birth to truth. In modern politics, politicians are not interested in helping to discover the truth: there is only victory or defeat. Ministers preparing to be interviewed are well aware of the complexities of the policies or decisions they are about to defend. They will have heard from their civil servants all the objections and will have been schooled by advisers on the pitfalls they must avoid and the points they must stress regardless of the questions they are asked. Resigned to these stubborn refusals to answer questions, Robin Day used to suggest the remedy might be to open an interview simply with the words, 'Minister, what is your answer to my first question?'

Nonetheless, the ambition of political interviewing when it began was high minded. Grace Wyndham Goldie, in charge of the BBC's news and current affairs, played a critical role in developing the technique. Wyndham Goldie believed in dialogue between politician and interviewer for the benefit of the viewer and she was never satisfied. After any interview she would conduct a post-mortem: Why didn't you ask this? Or follow up with that? She was remorseless in her determination to make political interviewing a serious part of the democratic process. This was long before parliament had let television cameras into its debates and committee hearings, allowing politics to be seen in the raw. At the time, newspaper articles, commentary and interviews were the only way in which political ideas reached the public. Wyndham Goldie saw television as an exciting way of engaging voters with the political process in all its murk. She would have been dismayed at what it has become.

Both sides must take some of the blame. Brevity may be the soul of wit but it is death to a political interview. The first answer to a question always needs a follow-up question springing from the answer, and the answer to that question a follow-up in turn. One of the difficult decisions an interviewer faces is when to leave one area of questioning and move on to the next. The pressure of time is their enemy and the interviewee's friend. The shorter the interview the less chance of the interviewee saying something they will regret. Short is sweet. And brevity seems to be what the broadcasters increasingly want as the attention span of audiences shrinks.

If brevity is the enemy of political interviewing, so is the sofa. David Frost's interviewing technique may have lulled politicians into saying what they did not mean to say, but the brief and breezy chat on the breakfast sofa plays into the politicians' hands.

It will never be an equal battle. Evasive answers are so often the politician's refuge both in parliament and outside. 'Why don't you get them to answer the question?' I am often asked. 'Because I don't have a gun,' is my woefully inadequate reply.

The BBC could do democracy a good service by restoring the long-form interview as a regular vehicle not just to politicians but to a wide range of people who influence our lives: scientists, thinkers, teachers. *Hard Talk* on the BBC World Service perfectly fits the bill but there is nothing similar on our domestic television screen, nothing to offer the drumbeat of regular thoughtful political talk and discussion, no Socratic process to help us through our difficult and disturbing times.

The fault lies mainly with politicians though. Television and radio are now served by a host of excellent political interviewers. Even those conducted on the sofa can be sharp and to the point. No one any longer seems nervous about going for the jugular. What is missing is the politicians.

Ministers' advisers do not ask themselves whether it is in the public interest for their minister to appear, but whether there is anything in it for them. The more senior they are, the less willing they seem to be to submit themselves to questioning. Junior ministers are regularly sent out instead of the big hitters to defend government policy and behaviour, expected to answer questions way above their pay grade, using all the techniques of obfuscation they have been taught by their parties' PR machines. Or no one appears at all and we have to put up with presenters forced to say, 'We asked the government for an interview but they said no one was available.'

There is nothing broadcasters can do to force a minister into a studio, and little they can do to shame them if they do not. The decision can be mocked by replacing the politician with, variously, a tub of lard (for Roy Hattersley) or a sculpture of ice, melting (for Boris Johnson). At the 2019 general election, Andrew Neil, faced with Johnson's refusal to be interviewed by him, said this, on air:

> *No broadcaster can compel a politician to be interviewed but leaders' interviews have been a key part of the BBC's prime-time election coverage for decades. We do them on your behalf to scrutinise and hold to account those who would govern us. That is democracy. We have always proceeded in good faith that the leaders would participate. And in every election they have. All of them. Until this one. We have been asking him for weeks now … It is not too late. We have an interview prepared, oven ready as Mr Johnson likes to say.*

What he went on to say probably explains Johnson's refusal.

> *The theme running through our questions is trust and why at so many times in his career in politics and journalism critics and sometimes even those close to him have deemed him to be untrustworthy.*

Or maybe it was, as his then adviser Dominic Cummings later said, because Johnson was a 'gaffe machine clueless about policy'. Whatever the reason, Johnson decided not to appear and did democracy a bad service, a habit that he has not abandoned. It is part of the business of democracy that those seeking and holding power are prepared to submit themselves to questioning, argue their case, meet objections to it, and let the public decide.

It is not good interviewers we lack, but politicians willing to be interviewed. Political debate no longer takes place just inside the House of Commons but in a host of places, every-where from news programmes to phone-ins to social media. By absenting themselves so often from these arenas, polit-icians are damaging our democracy. They have only them-selves to blame if they are increasingly held in something close to contempt.

5

Keep Talking

Q: How do you go so long without having a pee?

A: No idea. Probably adrenaline. Or maybe the studio lights are dehydrating.

Q: And what do you eat?

A: Difficult this. For my first election I checked what astronauts ate in space and survived on bananas. Then I tried chocolate. Robin Day put an end to that. Told to stop his interview and 'hand to David for important news', he did so. The camera caught me with my mouth full. 'Sorry,' I blurted out, 'I was just eating a Mars bar.' I thought this endorsement of the snack that helped you work, rest and play might mean a lifetime supply heading my way, but no such luck.

Q: How do you stay awake? I went to bed at two and you were still there when I woke up, looking bright as a button.

A: It is not that easy to fall asleep under floodlights, with a camera pointed at you, talking to a million people or more.

The English writer, H. G. Wells, called the election 'democracy's ceremonial, its feast, its great function'. The BBC, judging by the effort it puts into it – the lavishness of the studio sets, the hordes of producers and experts, the serried ranks of political researchers inputting results, the camera crews and reporters despatched to counts all over Britain, to say nothing of a gang of presenters and interviewers – thinks much the same. To be the master of ceremonies at this feast is the ultimate broadcasting thrill. Staying awake or resisting the urge to pee are the least of the problems.

I anchored ten British General Elections in all, from 1979 to 2017, covering dramatic changes in the balance of power. Impossible to forget Margaret Thatcher's trouncing Jim Callaghan in 1979. It heralded the greatest change in political policies and attitudes in my lifetime. Tony Blair's conquest in 1997, winning nearly a hundred and fifty seats from his opponents, marked another sea change, or as he put it a 'new dawn'. But both these election results were predictable and the predictable is the enemy of an exciting programme. It is the close-run contests that yield the best moments. Like the election of 2010.

On 6 May 2010 our coverage began as usual just before ten o'clock in the evening and ran with a brief break for eighteen hours until mid-afternoon the following day and for several days after that. The election-night exit poll had confirmed what opinion polls had been suggesting for some weeks: that no party would win a majority. What followed was exciting political theatre. Nick Clegg, leader of the Liberal Democrats, held the whip hand. Speculation ranged across a wide spectrum of possibilities, from a new government with Clegg in alliance with the Prime Minister, Gordon Brown, and Labour, to a coalition with the Tories under David Cameron. All weekend we followed the twists and turns of the story, the leaks about the talks that were taking place and the promises that were being made. It was not until five days after the election, by which time we had decamped from our glamorous election-night studio to College Green opposite the House of Commons, that pictures finally emerged of Gordon Brown quitting Downing Street and Cameron and Clegg embarking on their fateful coalition. Michael Heseltine was my guest in the studio as we watched Cameron and his wife going into Number 10 for the first time, the staff out on the street to greet them. 'Look,' said Heseltine, 'they have even got the chef out to welcome him.' 'No,' I said, 'that's Steve Hilton [Cameron's famously scruffy Director of Strategy], who's put on a clean shirt for the occasion.'

The election-night broadcast is perhaps best understood as an archaeological dig. You begin with a wasteland, the exit poll being the only clue to what you might discover as the night goes on. The first few results start to give shape to the political landscape waiting to be revealed. They may be from the safest of seats, but that doesn't matter. Just the shifts of support from the previous election – Tories up a bit, Labour down a bit, or vice versa, third parties taking crucial percentage points or not – provide the clues needed to predict the outcomes in other seats with some certainty. Slowly, count by count, the outline of the 650 constituencies emerges, until by the early hours of the morning, barring a close result, the new political landscape is exposed. This is the excitement of election night: watching the rise and fall of political parties and the human drama of success or failure played out in front of the cameras.

The way the results are announced – a charming anachronism in the age of instant electronic communication – adds to the sense of theatre. The candidates shuffle on stage in the town hall or school where the count has taken place, lining up like targets in a fairground shooting range. 'I, Joe Bloggs, the returning officer for the constituency of Castlebridge,' intones the mayor or whoever is appointed to the post, 'hereby give notice . . .' and what follows as the cameras alight on the candidates' faces and the number of their votes is read out, is the whole gamut of emotion, ranging from laughter as the Monster Raving Loony Party chalks up another hundred or so votes, to surprise where a minority party wins more than expected – this followed by loud cheers from their party workers – to the serious business of the announcement, the name of the actual winner. Impossible to forget the look on the face of the victor in Enfield Southgate in the 1997 election. After three o'clock in the morning, just as we were preparing to close our transmission, the returning officer declared the result. Stephen Twigg, an unknown, had defeated

Michael Portillo, the Secretary of State for Defence, and a man once tipped to be the next Tory leader. Portillo's previous majority had been over fifteen thousand in what seemed to be the safest of safe Tory seats, but the victory that was sweeping Blair to power had swept him away. Twigg's raised eyebrows and twinkling smile, Portillo's sombre face, told the story of the moment and encapsulated the scale of Blair's victory. 'Were you still up for Portillo?' people asked each other the next day and the phrase became shorthand for the Tories' defeat after thirteen years in office. Politics is a cruel business and never more so than on election night.

A good ceremony needs a grand setting. My first general election in 1979 was a relatively austere production. The set was meant to look futuristic but on the screen came across as dull: a beige background and graphic displays that look primitive compared to what came later. When the computers crashed, my producer resorted to passing me notes on the end of a stick. But over the years the BBC realised that election night was big box office. As technology developed, information was displayed in ever more sophisticated ways. It had begun with the simple magic of the swingometer, a pendulum that showed the effect on the two main parties of voters changing their allegiance. The first swingometer was a wooden arrow hanging on a board with one side of the board painted red for Labour, the other blue for the Tories. As the arrow was moved left or right it showed the number of seats that would change hands as voters changed their vote.

I liked the simplicity of the wooden arrow but as soon as technology allowed it gave way to a virtual swingometer with coloured lights that flickered blue or red. That in turn, with the invention of virtual reality, led to even more vivid ways of illustrating the results and keeping viewers amused. We entered the era of a simulated House of Commons with victorious MPs taking their place on one side or the other and Jeremy Vine apparently walking on the floor of the House, illustrating the effect of the election on the makeup of the new parliament; or seeming to walk along Downing Street, its paving stones revealing who would go through the door of Number 10. There were London buses and crumbling cliffs, and once, for reasons that I think escaped even him, Jeremy Vine dressed as a cowboy and speaking in an American accent. We risked being carried away by the brilliance of our technology. Some of the visual displays were of great complexity, and to my layman's eye did not seem to make sense. During rehearsals I would try to see them from the viewers' perspective, and badger the production teams to make them clearer or simpler. By 2015 we were calling on a host of different ways of explaining the story. Emily Maitlis, stood in front of a huge screen that showed every constituency and allowed her to give a thumbnail sketch of each; Sophie Raworth, stood outside Broadcasting House with a vast map of Britain projected on the pavement; and Jeremy Vine now had politicians as breathing avatars at his beck and call. 'On election night,' one paper said, 'you can't beat the BBC.' That was the endorsement we strove for.

Election studios were magical spaces to work in. The glamour of a lavish set inspired everyone: presenters, producers, researchers, inputters, the whole team, and I hope the viewer too. The effect of a good design is to say, 'This is important. It's exciting. And it's fun.'

To anyone using Twitter or other platforms, information, gossip and comment are now instantly available, often upstaging the results programme, which, a stickler for accuracy, waits until news is confirmed before it is broadcast. It is a far cry from earlier days when we would ask viewers who had questions to email or even, in 1979, send them in advance on a postcard. The BBC itself, quick to adapt to new media, now offers results in many different formats, but I suspect nothing will beat the verve and energy of a live studio transmission.

The job, then, is to present the results as fast and as accurately as possible and to explain what the political consequences are likely to be. To reveal the new political landscape. To take the threads and from them weave a political story.

The studio is full of experts, far more expert than me, expert in analysing the significance of particular results or trends in voting. They are the maestros who feed presenters with the facts and figures they need to tell the story. Every presenter has a producer helping to analyse this information, making sure what reaches the TV screen is accurate, and each presenter has their own special role: conducting political interviews, showing how the parties are doing and what their targets are, or analysing the constituency results one by one, pointing out the significance of what they show. The anchor's job is quite different. It is to keep a narrative flow, shaping the story so that all the elements come together coherently, and, of course, keeping the show on the road when things go wrong, which they almost always do.

The first highlight of election night is the exit poll. This is a complicated calculation based on polling thousands of voters on election day between 7 a.m. and 10 p.m. at a number of carefully selected polling stations – the same ones every time. Changes in voting patterns at these stations from one election to the next can, in theory, reveal what the country as a whole has decided. The pollsters are wary of explaining exactly how they do this and, naturally, refuse to disclose which polling stations they use for fear it would distort their findings. The psephologists working on the data do so in secret. If their findings became public prematurely it would not only be an offence against electoral law, it would allow anyone in the know to make a killing with the bookmakers.

Voting closes at 10 p.m. Only then, as Big Ben strikes, can we publish the results of our exit poll. The words appear across the screen and, in a moment of high drama, we tell the nation that this or that government will be back, or that they can expect a hung parliament, or that it is too close to call. For the broadcaster, 'too close to call' is the most exciting outcome. It means that every early result is important, revealing how one part of the country has voted and allowing the psephologists to predict from that what is likely to have happened elsewhere: the archaeological equivalent of discovering the first trace of the city wall.

I'm not a great fan of exit polls. The thrill of our electoral process is that we do know actual results only a few hours after the polls have closed. Other systems are different. Every four years we would traipse to Washington for the US elections and mount an entire evening's programme from there, with studio guests and graphics and gadgetry that only Peter Snow could understand, and psephologists and reporters scattered about America, usually to report on nothing much happening. Because in American elections nothing much does happen. It is not the States who declare the results, but the television networks, each with its own way of assessing, State by State, the way the day has gone not just for the presidential candidates but for the Senate and Congressional seats as well. The competition is between the networks to call the results first, using whatever model of analysing votes cast they have devised. The full and final tally of votes often comes many days later. On election night the excitement is limited to 'ABC calls Ohio for X or Y', 'CNN has just called Georgia for Z'. It makes American election programmes dull affairs compared with ours. No returning officers, no candidates biting their lip waiting for votes to be tallied at the count or making great speeches in victory or defeat. All we could show was people in the headquarters of one party or another, cheering to order. But they were still fun to cover. All elections are fun to me, like horse racing is fun if you like horse racing, or football matches if you like football, neither of which I do. But show me an election and my eyes light up. I even enjoyed presenting BBC coverage of an Australian election night, the dullest I have ever covered. Worse even than America. Nothing seemed to happen. We broadcast results posted on a screen in election headquarters in Canberra. No candidates appeared. No party headquarters. No voters. Just state by state voting numbers under a proportional representation scheme so complex that I gave up trying to understand it.

The glory of a British election is that 650 constituencies have to give their result individually and do so within a few hours of the polls closing. So what is the point of exit polls? As they become more accurate they drain the drama from the night, like revealing the denouement of what should be a play in five acts. I see no point in spending money predicting what is going to happen in a few hours' time rather than waiting for it to happen. The exit poll adds nothing and spoils the fun. If it is accurate and is confirmed by the actual results it makes the reality a dull affair, simply confirmation of what has been predicted. How uninspiring to hear a presenter say, 'the results so far confirm the findings of our exit poll'. Who cares? Why rob the real results of their impact? Why not wait for the truth, rather than guess at it? My editors think this is a curmudgeonly view and ask, quite sensibly, how would we fill the two hours between 10 p.m. and midnight if we did not have the exit poll to talk about? Fair point. Anyway, it is too late now to wish them away.

Pollsters are of course addicted to polling. Their day job is assessing public taste for consumer goods or the effectiveness of slogans that sell them. Polling politics, when it is accurate, enhances their public reputation. Psephologists are addicted to polling too. Without it they would lose their toolkit for analysing the rise and fall of politicians and their parties. Voters sensibly take most of this with a pinch of salt. Who really cares about who is a few points up or down in the polls? We know that opinions change all the time and it is only on election day, with real voters voting, that we know the truth.

I always enjoy it when exit polls go wrong. In the election of 1987 they went spectacularly wrong. I opened the programme announcing with a confident flourish the surprising news that according to our poll Margaret Thatcher, up against Neil Kinnock for Labour, might lose her majority. This prediction was based on polling done by Gallup on the eve and on the day of the general election. As the actual results started to come in it became clear that the forecast was about as wrong as it could be. Not only was Thatcher in no danger of losing control of parliament, she did not even come close to it. She ended the night with a majority of well over a hundred seats, and a ten percentage point lead over Labour in votes cast, a feat incidentally not achieved again by the Conservative Party for over thirty years, when Boris Johnson trounced Jeremy Corbyn.

Faced with this debacle, the BBC of course went into a tailspin. Solemn inquests were held. How could we have got it so wrong? A new way of assessing the vote for election night must be found. Margaret Thatcher's reaction to our error was predictable though irrational. She put it about that the poll demonstrated the BBC's prejudice against the Conservatives. It was an odd argument. What point could there be in deliberately predicting a Conservative setback knowing that within a few hours the truth would be out? But such was her distrust of the BBC that she and her allies would seize upon any weapon that came to hand.

The attack on the BBC so discomfited the pollsters that they overcompensated, with disastrous results. The occasion was an important by-election in Eastbourne in October 1990. Margaret Thatcher's close adviser Ian Gow, the Conservative MP for Eastbourne, had been killed by an IRA bomb planted under his car. These days by-elections caused by the murder of a sitting MP go uncontested by the main political parties, out of respect for the dead and in order not to give succour to the murderer. Not so in 1990. Eight candidates decided to fight the Eastbourne seat, Labour and the Liberal Democrats among them. In those days the BBC still took by-elections seriously. We would regularly broadcast a late-night by-election special, with political guests arguing until the early hours, when the returning officer finally came to the podium, cleared their throat and began to intone the time-honoured incantation.

Back then we still commissioned exit polls for by-elections too. In Eastbourne in 1990 it was expected that because the cause of the election was a cold-blooded murder by the IRA that was an insult to our democracy, the voters would feel honour-bound to return another Conservative. At about 9.30, the exit poll results were analysed. They revealed, shock horror, that the Conservative candidate appeared to have been defeated by the Liberal Democrat with a thumping majority of around five thousand. 'The poll must be wrong,' said our resident psephologist. 'We can't possibly say that.' Much argument followed. I mildly suggested there was no point in doing an exit poll unless you were going to use its findings. A few minutes before we were due to go on air the script was finally agreed. I said, 'Eastbourne may be about to spring a big surprise on us this evening.' Then I went to our pollster, who said, 'it really is too close to call'. Several hours later the returning officer stood up and announced that the Liberal Democrat candidate had been returned with a majority of 4,550 votes, almost exactly what the exit poll had predicted. Slightly embarrassed, our psephologist explained that the exit poll had been adjusted to take account of voters who had refused to tell the exit pollster how they had voted. For some reason, it had been assumed that these refuseniks were mainly Conservatives. The truth was, they did not believe the poll predicting a thumping majority for the Liberal Democrats, and did not dare risk further straining relations with the government if they had got it wrong.

Two years later came the 1992 general election. By now John Major had taken over the Tory leadership from Thatcher (defenestrated by her party just a few weeks after the shock of Eastbourne). I remember this election night well. The set was spectacular. The desk from which I presented was on a raised circular platform above the studio floor, reached by a set of stairs. Set designers use stairs to add a touch of glamour – a visual reference to the Café de Paris or Fred Astaire and Ginger Rogers. They may look good but they are a hazard. Going up them looks dull, which is why on *Strictly* the exhausted couples are forced to run up the flight of stairs after their dance, as though fresh as daisies. But coming down is worse, the risk of a trip and headlong fall outweighing any possible dramatic impact.

We announce the result of the exit poll, not as Big Ben is chiming, but after the chimes, on the first strike of the hour. That evening, as I climbed the steps to my podium and the chimes that led up to that first bong resounded in the studio, I still did not know what the experts had decided we could say. When I did speak it was to give yet another spectacularly wrong prediction: I said it would be a hung parliament at best for the ruling Conservatives with John Major forced to seek support from other parties to stay in power; I added that it was possible that Labour would be the largest party and Neil Kinnock could become Prime Minister. As the results started coming in it became clear that this prediction was wrong. John Major won, albeit with a significantly reduced majority of twenty-one. The pollsters once again had egg on their face. And the BBC of course had egg on its face.

By 2005 we had abandoned the claim to have our own BBC exit poll, in favour of a poll commissioned jointly by the BBC and ITN. Safety in numbers. If there was to be egg at least it would be on their faces too. Exit polls continued to keep us on our toes though. In 2010 – the knife-edge election that resulted in the Conservative–Liberal Democrat coalition government – the exit poll was almost perfect, but it was treated with scepticism in the studio. In 2015, when everyone including the Prime Minister, David Cameron, was expecting another hung parliament and another coalition government, the exit poll turned out to be more accurate than the opinion polls leading up to the election, though it still failed to predict a Conservative majority. It was this narrow victory that forced Cameron, unrestrained by a coalition with the Liberal Democrats, to call the referendum he had promised on Britain's membership of the EU. We were still nervous about putting too much trust in our exit polling. In 2017 – the election Theresa May had called to give herself a mandate to push through her Brexit deal – the exit poll knocked us all sideways by predicting that while the Conservatives would emerge as the largest party, Theresa May would lose her overall majority. 'We're going to be hung, drawn and quartered if we've got this wrong,' I said as I announced the poll. But this time we had it right.

Even so we nearly came to disaster with that poll but for a different reason. We had become paranoid about the exit poll leaking before the witching hour of ten o'clock. We were afraid that with social media now able to spread news worldwide within seconds, any leak would become known immediately. Quick-witted gamblers could have placed their bets, and we would have broken the law. We decided that the most severe restrictions must be imposed. I was ushered into a room with the then Director General of the BBC, Lord Hall; the editor of the programme, Sam Woodhouse; and Jeremy Vine. The door was locked behind us. Down the phone line from the secret exit poll headquarters came the voice of John Curtice, the leading psephologist who had been heading up the work on the poll. He told us the prediction. We talked about how to present it in simple but accurate terms and, once the wording was decided, with 10 p.m. fast approaching, went to open the door to return to the studio. It was stuck. We banged furiously. At last a security guard heard us and let us out just in time to catch the ten o'clock chimes. Fortunately this was not the real thing but our last rehearsal. When election day itself came we threw caution to the wind. Balancing the risk of being overheard in our private room against going on air not only with no exit poll but with no presenter either, we left the door unlocked.

Once the exit poll has been announced on the first stroke of Big Ben at ten o'clock there are two hours of television to fill before the first results come in. Keep talking is the mantra while everyone waits to see whether the exit poll has told the truth. Keep talking first to politicians from the main parties, who come to sit at the table and invariably say: 'Let's wait until we see what has happened.' Not helpful. If the exit poll is looking particularly encouraging, perhaps they might venture, 'It's looking good, but let's wait and see.' If it is particularly dire, 'The exit poll may be wrong. Let's wait and see.'

Time to take the temperature around the country. On a huge screen of monitors in the studio, reporters in the field are expected to answer inane questions. 'What's the mood in Cheltenham?' (or wherever). And the reporter replies, as cautious as the politicians, 'The Conservatives' (or whoever) 'are looking cheerful.' Or 'optimistic'. Or if the news is bad, perhaps 'tight-lipped'.

Then there is the sideshow of who will be first to declare. In an attempt to keep up the excitement there is the ritual battle to be the first of the 650 constituencies to deliver a result, a race that consists of footage of people running into the counting station with sealed boxes, the boxes being opened, the ballot papers being tipped onto tables, and the counters opening the ballot sheets and placing them in long lines, party by party. Two constituencies take the race very seriously. Sunderland and Newcastle Central organise practice runs from polling stations to the count in the days before the election. The winner needs to be a densely populated constituency with the polling stations all near the count so that the ballot boxes reach their destination within minutes of the polls closing.

There are other rituals. Senior correspondents, used to reporting from distant battlefields, will happily do a turn on election night, standing outside the house where a party leader is incarcerated with their team of advisers, describing how 'they arrived here an hour ago and are not expected to make a statement or give an interview until the outcome is clear'. Keep talking. I press the switch on my desk to speak directly to my editor. 'Where shall we go now?' 'We can go to party headquarters and see what the mood is there.' Reporter:

'They are looking glum here' or 'The mood here is optimistic, but it is, they are saying, too early to break out the champagne.' And so on and so on. Just keep talking, until that first result comes in, and is analysed by the brilliant psephologists, and the first glimmer of reality breaks through. 'If the swing in Sunderland is repeated throughout the country it looks as though . . .' Blessed relief. We are on our way.

The next three hours are the opposite of the first three. Now it is result after result to be analysed, the national trend illustrated in all the different ways that have been devised, the simulated House of Commons, the door to Number 10, a map of the country colouring up red, blue or yellow, interviews with surprised victors at their counts or famous politicians in the studio. Not so much 'keep talking' now but the opposite injunction: 'Wrap them up, we have to go to Heseltine who's been waiting ten minutes to get on air. He will go to ITV if we don't come to him now.' Helter-skelter all the way to four in the morning, or if it is a close-run thing, to four the next afternoon, with a couple of hours' kip as dawn breaks.

Anchoring a programme like this is an adrenaline-filled ride: marshalling all the information, all the detail, the bank of monitors, the interviews, the reporters in the field, but never losing the thread of the story being told: why and how the winner has won and what it says about the country and the voters, the people who matter.

The key is to have something pertinent to say at any moment, to fill gaps, to cover up mistakes or glitches, and to make the viewer feel at ease with what is being shown and able to follow the story. I learnt in the first general election I presented that it takes hard work and hours of preparation. During the rehearsals for that election in 1979 my editor took me to one side and said he was worried that I did not seem to know enough about each constituency and its candidates, and it showed on screen. Chastened, I realised more homework was needed. In those days we did not have the benefit of computer screens to show each constituency at a glance. Everything was on paper. That night and for two days that followed I immersed myself in a huge folder listing constituency after constituency in alphabetical order. Each constituency might matter in an election broadcast. Safe seats are as important as marginal seats because even a safe seat can reveal a national trend. The so-called early declarers, the results that come in first, are particularly important for the trends they reveal. I asked my producer and researcher to take turns in testing me. They would name a constituency and I would give a thumbnail sketch. Perhaps it had a prominent politician contesting it. Maybe there had been a particularly vicious local campaign. Or maybe it was one of the earlier declarers, to be milked for anything they might reveal about the national result we might expect. A little colour about the place helps too: its industries – famous for boots and shoes, or cheese, or once a coal-mining town – or a famous cathedral or castle or Civil War battlefield. Anything to fill the time while the returning officer shuffles their papers before giving the result. These details bring the programme alive and can make the presenter seem omniscient. I was far from that but with a good short-term memory and my card index I came through that 1979 election unscathed.

The arrival of fully automated computer graphics and screens made the job of presenting much easier. I only had to mention a constituency and all the details would appear on a screen in front of me – not just its electoral history but the names of the candidates, the local issues that might affect the outcome and one or two interesting facts or anecdotes to use while we waited for the result to be announced. It also helped that from the moment I started chairing *Question Time* in 1994 I was visiting many of these places, meeting the people who lived there and hearing first-hand about their problems and the issues that affected them. *Question Time* and election night complemented each other.

Crucial to the success of the programme is my own production team, people far better versed in politics than me, who could talk into my earpiece if I was lost. On my desk a series of switches let me talk privately to the control gallery where the editor and director sat or to my backup team, and let them talk to me. So a click on a switch and a panicked 'Why are we going to Dudley North?' from me would get a swift 'Because it's a Labour marginal' and without missing a beat and confidently adopting the voice of authority I could say 'Now we are going to Dudley North, a key Labour marginal. If they hold this it's further evidence they might win tonight.' During the rehearsals we would practise these routines. Alongside the switches, built into the desk in front of me would be the serried ranks of computer screens and television monitors, like the *Starship Enterprise*. They provided all the information I needed: the results in so far, the national swing and change in the vote, the result from each constituency as it came in, and the national tallies of seats won and lost. Other screens would show the scenes at the various places we had presenters and camera teams: a particular count where we were watching for the returning officer coming to the stage, or the door of the house from which a party leader might emerge. Mrs Thatcher for instance, arriving at her count at Finchley – or as I inadvertently put it, 'Mrs Finchley arriving at her count.' There would be helicopter shots on offer, shots of Downing Street, shots from inside or outside party headquarters. It felt like being master of the universe, though the real masters were the director and producer upstairs in the gallery, with an array of BBC bigwigs behind them, choosing which pictures to go to, which counts were most important, who should be interviewed. They kept an open microphone to me so that throughout the evening I had their voices in my ear asking me to lead to this or that scene, or this or that presenter. 'Peter Snow' – or in later years, Jeremy Vine – 'is ready with the state of play. Lead to him when you can.' Or, 'We are trying to get Mandelson for an interview in a moment, just keep talking.' Keep talking. Keep talking, the essential glue that held the programme together. As anchor I too had my own view of what we should be doing and brief exchanges, mostly unheard by the viewer, would take place between me and the gallery, usually me saying, 'Aren't we doing too much of this or that?' (maybe showing pictures of a front door with no one coming out of it) or 'Can't you get pictures from the pub, they seem very jolly?' and – actually said on air – 'Please, not more helicopter shots of the Mall.' It was probably irritating to them sometimes, but the partnership between the anchor and the production gallery was at the heart of the programme. They shaped the programme and trusted me to keep talking, ideally not spouting nonsense but explaining what was happening, what was significant, and what to watch for next.

Interviews with politicians are a crucial element in the programme. The campaigning is over, election night is underway, the politicians are free, suspended in time for a moment, to speak without their usual constraint about the campaign itself, why things are unfolding as they are, and what the future holds. A few could be grumpy and tetchy, especially if they were left waiting at their count to go on air. At one election I could see on one of my monitors an increasingly irritated Alex Salmond waiting his turn to be interviewed. A voice in my ear said, 'We have to go to Salmond now or he will walk.' As leader of the Scottish National Party at the time he obviously thought his status qualified him for special treatment. 'Next time,' he said, 'I will not give you priority. In fact I will do everybody else first and the BBC last.' Less pompous politicians were more amenable, however exalted their rank. Michael Heseltine or Paddy Ashdown or Robin Cook would happily come in and talk about the results, however gloomy the outcome looked for them. In 2015 Paddy Ashdown said he would eat his hat if the exit poll was right and the Liberal Democrats were in for the bad result it predicted; and Alastair Campbell then said he would eat his kilt if the SNP did as well as the exit poll was predicting. The following day they were both on our panel at *Question Time* and we had a chocolate cake baked into the shape of a hat, and another in the shape of a kilt, which they gamely ate on air.

Some of the interviews would be done by reporters on location, some by our studio interviewers, Robin Day, Jeremy

Paxman or Andrew Neil. Some would be done by me. I insisted on this. Without the chance to question politicians myself my performance would be vanilla, no more than a link man. I needed to be embedded in the events of the night. It was easier said than done. Day and Paxman and Neil would sit back, watch the coverage and work out what mischief they could make with their guests. I meanwhile was running full tilt with the flow of results, the linking of different scenes and counts, the reactions from party headquarters or from voters in clubs or pubs, or once, chaotically, on a boat moored on the Thames. Plunging straight into a political interview from dealing with all these pressures was not easy. I devised another system. I had an indexed chart with the names of all my likely interviewees, their political biographies, and a few questions to ask – one set if things were going well for them, one if badly. In the general chaos I would occasionally forget who I was about to interview even as their face appeared on the screen before me. Panic. Push down the switch to my producer sitting out of sight behind me: 'Who is this? Why am I talking to them?' and in a split second I would get the prompt I needed. I hope it looked effortless onscreen. In reality, as the broadcasting cliché has it, I was a swan sailing along seemingly serene but underwater furiously paddling.

There is an ambivalence about the way we treat our politicians. It is always said that in their constituencies MPs are treated with respect. They try to sort out the complex problems so many people face with everything from issues with social security payments or their landlords, to objections to new housing estates or town centre planning. They spend their weekends at fetes or bring-and-buy sales for local charities, at fundraising events of all kinds. And it's expensive. The amount of cash a prospective parliamentary candidate has to find each week to avoid being seen as a cheapskate by the local electorate actively deters people from going into politics. They cannot afford it. Yet put these paragons of virtue, these pillars of their community, in the House of Commons and they become the subject of almost universal derision and contempt. The sight of the House of Commons at Prime Minister's Questions does nothing to discourage those who say, at election time, 'Don't vote, it only encourages them' or 'Bloody politicians, they are all the same.'

Having seen them at close quarters for many years, including in those moments of great triumph or despair, they don't all seem the same to me, although most of them, at the start of their careers, have one characteristic in common: the belief that by going into parliament they can make the world a better place together with a sneaking feeling that they just might, just might, be Prime Minister one day. In most other respects, 650 MPs, to say nothing of several thousand wannabe MPs, have their own motives for paying their cash deposit and asking the voters to choose them. There is no contradiction in their minds between working to serve the public good – to make the world a better place – and being ambitious for power and influence. One cannot be achieved without the other, which is why politicians are obsessed with political gossip: who is up and who is down, who to make a friend and who to avoid, the power struggle within parties being much fiercer than the battle between parties. Only if you come out top in your party can you effectively defeat your enemies on the opposition benches.

If election nights are almost always exciting the three-week campaigns that go before them can seem interminable and boring. No one believes campaigns change minds. Most voters have decided where their loyalties lie long before they put their cross on their ballot paper. But for the three weeks running up to polling day the broadcasters operate under strict Electoral Commission rules designed to provide balance, supported by stopwatch evidence that fair time has been given to each party. The parties for their part have to try to offer something each day for the television networks to show. Hence Margaret Thatcher improbably cuddling a calf, or Tony Blair offering an embarrassed Gordon Brown an ice cream cone. And hence Boris Johnson driving HGVs in a high-vis jacket rather than sitting down to an interview with Andrew Neil. Whatever absurd photo opportunities the party leaders offer, the television networks are bound to show, while the viewers are bound to despair. In the meantime, the candidates in their constituencies are wasting their time knocking on doors and palming off on whoever answers the door, which many sensibly refuse to do, their party propaganda leaflets. There is, the political pundits will tell you, no evidence that this canvassing activity has any effect on the outcome of the election, but it does give the hopefuls something to do as they while away the time to polling day.

One relatively recent campaigning innovation, imported from the United States, is the so-called head-to-head debate between party leaders. It has not been a great success. I chaired one of the first of them, between David Cameron, Gordon Brown and Nick Clegg, in 2010 at Birmingham University. It was the series of debates that became known for the phrase 'I agree with Nick'. The rules for these debates were absurdly tight. There were seventy-six different rules covering everything from the selection of the questions to the role of the audience to when the three participants should shake hands.

The questions were submitted by the audience and chosen by the producers, the three leaders of course not knowing in advance what they would be asked. Selected members of the audience duly put their questions, but apart from this the audience had to observe Trappist rules – they were allowed no follow-up question when the answers were evasive, nor were they even allowed to applaud points they liked or boo those they did not. As Chairman or moderator I was also under strict constraint. No follow-up questions, only questions if they were needed to clarify what one of the three had said. The teams for each party leader had an open line to the programme's editor. At my first intervention to 'clarify' a point, a voice in my ear said, 'They have complained about what you just asked.'

Debates between candidates developed until there were absurd programmes where seven different party leaders appeared, each behind their little pulpit. Needless to say, no light was thrown on their characters or their policies. There are two forums that do help to elucidate policy and test the mettle of the candidates: the straightforward long-form interview, of the kind I did with Tony Blair in 1997 and Andrew Neil did for the BBC at the 2019 election, and an appearance before a no-holds-barred *Question Time*-style audience. The one-on-one interview is so effective that Boris Johnson refused to appear with Neil in 2019 when he was Conservative

Party leader, aware that the lies that are his stock in trade would be exposed. *Question Time* audiences make their own powerful impact. There is no trotting out pre-prepared lines in a calm studio, and no complacent brushing off of difficult questions with the irritating suggestion that 'That is not what the public is interested in.' The public is right there, and it will be the judge of what interests it. David Cameron, Nick Clegg and Ed Miliband appeared one after the other before an audience in Leeds during the 2015 election campaign. It was remembered wrongly for Miliband tripping as he walked off the set, a trivial issue magnified by the press to try to suggest incompetence. In reality it was a powerful hour and a half of television in which both candidates were roasted by the Yorkshire audience, always to be relied on for blunt speaking. Cameron, politely disagreeing with an audience member, was told, 'Well you're wrong.' Miliband was asked, to applause and cheering, 'If that's the way your party wants to treat the economy, how can we trust you?' and was told, 'That is absolutely ludicrous. You're frankly just lying.' To Clegg, 'I'm just wondering if you've got plans for a new job after next week when you become unemployed and your party becomes an irrelevance.' 'Charming!' he replied. 'No, I don't.'

Election nights are a celebration of our democracy. But they also expose its flaws. One of the weaknesses of our First Past the Post system is that many voters put their cross on the ballot paper with no hope of their choice ever being victorious. In dead safe Labour or Conservative seats, votes against the dominant party are cast in vain; and supporters of smaller parties have scant chance of ever being represented at

Westminster. The Green Party, for example, had over a quarter of a million votes cast for its candidates in the 2010 election, but only one MP returned to parliament, Caroline Lucas. Fast-forward to 2019. The Green Party's votes had tripled to over 850,000, nearly 3 per cent of all votes cast in that election, but still it was only Caroline Lucas returned for the Green Party to the House of Commons. The Greens' share of the national vote, at 2.7 per cent, would have given them seventeen seats if every vote counted equally. To argue that this is unfair is heresy to believers in the present system, whereby each MP holds their seat by virtue of winning a majority in their constituency. But the system disenfranchises many voters. It would self-evidently be fairer to have a system that more accurately represented the views of all voters. It would mean coalition governments and opponents of proportional representation think coalition makes for bad government. I am not so sure. They point to the 2010–15 coalition of Conservatives and Liberal Democrats under David Cameron and Nick Clegg as a demonstration of the weakness of coalitions. It certainly involved some compromises. Liberal Democrats themselves were angry when their leader, Nick Clegg, dropped his flagship policy of free tuition fees for university students. He was never forgiven. But compromise is, I would argue, the essence not only of coalition government but of good government in general, and of a healthy democracy.

There was a half-hearted attempt under the Cameron–Clegg administration to introduce a very modest form of proportional representation. A referendum was held in 2011. Few voters understood the Alternative Vote system that was being proposed, few voted, and the proposal was rejected by almost 68 per cent of those who did.

Proportional representation certainly makes for duller election nights. We would miss out on the nail-biting cliff-hangers, the precipitous rise and fall of one party or another. But that would be a small price to pay for allowing all voters to believe that their vote counts. And do coalitions really produce worse governance? Is Germany less well governed than Britain? I don't think so.

There is, however, one aspect of a general election that we would be denied by proportional representation and the convoluted negotiations to form a new government. That is the ceremony's final act. Unlike the visit of the newly elected Prime Minister to kiss hands with the Sovereign in Buckingham Palace it takes place in public. It is sometimes glimpsed on television, but not given the wall-to-wall coverage of the glitzy State Opening of Parliament. Yet it is at the heart of our parliamentary democracy. You have to be up early, the morning after the election, to catch it. A removal van manoeuvres gingerly into Downing Street and men in brown coats go inside Numbers 10 and 11, emerging carrying suitcases, boxes, odd pieces of furniture and other personal possessions as the old incumbent makes way for the new. It is a curiously intimate, even intrusive moment, this changeover of power, but in a strange way deeply affecting. A sign that our democracy is at least in this one respect alive and well. We know how to kick them out.

6

Stay Silent

There are many ways of commentating on state occasions. Some commentators gush with enthusiasm. Others try to prompt the viewer into an 'appropriate' reaction, telling them that a particular moment is poignant or moving. I try a different approach. I imagine myself sitting on the sofa beside the viewer, as though we are watching the event together, only speaking when there is something that needs explaining, and trying to curb my instinct to keep talking. On election nights my job is to keep talking. The secret to good commentary is knowing when to keep silent, and letting the event speak for itself. It's the silence not the words that count.

As I write, I have on my desk a book of 183 pages, bound in red Morocco leather and embossed in gold with a Royal Coat of Arms and the title *Coronation of Her Majesty Queen Elizabeth II*. Underneath, the subtitle reads *The Form and Order of Service and the Music Sung in the Abbey Church of St Peter Westminster*. Coronation Day. 2 June 1953. I remember the day well. My mother, my father and I (aged fourteen) had spent the night on our Dutch sailing barge, moored on the Thames just above Westminster Bridge. My father liked idiosyncratic arrivals and departures. For a royal tour he would have his Rolls Royce shipped abroad so that he could travel in style. For the Coronation he had persuaded himself that no hotel rooms would be available in London, at least not near Westminster Abbey where he would have days of rehearsal. Naturally the solution was to have *Vabel* brought round from Itchenor in Chichester Harbour to be moored in solitary splendour in the middle of the river opposite the Houses of Parliament. At four o'clock on Coronation morning, in the cramped cabin, he was changing into morning dress: striped trousers, tailcoat and top hat. At half past four, in the early light, a police launch came alongside to take us to Westminster Pier. We disembarked and went on foot down the empty roads to the abbey. On the pavements to each side thousands of people had camped out all night, some even for two or three days, to catch a glimpse of the Queen. Instead, at five in the morning, they caught a glimpse of my father and a cheer went up. He raised his top hat to acknowledge it and bowed in mock solemnity. My mother and I left him armed with his Order of Service at the abbey. We walked on to Regent Street where we had seats on the first floor of a shop to watch the programme on black-and-white television and to see the two-mile-long procession that followed the service with our own eyes.

The broadcast of the Coronation was spectacular. Thousands of families had bought their first television sets to watch it at home. Others watched with neighbours, or in village halls and pubs across Britain. It is said over half the country was watching. It was the most important broadcast my father had done since the end of the Second World War. Those reports had dwelt on the barbarity of war, bombs falling on Germany and the horrors of Belsen. Now he was having to describe the symbols of peace and stability, a coronation heralded as the dawn of a new Elizabethan era for Britain. The events could not have been more different, but the professional skill it called for – the power of vivid description – was the same.

The Coronation Service itself, planned by a committee chaired by the Duke of Edinburgh, was full of symbolism referring back to Britain's past. The Queen's throne was set high on a dais, recalling, as my father noted in his commentary, the time when the early kings sat on a mound of earth to be crowned and were then raised up on the shoulders of the nobles 'so that the people might see them'. Homage was paid in descending order by Dukes, Marquesses, Earls, Viscounts and Barons. A sword, in a custom that my father described as going back six hundred years, was received by Lord Salisbury in return for one hundred silver shillings presented to the

Dean of Westminster in a golden bowl. The Queen's Robe, he said, 'may well be descended from the imperial cloaks of the Byzantine Emperors'. These details of ceremonial, revived for the twentieth century, seem arcane. But my father relished them: he believed in the importance of tradition as a construct-ive and unifying force. His commentary was typed out and pasted inside the book, episode by episode, with reminders to himself in the margins about the important pacing of his words: *Talk slowly. Start smartly. Wait on actions and Wait until Canopy well on way.* (The canopy was the cloth of gold held over the Queen's head for the anointing, to conceal this sacred moment from public gaze.) The language he used was simple with occasional archaic forms of words to match the ceremonial. 'The ring *wherein* is set a sapphire' and, memora-bly, 'The moment of the Queen's crowning *is* [not has] come.' At the moment of the crowning he put down his microphone and, wanting to record what he could see for posterity, picked up his cine camera and filmed the event. A blurred shot from high up in the gallery of the abbey, above the nave, shows no Queen, no crown, only the blazing lights of the chandeliers that blocked his view. It was a pity he could not record it because he had orchestrated this part of the Coronation himself. Noticing in rehearsals that the Archbishop of Canterbury was placing the crown on the Queen's head rather abruptly, not milking the moment for its significance, he had persuaded him to raise it above her head and then, like a soldier practising arms drill, count 'two, three' before lowering it. The Archbishop, to my father's delight, obeyed. A minor episode, which could now become another part of Coronation ritual. 'The crown is raised,' future commentators can say, 'and by tradition, a pause, for television viewers across the land, before it is lowered to the Sovereign's Head.'

Television has shaped our image of the monarchy. The BBC has not simply observed events. It has not simply commentated. Rather, it has been used to enhance the monarchy, glorying in the theatre of ceremonial and even helping to create it. In return, the monarchy has provided the BBC and its viewers with a steady stream of news and entertainment. The quantity of coverage has declined in recent years: in the 1950s and 1960s all kinds of royal events were televised, from the annual Maundy Money service to the Queen Mother opening a needlework exhibition. But still today, news stories relating to the Royals can dominate the BBC news. And when the Queen's Jubilees are televised, or the wedding of Charles and Diana, or almost any ceremony you can think of, the interaction between these two totemic pillars of the British establishment is intense. The BBC acts almost as a stage manager for these occasions, finding the most effective and dramatic way of showing them and even occasionally offering the Palace hints on how a small change here or there could make the television offering more effective. Today it also packages them, with guests commenting on the event and its significance from elegant portable studios erected to overlook the site.

In my father's day there were no such studios but that did not mean he was not required to package an event in commentary. When the Queen Mother came to open the needlework exhibition at Clarence House the producer of the programme asked my father to give viewers a guided tour of the artefacts as the precursor to the Queen Mother's arrival. He knew nothing about needlework but did his homework like a true professional and started the programme with an elegant description of the works on show. The Queen Mother was late. He went on talking. She still had not arrived. By now he was on the verge of panic. He had said everything he knew about needlework and indeed was probably hoping he would never see embroidery again. At last she came in and the opening ceremony started. He was back on safe ground. After the programme was over he was by chance in an outer room when she came over to him and said, 'Oh Mr Dimbleby, I am sorry I was so late. I hope it was not inconvenient. I was watching your commentary on a television outside and I was so fascinated by what you were saying that I could not tear myself away.'

The BBC handles the monarchy with respect and reverence – seeing the enhancement of the institution, and reflecting its popularity with the public, as part of its remit. It has its own senior member of staff, the Royal Liaison Officer, whose job it is to maintain a smooth working relationship with the Palace, and who is customarily made a member of the Royal Victorian Order (an honour in the gift of the monarch) on leaving office. In theory, no contact with the Royal Family is allowed except through that office, whose purpose, among other things, is 'to coordinate bids from BBC programmes for interviews with members of the Royal Family'. There have been only two notable exceptions: Martin Bashir's 1995 interview with Diana, Princess of Wales, achieved by subterfuge; and Emily Maitlis's 2019 interview with Prince Andrew, which he agreed to when invited by Maitlis, after he had, apparently, checked with the Queen. So much for the Royal

Liaison Officers, excluded from the two most explosive interviews ever given by Royalty.

Each institution, BBC and monarchy, at times seemingly bound in an incestuous relationship, grapples with a conundrum. For the monarchy it is how to combine the pomp of a head of state with popular appeal. Are our monarchs meant to be symbols, aloof and separate? Or are they meant to be human beings just like us who happen to have been given the responsibility of being head of state? Which approach will best ensure the monarchy's continued acceptability and popularity? For the BBC the issue is the degree to which it should be a disinterested observer of monarchy or the vehicle for its promotion.

In 1968 the Queen decided that the Royal Family should attempt to project themselves as an ordinary family. It was an approach that had worked well for her grandfather, George V. His Private Secretary, Lord Stamfordham, had argued that the monarch should be seen out and about among the people – that he should become a person the public felt they knew. He urged the king to allow his family to be exposed to the public gaze, to enhance the public interest in the Royal Family. They were duly despatched to various parts of the Empire on visits designed to staunch the incipient appetite for republicanism that was taking root at the end of the First World War. Stamfordham also introduced the royal Christmas broadcast. These innovations took monarchy to new heights of popularity. George V, surprised, said that Stamfordham 'taught me everything about how to be King'. To match George V's success has been an ambition of the Palace ever since.

In 1969, in a ninety-minute film made by the BBC and the

Royal Family over the course of a year and watched by over thirty million people in Britain, the family was seen joshing at a barbeque, watching television, practising music and buying ice cream, all interspersed with a variety of official engagements: formal lunches, garden parties and a tour of South America. An ordinary family just getting on with the job. This was before multiple divorces and adulteries, before Prince Harry's abrupt departure from the firm and before Prince Andrew was embroiled in the Epstein saga. It would not work so well today. In any case, you are forbidden to see it now. It was last shown in 1977 as part of the Queen's Silver Jubilee celebrations and then abruptly withdrawn from circulation by the Queen herself who owned the copyright. Perhaps, in the light of growing evidence that the Royal Family was indeed a family like any other and by no means perfect, she had finally heeded David Attenborough's advice. As Controller of BBC Two at the time the film was made he had written to the producer of the film to say that he was 'in danger of killing the monarchy'. He continued, in suitably anthropological mode: 'The whole institution depends on mystique and the tribal chief in his hut . . . if any member of the tribe ever sees inside the hut then the whole system of the tribal chiefdom is damaged and the tribe eventually disintegrates.' Or as Walter Bagehot, the Victorian writer on the constitution, famously described monarchy: 'Its mystery is its life. We must not let daylight in upon magic.'

The Queen herself acknowledges that it is not always an easy role to fulfil. Fifteen years after the final outing of that film showing the family in perfect harmony she was bewailing her '*annus horribilis*' in a speech in the City of London.

'*Horribilis*' because 1992 had seen the public breakdown of three of her children's marriages: Prince Andrew in March, Princess Anne in April and Prince Charles in December. These events were followed by public anger at reports that the taxpayer at a moment of economic uncertainty would have to stump up thirty-seven million pounds for the restoration of Windsor Castle after a fire. In her speech at Guildhall she acknowledged the strains and pressures of her job. She asked for 'moderation and compassion' from commentators rather than a rush to judgement. 'Most people,' she said, 'try to do their jobs as best they can even if the result is not always successful.' She acknowledged that 'criticism is good for people and institutions that are part of public life. No institution – City, Monarchy, whatever – should expect to be free from the scrutiny of those who give it their loyalty and support', adding 'not to mention those who don't'. It is a challenge the BBC resolutely refuses to accept. Happy to portray the monarchy on its own terms, it is less comfortable scrutinising the institution or asking whether it is fit for purpose.

Queen Elizabeth's resolute determination to carry out her public duties and refrain from controversy or, with the exception of occasional cryptic remarks reported by others, show any sign of political partisanship, has set a high standard for the institution of monarchy in a fractious age. The conventions of keeping opinions private and not complaining about the constraints of being born into the Royal Family have been less well observed, or deliberately flouted, by some younger members.

To be born into this institution does seem an unnatural punishment. I once asked Lord Charteris, who had been the Queen's Private Secretary for many years, whether he did not feel sorry for the Royal Family. 'Sorry?' he said. 'For people who have someone to clean their shoes every day? Certainly not.' But I cannot think of many worse fates than having your one life on earth set in stone, preordained by birth. The advantages of a life of luxury pale against the obligation to conform to constitutional ritual – unless like Edward VIII or Prince Harry you decide to break away. You only need to read the Court Circular with its daily round of duties imposed on the Queen and the so-called 'senior' Royals, and imagine for a moment what it must be like: investitures, ambassadors to be welcomed, hospitals and schools, factories, laboratories, regiments, girl guides and boy scouts to be visited; and each visit preceded by a briefing on who will be presented to you, and why they matter; with each person needing to be listened to; and all under the constant eyes of admirers straining to catch every word, or even a glimpse, of this bird in its gilded cage.

Some of them do the job impeccably. I was once president of a charity that gave support and training to young people living in the poorer parts of south London and saw the Royal Family in action for the first time. Princess Anne became our Patron and her diligence was extraordinary. She not only engaged with our members, talking to them earnestly about their lives and ambitions; she also made thoughtful, well-informed speeches about our work, without notes. It was a masterful performance and it raised the morale of everyone involved. But why? Why do we need this affirmation? And is it right that we should require from this family that they give up the one freedom the rest of us have: to decide how we want to live our lives?

The idea of Britain abandoning the monarchy is pie in the sky, not only because there is still widespread support for the principle but because republicans do not have the slightest idea how they would bring a republic about. Maybe a referendum, like on Scottish independence or Brexit. And then what? Years of wrangling over a written constitution.

We have always prided ourselves on the merits of our unwritten constitution, superior it is said to the constitutions written down by revolutionaries in America or France. But its strength depends upon its conventions being observed. A government that treats precedence and convention as no more than hurdles to be overcome in pursuit of its aims makes an unwritten constitution seem positively dangerous. If you knowingly lie to parliament as Prime Minister, our convention says you must resign. But if you knowingly lie and choose not to resign, it seems no one can lay a glove on you.

The practical difficulties in creating a republic are daunting, as Australia found when it held a referendum on whether to give up the Queen as head of state in favour of an elected president. I chaired a *Question Time* debate there on the eve of the vote in 1999. It seemed an extravagant trip for *Question Time* but I learnt later that the BBC wanted us to cover it because questions could be raised abroad about the desirability and efficacy of monarchy that the BBC could not comfortably discuss otherwise. We built an open-air studio just by the

Sydney Harbour Bridge – a dramatic location but not an easy place for a broadcast: our discussion was conducted against a constant background of bellowing foghorns from the ferries trundling in and out of the docks below us. What came through clearly though was how complex writing a new constitution would be, and a fear that it would be manipulated by politicians pursuing their own ends. Australia duly voted for no change.

All that said, I find deference unsettling. The bowing and scraping. I blame an incident in my childhood. I was in my mid-teens and I remember the day well, although it was nearly seventy years ago: a warm summer afternoon in a park set below the forbidding walls of Windsor Castle. We had come as a family to the annual Royal Windsor Horse Show. I took only the mildest interest in horses, but my younger brother Jonathan was a horse fanatic and where he went we followed. Early in the afternoon the Queen was driven down from the castle to watch the event. There was a stir as she approached, everyone craning their necks to catch sight of her. As she entered the showground, trumpets blared out from the loudspeakers. Suddenly from behind me a hand grabbed at my cap. I turned round. It was my father who had snatched it off my head without saying a word. I asked him why he had done it. 'It's the Royal Salute,' he said. I knew to take off my cap when the National Anthem was played but had never heard of a Royal Salute, and had no idea what it meant. I remember feeling angry and humiliated, or perhaps angry at being humiliated, treated like a child in front of the crowd of spectators, who would all have recognised my father and seen what he had done. I suppose his keenness to ensure a public display of loyalty, of respect for the Queen, overrode any qualms he had about treating me like a child, embarrassing me in front of everyone. If it was meant to teach me respect it had the opposite effect. It made me resentful and suspicious of these hollow gestures. Even as I write I can feel the incomprehension welling up in me again. Why should one person feel bound to bow or curtsey to another? When the monarch wielded real power it may have been prudent. It would have been foolhardy not to prostrate oneself in front of Elizabeth I. But Elizabeth II, who we are told has no power? Who is simply a constitutional head of state? Why the need for obeisance? Why the fuss?

All of this may make it seem strange that I have done so many royal commentaries, from State Openings of Parliament to Royal Weddings, Royal Jubilees and Royal Funerals. Holding these somewhat ambivalent views, how could I have been part of the support system of the monarchy?

I don't know the answer, but perhaps it is that royal events are among the most difficult and challenging tasks a broadcaster can face, and therefore irresistible. I suspect they rank alongside sports commentary for their complexity and excitement. I could never have covered sport. I do not follow cricket or tennis or football or Formula One. The triumphs of World Cups pass me by. The Olympic Games, except for the opening ceremony in London in 2012, go unwatched. I was once presenting the political segment of the news during an election campaign and was told to hand over to my fellow presenter at the end of the bulletin for a football result. 'It's okay,' I said, 'I can do it.' So poor was my understanding even of football scores that I announced the result as 'three-love'. The BBC's sports department, sensitive about their patch, were furious and thought I had done it deliberately to mock them. I had to explain that I was just trying to use what I thought was their jargon.

Royal events are live, they are complex, and they are important to those who watch. That makes them uniquely exciting and difficult to broadcast. The first rule is that things almost always go wrong: not necessarily very wrong, but usually a bit wrong, so however much you prepare you can never prepare enough. A slip of the tongue is out and away and cannot be called back. I still blush at the thought of one of my *faux pas*. In 2000, the Queen Mother celebrated her hundredth birthday. The Band of the Irish Guards played 'Happy Birthday' and there was a forty-one-gun salute fired by the Kings Troop Royal Horse Artillery. The Queen Mother was driven in an open carriage drawn by two handsome white horses, properly known as the Windsor Greys. 'The Queen Mother comes through Horse Guards Arch,' I intoned, 'drawn by two Windsor Gays.' No elegant way of correcting myself. It would only make things worse. The perils of live broadcasting.

Other mistakes are less easily explained. Why did it come into my head to describe the Duke of Edinburgh – wearing a shiny black top hat and sitting in an open horse-drawn carriage being driven up the hill towards Windsor Castle, with Lech Wałęsa, the former shipyard apprentice who had led the Solidarity movement and was now the first elected President of Poland, sitting beside him – as 'looking like Count Dracula'? It was a happy occasion, the crowds were cheering, and I was trying to enter into the informality and general air of goodwill. The tabloid press took offence – the *Daily Mirror* nominated me Twit of the Week – as no doubt did the Duke. The BBC duly apologised and I was rapped over the knuckles.

Given that things always go wrong, the second rule is that preparation is key. The system I developed for the rigours of twenty-four-hour general election broadcasting marathons works just as well for royal events. I like to have all the essential information – names and biographies of all the major and minor participants, descriptions of any buildings and statues that might be seen, names of any regiments involved, names of senior officers on parade, and so on – written on cards, and the cards put into a numbered and indexed flip-book, so that whatever happens the facts are always to hand. Probably sixty or more reference cards for any broadcast, all carefully read with key dates and words highlighted. The flip-books themselves were invented for warehousemen before computers, for stocktaking. Peter Snow first introduced me to them, and they are the envy of everyone I show them to. These live broadcasts are teamwork. Everyone matters: camera crews, sound operators, studio managers, vision mixers, tape editors and one key production assistant, with an ear for music, counting the bars and telling the director when to cut from a shot of trombones to the trumpets or the drums. There is a trio at the heart of it all. Director, researcher and commentator. The director in the scanner – the mobile control room – tells me what shots we are going to show next, nudges me when to lead to the next sequence, and passes on crucial information about delays or changes to the planned programme. The researcher has not only prepared all the cards with all the information I need to know but has to have each one ready at the right moment for me to keep up a steady flow of relevant commentary. I am particularly bad at distinguishing one royal duchess from another, and seeing the camera close in on a face I point at the screen mouthing silently 'Who's that?' In a trice the researcher will have the card to hand jabbing furiously at the name of the duchess just in time for me to offer the smoothest of identifications. The first researcher I had for the State Opening of Parliament, a Papal visit, an inauguration of an Archbishop of Canterbury as well as the Cenotaph Service had an encyclopaedic knowledge of the structure and politics of the Church of England. If I ever made a mistake she had an endearing habit of kicking me hard under the table. I soon learnt.

You can never have too much research. This was another lesson I learnt from my father. After Princess Margaret's wedding service, the car taking her and her new husband Tony Armstrong-Jones from Westminster Abbey down to Tower Bridge to join the Royal Yacht *Britannia* was held up for over an hour in a traffic jam. My father, doing the television commentary, had exhausted every nugget of information he had about the Strand, and the Law Courts, and all the other buildings on the route, when a brilliant idea came to him. 'I don't know what is going on,' he announced. 'I will just go down into the crowd and see if I can find out.' He switched off his microphone, turned to his producer, put his feet up on the table and said, 'Time for a cup of tea.' Five minutes later, microphone back on, he said, 'No one seems to know anything,' and carried on with his commentary refreshed.

And the third rule is never to try to use all the material you have slaved over. Do not speak when you do not need to. Do not show off what you know. Do not let the commentary dominate the event. Be less ringmaster, more friendly guide.

My introduction to commentating was the annual State Opening of Parliament, which I covered on and off for twenty years from 1981 to 2002, until I relinquished the role because my enthusiasm for the event itself was waning and I thought it might become obvious to the viewer. The ceremonial for the State Opening does not, despite appearances, date back to the reign of Elizabeth I or beyond. It was the creation of a Royal Commission set up in 1902. Queen Victoria in her widowhood had abandoned the State Opening and many other public appearances. On her death in 1901, her son, Edward VII, inherited a throne that had become remote from the people it was meant to serve. He worked with his Private Secretary, Lord Knollys, to restore to the monarchy some of the lustre that Victoria's absence from public life had eroded. The ceremony we see each year, full of complex and arcane detail, is the result of their endeavours. It begins with the search of the cellars of the Houses of Parliament by the Yeoman of the Bodyguard, checking that a latter day Guy Fawkes has not planted explosives in a bid to eliminate parliament and sovereign. Once their work is done the ceremonial proper begins. It is complex and sometimes incomprehensible. Even the experts on the procedure in the House of Lords differ in their explanations of its significance, and it is a commentator's nightmare to offer an explanation for what is going on. It is simple enough to explain that the Queen's crown is brought to Westminster in a coach with the Queen's

Jeweller in attendance. But who is the Queen's Jeweller and what does he do? Woe betide you if you forget to point out that the coach is accompanied by two Royal Bargemasters who sit at the back of the coach instead of the usual footmen, there because the crown used to be brought to Westminster from the Tower of London by river. Who, what and why are Ladies of the Bedchamber? Most mysterious of all, what is the Cap of Maintenance, a scarlet velvet cap fringed with ermine, vulgarly known by the ceremonial experts as the squirrel on a stick. No one quite knows what it is doing there. The accepted version is that it was given to Henry VIII by the Pope in gratitude for his valuable support for the Vatican, a gift that needless to say predates Henry's insistence on divorce and the separation of the English Church from Rome. Why it should still be paraded after that debacle is a mystery.

The most awkward part of the ceremony is the emergence from the Robing Room in the House of Lords of the Queen, wearing her train, with her pages behind her and the Lord Great Chamberlain walking in front. When I began doing these commentaries he had to walk backwards so that he faced the Queen: turning his back on her, I was assured, being *lèse-majesté*, or contrary to the dignity of the sovereign. Watching the Lord Great Chamberlain walk backwards the full length of the Prince's Chamber did add a small element of drama to the occasion. Would the Lord Great Chamberlain go off course? Or worse still fall over? No matter. It was an important tradition, part of history, that he should walk backwards. Until suddenly one year, with no explanation, he was allowed to walk forwards. So much for tradition. The procession makes for a slow and in television terms rather boring journey from the Queen's Robing Room to the Lords Chamber. I once suggested to Black Rod, the House of Lords official in charge of the event, that an orchestra could play Mozart to cover this *longueur*, a proposal that fell on very deaf ears.

Another event I used to cover as commentator was the annual Trooping the Colour ceremony on the Queen's official birthday in early June. There would be over a thousand soldiers and mounted military bands circling and wheeling and fast marching and slow marching and then an RAF fly past. The detail of the event is complex (over a hundred military commands are given) and, like many state occasions, however carefully planned it is, it can sometimes go awry. Split-second timing is easy on paper. In reality the slightest upset can destroy the pattern of events and leave the commentator and the director scrabbling to work out what will happen next. Military experts love these occasions but for me they were testing. I knew that the position of the buttons on their tunics was the surefire way of identifying which guardsman was which – Welsh from Irish, Coldstream from Grenadier – but I could never remember which button position went with which Guard. Any mistake was rightly seized on as incompetence. The Head of Events at the BBC once asked me whether I really cared about the order of the buttons and I had to confess it was not top of my list of interests. I think he was trying, none too gently, to suggest I should give up these formal ceremonies, that they were in conflict with the 'political' work I was doing at elections and on *Panorama*.

There is one broadcast each year that I take very seriously, and that has silence at its heart: the annual ceremony at the

Cenotaph, with the laying of wreaths, the march past of veterans, and the two minutes' silence at eleven o'clock, marking the moment in 1918 when the guns stopped firing on the Western Front. It is watched by millions of people who want to share the commemoration of those killed and injured in war, and want too to remember the bereaved families. The Cenotaph ceremony is unlike any other state occasion because as commentator you are not simply observing the event, but become part of it, embedded in it. The words you speak and the tone you take are part of the commemoration. The preparations for it are extensive. There is the usual research to be done: who will be there from the Royal Family, which politicians will be laying wreaths, who the Service chiefs are, who the high commissioners and ambassadors and participants in the brief service, including the cross bearer and the choir of the Chapel Royal, the names of all the religious leaders attending – which has grown longer over the years – which bands are playing and who is conducting them, which contingents from the army, the navy and the air force will form the 'hollow square' around the Cenotaph, the names of all the statues that might come into shot, the architects of the buildings on Whitehall and their dates, and of course the history of the design and building of the Cenotaph itself. So far, so normal. Masses of information, most of which will never be broadcast, but all there in case it is needed – in case things go wrong and there are delays to fill. But that is only the start of the preparations. It is the march past organised by the royal British Legion that is really complicated. In 2021 there were 274 different contingents marching. They come in a steady stream down

Whitehall, each contingent with a wreath to lay as it passes the Cenotaph with an 'Eyes Left'. Our cameras cannot pick up each of the 274 contingents, and we do not know in advance which will be shown and which not, so we have to be ready to identify any one of them at the moment they appear. For weeks before, a researcher tries to contact each contingent, to discover who is in their group and what brings them together. It might be the crew of a particular warship, or pilots from a now-defunct aeroplane, or representatives of long-merged regiments who want to keep their name alive. There are contingents of those honoured with medals for bravery, or for taking part in a particular campaign. There are dog handlers, military police, war widows, people evacuated from the Blitz and service support charities of many different kinds. Of all these, some are easily identifiable: the Royal Hospital Chelsea contingent in scarlet uniforms or the wheelchair contingent or the blind veterans guided by a companion. Others are more difficult. Each has an important story to tell but as the commentator there is only a split second in which to both identify them and tell their tale. And of course you do not want to get it wrong. In 2021, for example, seventy members of the Type 21 Association were marching as the 34th contingent of Column E. Their name comes from the Type 21 Amazon Class warships that formed the 4th Frigate Squadron in the Royal Navy. These ships were powered by the same Rolls Royce engines that powered Concorde and were known as the Porsches of the fleet, with a top speed of 30 knots or 35 miles an hour. Two of them, HMS *Ardent* and HMS *Antelope*, were lost in the Falklands War. As the contingent came into view I glanced down at my research notes, quickly assimilated what to say, and then said they represented not the 21 but the type 2 frigate. A moment's inattention, a slip of the tongue, but this is live and the words cannot be recalled. Fortunately, there was no official complaint (as there always is if you dare call the St John Ambulance the St John's Ambulance) and I heard later that the Type 21 Association laughed it off.

Throughout the programme, the production team in the scanner, and I, can talk to each other. The director will tell me what shot they are going to next, or ask me to lead them in commentary to a particular sequence. I will ask for shots to cover something I want to refer to. I have two buttons in front of me. If I push one, what I say goes out on air. When I push the other, only the production team in the scanner can hear. Only once has the system broken down. The director that year was confused about where we had reached in the two minutes' silence. He was waiting to put up the shot of the Royal Horse Artillery on Horse Guards Parade, who end the silence with a round from their guns. Wanting to help, I said, '45 seconds to go'. Unfortunately, I had pushed the wrong button and the words were broadcast. What the audience made of this strange injection into the most solemn moment of the ceremony I never knew. I just hope they passed it off as a technical glitch and did not recognise my voice.

The perils of speaking out of turn in live commentary are ever-present. At the Queen's Diamond Jubilee celebrations in 2012 a chain of beacons was to be lit across Britain. The chain was to start with a beacon lit by the Queen from a platform in St James's Park. We were broadcasting live and had rigged loudspeakers and monitors in the park for spectators who had gathered there to be able to watch the evening's events as they unfolded around the country. I was in a studio built outside Buckingham Palace looking out over the Victoria Memorial and the park itself. Every time I spoke, I could hear my voice coming back to me from the loudspeakers in the park. The Queen duly arrived, ready to light the first beacon, but I realised that we had failed to switch off the loudspeakers in the park for this part of the evening. The Queen was going to hear every word I said. 'Lead to the beacon-lighting', came the instruction from the scanner. Silence from me. Then, more urgently, 'Please lead to the lighting, David.' Still silence. For a moment I thought of saying, 'I am sorry Your Majesty. I know you can hear my voice. I am explaining that you are about to light the chain of beacons.' Mercifully, at the last moment the sound engineers realised what was wrong, cut out St James's Park, and I was able to carry on.

One of the most challenging state occasions I was ever involved with was the funeral of Diana, Princess of Wales. Her death was shocking, the days that followed had to be handled with great sensitivity, and there was no tradition or ritual to fall back on. It highlighted, perhaps more than any previous event, the tension for each member of the Royal Family between their role as symbol and their reality as human beings.

The build-up to the event had preoccupied the country and the BBC. The news of the car crash in Paris came through early on the morning of Sunday 31 August 1997. I was woken at 6.05 that morning by my BBC boss. Like many others, I had spent the previous night celebrating the last weekend of summer, but the news shook me back into sobriety. There was work to do. That evening we broadcast a two-hour-long tribute to Diana.

The week that followed was difficult for the Royal Family. Their first reaction was to maintain a dignified silence, remaining at Balmoral in Scotland and sheltering Diana's young sons William and Harry from the public gaze. The public reaction was different: an extraordinary outpouring of grief. Within hours of the news of Diana's death the first flowers were laid outside Kensington Palace, Diana's home. The whole area soon swelled into a great bank of colour, of handpicked bunches and formal bouquets, many with messages, which all said in their various ways, 'We love you Diana.'

Some thought this outpouring of public grief was mawkish, that the grief was phoney, a sentimental display of attachment to someone none of them really knew. An American colleague sent over to cover the event for one of the US networks said to me, 'Your country has gone mad.' Two days after Diana's death I went to Kensington Palace to see the scene for myself and found the sight not mawkish but moving. For whatever reason, each of the families standing there, some with their children, were mourning someone who had touched their hearts. Diana had her critics, but there were many who had seen her as an inspiration and, until her divorce and exile from the Royal Family, as a fresh and welcome face in the stuffy world of courtiers and their protocol. Rightly or wrongly they thought she had been hard done by, not cared for, and they wanted to show their feelings.

The events that followed revealed the Royal Family trying to catch up with the public mood, which was verging on hostility at the absence of any royal reaction. Every family deals with death in its own way and should be allowed to do so in private. But the Royal Family is a public family too, whose role is to embody the nation's emotions. As the days passed, public irritation with its failure to do so became palpable, finding its harshest expression on the front pages of the tabloid press. The *Daily Mail* said, 'Let the flag fly at half mast.' The *Sun* asked, 'Where is our Queen? Where is her flag?' The *Mirror* said, 'Your people are suffering. Speak to us, M'am.' The *Express*, 'Show us you care.' It was not until the end of the week, Friday, that the Queen returned to Buckingham Palace. She mingled with the crowds outside the gates, ordered the Royal Standard to be flown at half-mast and then, sitting in front of a window through which the crowds outside on the Mall could be clearly seen, paid a moving tribute to Diana. It showed the Queen as head of a mourning nation and as a person struggling with her own emotions and concerned for her bereaved grandchildren. 'We have all,' she said, 'been trying in our different ways to cope. It is not easy to express a sense of loss, since the initial shock is often succeeded by a mixture of other feelings: disbelief, incomprehension, anger – and concern for those who remain.' And, in its warmth for Diana – 'an exceptional and gifted human being' – and its acknowledgement of how many people were feeling about her loss – 'millions of others who never met her, but felt they knew her, will remember her . . . I share your determination to cherish her memory' – it showed the Palace was back in tune with what the country was feeling.

At the BBC there was work to do. Diana had died in the

early hours of Sunday morning and her funeral was to be held on the following Saturday, giving us only six days to prepare. There are plans for deaths of senior members of the Royal Family on file at the BBC, each given cryptic code names. But with six days to go it was clear there was no plan for Diana's unexpected death. For these events the detail is everything. How would the coffin be carried? Where would the service take place? What military involvement would there be? Who would be in the congregation? What would the Order of Service be? Who would speak? Looking back it was extraordinary that so much was done in so little time. At the BBC there were daily planning meetings to decide on the complex technical arrangements, all very efficiently carried out so that by Saturday you might have thought this funeral had been a year in the planning.

There was one aspect of the planning that I did not understand: a discussion about what tone the BBC should set. I said repeatedly that the tone would not be set by us but by the event. As with all broadcasts of this kind, our job was simply to observe, and guide the viewer through the day, not set any particular tone. What tone could we set in any case? Mournful? Celebratory? What did it mean? Just as the Palace had, albeit late in the day, responded to and reflected the public mood, so on the day of the funeral we should take our cue from the public. Over a million people turned out to line the streets of central London that day, thronging the funeral route from Kensington Palace past Buckingham Palace and on to Westminster Abbey where the funeral service took place, and then again along the road the hearse would take from the abbey through north London to her family's house, Althorp, in Northamptonshire, where she would be buried. As the horse-drawn gun carriage with the coffin draped in the Royal Standard emerged from Kensington Palace, it was clear what the tone was going to be. 'God bless you Diana,' was the first cry I heard from the crowd, and all the way along the route there was applause. Flowers were thrown at the coffin – so many flowers that later, when the hearse was creeping through the crowded city streets, the driver had to turn on his windscreen wipers to clear the view. It was a striking image and we held the shot, a picture more powerful than any words.

The event illustrated the difference between the BBC and other broadcasters in their coverage of monarchy. While I was commentating on events outside the abbey, the television director of the service in the abbey decided to treat it as any other state funeral, ignoring the fact that this was a congregation packed with famous faces. ITN had briefed its staff that it wanted its coverage to be 'authoritative but people-based'. When it came to the service ITN therefore concentrated on the film stars and the celebrities; the BBC on its usual elegant slow pans down the stained-glass windows. At BBC HQ, where the controllers were watching both channels, a furious row broke out, with instructions to the director in the abbey to show more of the starry congregation and fewer of the traditional images.

I was very moved by Diana's funeral. I liked and admired her. I had met her at dinner parties a couple of times and danced with her once (jived I think). She was warm and funny and friendly. In all the troubles that she had been through – the horror of her marriage and divorce – I had always been what you might call on her side. So her sudden death was, for me, sad and shocking. I shared the emotions of so many members of the public and felt insulted by the stuffy columnists who thought it all phoney, or claimed they did, stuffy columnists having to put bread on their tables by being contrarian. I managed to get through the day without my emotions breaking through except for one unprofessional moment when my voice began to crack as I read out the single word on a wreath of white flowers on her coffin. 'Mummy'.

In Britain there is still majority support for monarchy among the older population, but not necessarily among the young. In 2019, according to YouGov, nearly half of eighteen- to twenty-four-year-olds were in favour of monarchy and only a quarter wanted an elected head of state. Two years later by 2021 that position had reversed: 41 per cent wanted an elected head of state with only 31 per cent wanting monarchy to continue. In the country as a whole though, 60 per cent of the population still supports monarchy, with just under a quarter preferring an elected head of state. The shift of opinion among the young will have been noted at Buckingham Palace, I suspect with some alarm.

Perhaps it is time to scale things back. It is often said of our state ceremonial that we do these things better than anyone else. And it's true. But is it still something to be proud of? I wonder. We are after all no longer an empire, as we were when much of this performance was invented. We are a middle-ranking power struggling to define our place in a global world, struggling to come to terms with the result of the Brexit decision, struggling to hold the country together. Does the glorification of monarchy, and the obsession with gossip about the Royal Family, serve a useful purpose? Maybe it is time for a less ostentatious display: a scaling back of the extravagance, a redefining of the role.

We are told this is something Prince Charles will want to achieve when he becomes king. His Coronation will be the first chance to see what he intends. The forces of conservatism will be ranged against him. He is not offered a blank slate on which to write his idea of a modern monarchy. Our history with its encrusted traditions will not be easily discarded. Will loyalty still be sworn to him by a gaggle of aristocrats from Dukes down to Barons via Marquesses and Earls as it was at his mother's Coronation? Watch this space.

"I WISH YOU WOULDN'T WATCH 'QUESTION TIME'..."

7

'You in the Red Shirt'

Question Time was invented on the back of an envelope. The BBC had a gap in its schedules and decided to try out a cheap format for a few weeks only. That was in 1979, over forty years ago. Like *The Mousetrap* it has run and run. The first Chairman, Robin Day, was chosen because he was kicking his heels, with a contract to fulfil but not enough work coming his way. After ten years in the chair Robin (by now Sir Robin) asked for an increase in his fee. Never an agile negotiator, he told the BBC that if they didn't up the money he would leave. To his surprise the BBC said, Okay. Leave. He did not know that they were trying to seduce Peter Sissons, a newsreader from Channel 4, to come over to BBC News. *Question Time* was offered to Peter as the cherry on the cake. When Sissons' time was up it was decided to hold auditions for the new presenter. I was told that my name was in the running but an audition was not necessary because they knew how I would do it. I could not imagine how they knew. I had last done an audience programme nearly twenty years earlier, when the people making this decision had been at the start of their careers. I lay in bed wondering whether this was just a way of keeping me sweet while giving the programme to one of the other candidates – Jeremy Paxman or Sue Lawley. I rang back the Head of Current Affairs and asked if I could do an audition too.

Auditioning between three of their regular broadcasters seemed a weird decision, as if the BBC did not know who they had been employing all these years or what their strengths and weaknesses were.

I spent time in the run-up to my audition thinking about the programme and how I could break a formula that, after fifteen years, had become stale. I decided that the audience should play a bigger part. Previous chairs had allowed them to ask one question and then, if they were lucky, put a supplementary. Occasionally a member of the audience would be picked at random for a quick comment, but that was it. I wanted the audience to be much more involved, to take part in a real debate on each topic. It had become very much a programme where the politicians talked to an audience. I wanted to reverse things and make it the audience talking to the politicians.

Audition day came. Sue Lawley was offered but declined to do an audition. So it was Jeremy Paxman against me. An audience had been recruited and two panels assembled. Paxman did his routine in the morning. My turn came in the afternoon. My panel of speakers was made up of aspirant politicians, provided by the political parties to give them an idea of the pressures of television performance. The Conservatives had put up a young man from their research department: a chance for him to try out his skills as a communicator. His name was David Cameron. When he was running for the leadership of the party on a *Question Time Special* twelve years later in 2005, he reminded me of this previous encounter, his first television outing.

To make my point about the need for the audience to be more involved I left my seat in the middle of the panel and walked across to the audience, the better to engage them. That may have done the trick. I was offered the job. It was a relief because I had decided that if I didn't get the job – the only one I still really wanted to do at the BBC – I would have to leave.

All broadcasting makes me nervous. It's not the nervousness of actors or singers who claim to be physically sick before going on stage. It's a tensing of the stomach, and being on edge until the job starts. I feel it even recording a trail for a programme. It's all performance, and the adrenaline rush is part of the excitement. David Frost used to say that if he ever felt nervous going on television he would give it up. I always thought the opposite: that I would give it up if I did not feel nervous.

A typical *Question Time* day would start mid-morning at a London railway station, where the editor, the director, two or three producers and researchers, and I would meet before setting off for Aberystwyth or Grimsby, Middlesbrough or Bradford, Cardiff or Truro. The technical crew would have gone in advance, often the night before, to set up the venue. Every week a different place and a different audience, but the same routine. On the train, read the research briefs on the topics we think might be raised and that we have discussed in the midweek programme meeting. Look longingly at passing woods and fields and wish I was out there instead of on the train. Argue about politics. Answer some questions from train staff and fellow passengers: 'Where are you coming from tonight?' 'Who is on the panel?' And the almost inevitable, 'Why can't you get them to answer the question?' Arrive at location, sometimes a grand Victorian town hall, with marble staircases leading to a council chamber hung with bad paintings of ancient worthies. More often a desultory school gymnasium with a side office where the whole team assembles: the director, the audience booker, the organiser, already working on next week's location or the one after that, the researchers, crouching over their laptops for the latest news, and, at our own table, the editor and me. Tea and coffee and too many chocolate biscuits and a long afternoon ahead.

There is a brief rehearsal. First with cameras, doing my opening and closing routines. Then, to check the sound, the camera crew leave their cameras to pose as audience members. They might chat to me about what is going on in their lives or have a political argument. One member of the crew will tell his weekly joke, usually incomprehensible, often unrepeatable. If we are at a school, it might have provided a team of sixth-form politics students to sit on the panel for rehearsals, with a scattering of teachers and students sitting in for the audience. Remember to tease the teachers remorselessly to cheer up the students. A few selfies with the pseudo-panellists who, on good days, will have been articulate and provocative. Then back to the office, apprehensive now, reminding myself that I know how to do this.

Early evening. The audience starts arriving. About a hundred and fifty people. They have been carefully selected, usually from about five hundred or more applicants. It is a special skill, at which our audience booker is adept. Our template requires political balance between the main parties according to BBC rules: a balance between Labour and Conservative supporters, rather fewer supporters of the Lib Dems and UKIP. A smattering of Greens. And of course, when we are in Wales or Scotland, representation of nationalist opinion. That is only the start. Rough gender equality matters and a racial mix that matches where we are. Mostly white faces in Cheltenham. Many black and Asian faces in Bradford.

An hour to go. I wade into the audience area outside the studio – the holding area we call it – to explain how the programme works. 'This is your programme,' I say, 'not mine, not the BBC's. Everything comes from you. We pick the questions from those you have submitted, not the questions we would like you to ask. The reason is that there is no point in picking a question none of you want to argue about.' And 'The panel is here for you, not you for them, so lay into them, say what you think, fight your corner, speak up. This is your chance.' I take questions, often: 'Who is your favourite panellist?' I never say, but talk about our regulars and do an imitation of Tony Benn, which usually gets a laugh. And then there is the joke. Always the same joke, wherever we are, a rough way of testing how lively the audience is: Norwich compared with Liverpool, Aberdeen against Croydon. It's not actually a joke. It is a true story from an earlier edition of *Question Time* that I tell to emphasise how personal experience can be used to make a point. I explain that, on a previous occasion, we were debating whether hanging was a deterrent to murder. A man in the audience kept waving his hand, desperate to get in. Eventually I called on him and he said, 'I know about this. Because I've *been* murdered.'

Back in the office, lively debate about which questions to take. The phrasing is as important as the subject. Is it clear enough for me to use it against an evasive panellist? 'That's not what the questioner asked.'

Finally the recording begins. The exhilarating signature tune starts, setting the tone with its suggestion of urgency. Take a deep breath. Smile. Remember this is meant to be fun. But it's all up to you. An exciting hour: a rollercoaster ride, trying to judge how long to spend on each question, making sure every panellist has spoken, shutting them up if they go on too long, picking a variety of speakers from the audience, trying to judge from their appearance which side of the fence they are on. Finally, 'That's it for this week. Next week we are in Oldham.'

After the programme, dinner. That must be the most interesting part, people say, when the politicians let their hair down and tell you what's really happening. The trouble is it all goes over my head. My adrenaline is still doing whatever adrenaline does and I can barely speak a sensible word let alone hear one. The following week the editor will sometimes say, 'Wasn't so-and-so fascinating?' I will have no memory of it. The panellists from opposing parties usually chat and gossip amiably over their glasses of cheap Merlot. Only occasionally does it become too spirited. Alastair Campbell's confrontation with John McDonnell – old new Labour against new old Labour you might call it – was legendary. Their argument became so heated that a producer was sent to make sure they didn't come to blows. Boris Johnson, when he was running for Mayor of London, fuming that he was asked a question about his personal morality, until his then father-in-law, the great BBC correspondent Charles Wheeler, shut him up. 'Of course that question had to be put.' For myself, the sooner I can leave to go back to my hotel the better. I need the time to figure out how the shower works before crashing out. Every hotel in Britain seems to have different controls. A guide to hotel showers would be a best-seller.

I rarely watched the programme back, indeed I would forget about it once it was done until our post-mortem the following week. There, we would analyse it in detail. First, the obvious questions. Had we chosen the right topics? How long had we spent on each? Then, how long had each panellist spoken for? Had the balance between them been fair? And lastly, what share of the programme had been given to the audience and what was the gender balance of those who had spoken? We wanted vigorous debate, but fairly conducted. Our post-mortem was based on a statistical breakdown of all these issues and helped us measure how closely the programme matched our intentions. It also provided an analysis to use against our critics, of whom there were always a few, usually political or public relations advisers claiming unfair treatment.

The most common complaint from bruised or over-sensitive politicians was that the audience had been biased against them. There *was* a problem with audiences (until the Brexit referendum changed the dynamic). The problem was that those on the left – not the far left only but the moderate, slightly left of centre – wanted change and could fluently articulate the change they wanted. Those on the right (what clumsy words they are) tended to be more cautious, less vociferous: in Walpole's famous dictum, 'letting sleeping dogs lie'. This natural inbuilt imbalance worsened in the mid-1990s, during the last days of John Major's premiership. With the government in its death throes, and Tony Blair's carefully constructed 'new' Labour story – red roses not red flags and Mandelsonian moderation in all things – taking hold, *Question Time* audiences started to display an open contempt for the Conservatives. We were still balancing our audience guests evenly, half and half Tory and Labour supporters with a smattering of others, but the Tories were no longer lovers of their government. In vain we tried to explain this to Major's Downing Street staff, but to no avail, until one week a senior Tory minister came on the show. Heckled and booed, we expected him to make the traditional complaint about lack of balance. To our relief, he said, 'They really are all against us aren't they? Our own people I mean.'

Some panellists never complained. Ken Clarke, Shirley Williams, Tony Benn, Michael Heseltine. They were the *Question Time* warhorses, and our heroes: always willing to come, always keen to argue with the audience, and not afraid of confrontation. They knew the game and how to play it. Tony Benn would adopt an air of sweet reasonableness, however controversial his views, as though butter would not melt in his mouth. His only complaint was that he was not allowed to smoke his pipe in the studio. Shirley Williams would argue politely with her opponents in the audience, only once rounding on a hapless young student, telling him that he did not know what he was talking about and should just listen to her. Michael Heseltine, smooth as they come, unfazed when his iPhone rang in the middle of the programme, coolly killing the call and then carrying on. 'My wife,' he explained to us later, 'asking where we were having dinner.' And Ken Clarke, always a bruiser, defending whatever he said as being the voice of common sense. His most memorable appearance was in 2011 when he was Justice Secretary. The programme came from Wormwood Scrubs prison, where the audience was made up in part of members of the public but also of prison warders and serving prisoners. It would have been a strange evening at the best of times. But Clarke had to defend and explain remarks he had made a few days earlier in which, referring to 'serious rapes' and differentiating them from other categories of rape, he had appeared to suggest that not all rapes were serious crimes. The press and social media had laid into him. This was his chance to explain himself, which he did, apologising for the way he had spoken but reiterating that some rapes, particularly prolonged and violent assaults, deserved longer sentences than others. A fairly obvious point but one that highlighted the care with which politicians have to pick their words.

Ideally in a democracy every voice should be heard and ideally a programme like *Question Time* should be the Athenian forum of debate. *Question Time*, like the BBC itself, was committed to impartiality or fairness or balance or whatever word you choose. It did a better job than so-called vox pops – the random questioning of people in the street – ever did. I am dubious about this approach as a vehicle for hearing from voters. Too often it reveals little more than that some agree and some disagree. *Question Time*, on the other hand, took great care to make its audience as close as possible to a cross-section of the voting public. It also forced the audience to listen to what other speakers said, and react to that.

Working in Bristol back in 1962 I had chaired *It's My Opinion* – an ill-fated attempt to transpose the long-running radio programme *Any Questions* to television. *Any Questions* is a stalwart part of the BBC's political coverage but it is different in two important respects from *Question Time*. The most obvious is that it is on radio and therefore the audience cannot be seen, their reactions only gauged by applause or murmurs of disapproval. But much more important is that its audience is not selected for political and social balance. When a venue is chosen the host school or institution is simply asked to invite an audience to hear what the panel has to say. When we tried to put *Any Questions* on television we, like them, just filled the hall with those who wanted to come, taking no account of their political disposition. As a result we could not and did not engage them in the debate, confining them to asking a question and maybe allowing a follow-up along the lines of 'Does that answer your question?'

Comparing it to *Question Time* was comparing chalk and cheese.

For a time in the 1970s I was involved in a different attempt to engage the public in debate. It was a programme in the early days of BBC Two called *The Dimbleby Talk-In*, and it opened with a touch of show-business pizzazz. I came down the stairs through the audience to a signature tune whose beat matched the appearance of the words on screen – *The Dimbleby Talk-In* – De da da de dum dum. But the programme was deadly serious. The studio audience was made up of people with experience of the topics we covered. I was briefed in advance on what each one of them wanted to say. We took one topic a week and for an hour discussed it in detail. Among the many subjects covered were the ground-breaking (depression, abortion – with women talking about their experiences), the dated (women talking about how a man should come home to beef for dinner, not chicken) and the perennials (discipline in schools, housing, MPs' greed and corruption). Each topic was given an airing for a full hour, far more than the quarter of an hour or so they would be allowed on *Question Time*. It was a pity when it ended.

But, as was no doubt also true in Athens, those who do not speak cannot be heard. I was less worried by the political balance of our *Question Time* audiences, which we were at pains to make fair, than I was by the social mix. At the end of each edition, heaving a sigh of relief, after 'That's all from *Question Time* for this week. Next week we will be in Chelmsford,' I would say, 'If you want to come, this is how to apply.' The consequence was that only those who had watched to the bitter end, which was usually approaching midnight, knew where we were going next, and so could decide whether to come. It meant the *Question Time* audience was made up mainly of *Question Time* viewers, a self-selecting group broadly taken from what, for want of a better word, we call the middle classes. We did not hear enough from people on low incomes. Those who did come and put up their hands to speak tended to be well-versed in the current political debate because they watched the programme each week. They were not necessarily representative of the country as a whole.

Question Time is often accused by those who voted Remain of having unduly promoted, even created, the architect of Brexit, Nigel Farage. Farage first appeared on the programme in the late autumn of 1999. He was by then the leading light, although not yet formally the leader, of the UK Independence Party, UKIP. He had just been elected a Member of the European Parliament and his party had beaten the Greens, who usually did well in European Parliament elections, into fourth place. Waiting to go on stage, while other guests sat silently in the Green Room, or nervously consulted their advisers for last-minute tips on what to say, Farage would have a glass or two of red wine and sneak outside for a last-minute fag. He was an immediate success as a panellist: articulate, amusing and engaging with the audience. They took to his man-of-the-people, no-nonsense style of speaking. He would invigorate any programme he appeared in.

He was not the first politician to build a reputation by appearing on the programme. Michael Heseltine, the first Cabinet Minister to agree to appear on the show, used

Question Time to help make himself a household name, as did Shirley Williams and Boris Johnson. Peter Mandelson in his memoirs says he was bowled over by Tony Blair's early appearances.

Farage appeared on *Question Time* when I was chairing it thirty-three times over nineteen years. The BBC has well-established rules for the number of outings on *Question Time* each political party should be given, depending on their strength in the UK and European Parliaments. To keep to the rules we had to invite UKIP onto the programme a certain number of times each year. As with the other parties, our instinct was to choose the most effective speakers. We were, after all, putting on a political debate programme. Farage was always articulate and forceful and there is no doubt that he won a following by his performance, but I do not believe he – and *Question Time* by association – swung the referendum vote for the Brexiteers. It is too simple an argument. The result was not the work of one man. And it's notable that the official Brexit campaign did not allow Farage to play any part in their team. He was ostracised. To blame *Question Time* for Britain's leaving the EU, which ardent Remainers sometimes tend to do, is absurd. What is not absurd is to credit him for the referendum being held in the first place.

Farage's fourth appearance on the programme was in the autumn of 2004 in Poole. With him on the panel was a Tory backbencher, the thirty-eight-year-old David Cameron, a politician coming up fast on the rails. At this point, in October 2004, Cameron had only just joined the Shadow Cabinet, but by the end of the following year he had become leader of the Conservative Party and five years later in 2010 he was, of course, Prime Minister. In Poole he was sitting on the panel with the man who would become his nemesis. 'I thought that having secured nearly three million votes in the European elections on June 10th and having come third in the Hartlepool by-election ... perhaps the political mainstream would listen to what UKIP were saying,' said Farage. I asked: 'So David Cameron, has Michael Howard [then the leader of the Conservative Party] given sufficient enticement to lure back Tory defectors and kill off UKIP?' In response he said, 'I think setting a date for the ... referendum ... is actually a powerful reminder that we are going to be accountable ... I think on an issue of great constitutional importance it is right to ask people what they think.' It was the threat to the Conservative majority posed by UKIP under Farage's leadership that persuaded Cameron to call the referendum on Europe.

The political balance of a *Question Time* panel is not in the hands of the editorial team but decided far away in the mysterious heights of the BBC's political secretariat, where the Director of Editorial Policy and Standards lays down the law. It was only when we had his agreement that one of the most controversial *Question Times* ever was broadcast. By the autumn of 2009 my editor and I had been arguing for several months that Nick Griffin should come on a panel. He led the British National Party, whose policies on immigration and on repatriation of black and Asian Britons were gaining ground in local elections, particularly in areas of Britain that had large immigrant communities. We felt that he should appear because he was clearly a political force to be reckoned with and ought to face the challenge of arguing his corner in front of a *Question Time* audience. He had appeared on television from time to time, usually during election programmes, so we saw no reason why he should not be invited onto *Question Time*. The BNP, however, did not meet the BBC's criteria for a *Question Time* outing, which was that the party should have won a seat in either the UK or the European Parliament. The BNP had been winning seats on local councils, but it was not until June 2009 that they won two seats in the European Parliament. They were now entitled under the BBC's rules to appear on *Question Time*. When the decision was announced there was uproar. Diane Abbott, at the time one of the country's few black MPs, worried that his appearance might make him more popular because *Question Time* was 'politics as entertainment'. Peter Hain, the Secretary of State for Wales and prominent anti-apartheid campaigner, and others, asked us to think again. But, supported by no less than our own Director General, Mark Thompson, we stuck to our decision. On the eve of the programme Mark Thompson wrote an opinion piece for the *Guardian* arguing that the BNP had met the criteria for appearing on *Question Time* and it would be censorship to prevent it. 'Democratic societies sometimes do decide that some parties and organisations are beyond the pale. As a result they proscribe them and/or ban them from the airwaves. But,' he went on, 'that drastic step can only be taken by government and parliament. Political censorship cannot be outsourced to the BBC.'

For ten years, under Nick Griffin's leadership, the BNP had been attempting to present a more moderate agenda than it had under its previous leader, John Tyndall. Tyndall was an overt admirer of Hitler, and a believer in a whites-only Britain and the enforced repatriation of anyone of colour. He was also anti-gay and anti-Semitic. Griffin had tried to tone down the rhetoric to make the party less obviously obnoxious to voters. The result had been the improvement in support that had led to his election as a Member of the European Parliament. Griffin was trying to present himself as an established political force, to be taken seriously as a contender for a seat in the Westminster Parliament.

At *Question Time* we devoted the whole week to preparation for this edition. We researched everything Nick Griffin had said about race and immigration in the past. As with any other politician, on the panel or in an interview, I saw my role as attempting to reveal the truth behind the mask. I thought he had escaped lightly from cross-examination on other programmes, but equally I did not want the *Question Time* audience to simply shut him down. On the night of 22 October 2009 it was we who were nearly shut down, not Griffin.

We had decided not to hold the programme in one of our usual venues. A town hall or school in Burnley or Barking or any of the other towns where the BNP had been gaining support would have been a natural choice, but was not sufficiently secure for such a controversial programme. We knew that anti-fascist groups were planning to protest and if possible prevent the programme from being broadcast. We decided that the safest venue would be our own BBC studios in White City, the imposing building designed, appropriately for us, in the shape of a question mark when seen from the air. The Television Centre was supposedly secure, with gates at each entrance and BBC passes required for access. It had survived most attempts at incursion, or the disruption of its output, for over forty years. Not, however, on the night of Nick Griffin's appearance. The *Question Time* team and the audience were all escorted into the building in the late afternoon. Nick Griffin and his escort of heavies were, by special arrangement, brought in by a back entrance. It had been agreed with the police that the protestors would be kept on the pavement opposite the front of the Television Centre, with the main road between them and the building. There, armed with banners and slogans, several hundred protestors could make themselves seen and heard without being able to prevent the programme from happening. They listened to speeches railing against the BBC from, among others, a little-known Labour back-bencher called Jeremy Corbyn. Everything was going to plan. Then for some reason, never explained, the police failed to do their job. The protestors swarmed across the road and forced their way through the gates into Television Centre itself. We were busy working on the last details of the programme in an office set on one of the centre's circular corridors when we heard a shout: 'Lock your doors. Stay where you are', followed by the sound of feet stampeding round the corridor outside and shouts of 'Where is he?' The protestors had breached our fortifications, but, like so many visitors to the Television Centre over the years, had discovered getting into the building was easier than finding your way around once you were inside.

Somehow a combination of the police and the BBC's own security managed to corner and expel the protestors. I assumed at the time they were looking for Nick Griffin, but I was told later that their aim was to find and kidnap me so that the programme could not go on. The doors were unlocked, and we carried on with our preparations as usual.

I talked to the audience and explained that the format would be like a normal *Question Time*, which was either naïve of me or meant to reassure them. I am still not sure which. I found Griffin in his dressing room. He had refused to meet the other panellists – the Justice Secretary Jack Straw, Sayeeda Warsi for the Conservatives, Chris Huhne for the Lib Dems and the playwright Bonnie Greer – and they had refused to meet him. One of his henchmen stood guarding his door. Two more were inside. Griffin was nervous, his guards unfriendly.

Griffin's reputation was destroyed by his performance on *Question Time* that night. Watched by nearly 11 million people, he came across as deceitful, his racist views and rampant hypocrisy exposed. A key moment was when he tried to claim that the BNP under his leadership was a moderate party and that it was hated by British Nazis and the Ku Klux Klan in the United States. I read out a letter he had written to the leader of the Klan explaining the BNP's policy on race and how they meant to achieve their aims. 'If you put [expelling all black people from the country] as your sole aim to start with, you are going to get nowhere. So instead of talking about racial purity we talk about identity. We use saleable words: freedom, security, identity, democracy. Nobody can come and attack you on those ideas.'

Griffin claimed afterwards that it was not a normal *Question Time* but 'a lynch mob'. He complained that we had not taken our usual range of questions – I think in particular that we had not raised the issue of postal charges, which were the subject of debate at the time. There are some programmes, however, where one topic is so contentious that it takes over the hour. Not surprisingly, both the audience and the panel only wanted to debate Nick Griffin and the BNP that night, as he must surely have understood. One person's 'lynch mob' is another's debate with an angry audience – where the audience wins. His disastrous performance led to his demise and that of his party, and I make no apology for it.

In any programme that offers members of the public the chance to display righteous anger, there will be moments of tension. It had happened earlier that year, when the so-called expenses scandal broke. The *Daily Telegraph* had published MPs' claims for expenses, all properly approved, but which, when exposed, outraged taxpayers who were footing the bill. It seemed that the House of Commons authorities had been interpreting the rules on expenses liberally to make up for what were seen as relatively low MPs' salaries. If MPs thought the issue would die away, *Question Time* from Grimsby in May 2009 would have made them think again. Margaret Beckett, the former Foreign Secretary and at that time Labour's Housing Minister, was on the panel. The *Telegraph* had revealed that among her claims was £600 for pot plants and hanging baskets for her constituency home in Derby. Admitting it was a mistake she nevertheless said she would not be paying the money back, a remark greeted with sustained boos and jeering. She should have been warned. Four weeks earlier Eric Pickles, the Chairman of the Conservative Party, had tried to explain why he needed a second home in London at taxpayers' expense when he lived less than forty miles away. 'If I could just make this brief contribution to "hang an MP week", he began, to loud boos, 'I have to be there in the House of Commons.'

'You mean like a proper job?' I asked.

'Yes exactly like a job,' he replied, to jeers and laughter. I met him by chance recently and he said he would never forget that edition of the programme, adding ruefully, 'It was not my finest hour.'

Being an MP can be a tough job (however well or poorly paid) and appearing on *Question Time* is a perilous outing. I respect those who see it as a public duty to accept an invitation, however difficult the outing is likely to be. I particularly respect those who come on the programme despite having being told by their party that they should steer clear. The BBC always insists that *it* invites who it chooses to be on the panel, not the political parties. Which does not prevent the parties from trying to push their own choices. We were rung by the Number 10 press office one week to be told that Kenneth Clarke, who for some reason was out of favour with the party, would not be able to appear as he had flu. Instead they suggested another minister. They forgot, however, to tell Clarke of his indisposition. When we spoke on the phone, he said, 'Flu? Me? No. They told me you'd double-booked and didn't need me. I'm on my way', and to the discomfort of the Number 10 machine he duly appeared.

On another occasion during the Conservative–Lib Dem coalition government of 2010–15 we had invited Alastair Campbell to appear for Labour. It was an important week. The government had just announced its legislation for the next parliament in the Queen's Speech. Number 10 said they would not allow a minister to appear if Campbell was on the panel. The BBC stood firm, saying it was not for political parties to determine who was invited to appear. We couldn't force a minister to appear, any more than we could force a panellist to answer the question, but we had other cards to play. In the absence of a Conservative minister, John Redwood – by then a maverick Tory backbencher – appeared instead.

Frontbench spokesmen, for understandable reasons, consistently refused to appear with backbenchers from their own party who opposed the party leadership. Since frontbenchers did generally agree to appear, this meant that these voices beyond the mainstream were only rarely heard. The result was a narrowing and stifling of political debate: an exclusion of certain voices, certain opinions.

For many years *Question Time* had a panel of four guests: three politicians and one layman, usually a journalist or political commentator. The format favoured the politicians, who could sideline the one layperson on the panel by ganging up on them or ignoring them altogether. By the late 1990s the format was becoming worn and we noticed that our viewing figures were declining. *Question Time* is produced not by the BBC itself but by independent companies, and a new company taking over the production decided to make a change. They would have not four but five guests on the panel. It may seem a minor adjustment but in the complex chemistry of the programme it was revolutionary. It meant we could have two laypeople who could work together against the politicians. It also allowed us to be bolder in our choice of guests. Billy Bragg, Tracey Emin, Ian Hislop, Sandi Toksvig and Benjamin Zephaniah brought iconoclastic voices to the table. Boy George appeared in a spectacular broad-brimmed hat. And there were comedians too, though theirs was a difficult role. If they were funny, critics would say they were not serious enough for a once-reputable programme of political debate. If they were serious the complaint would be that they were not much fun. Eddie Izzard was brilliant but unstoppable. Russell Brand came on with Boris Johnson, silencing the then London Mayor with a torrent of not entirely comprehensible theories about the working of the monetary system. The change worked well. It added variety and brought in a new viewing audience. Some politicians complained it was less serious than before, but the cannier ones recognised that politics is itself partly show business, and welcomed the stimulus of appearing with the provocative new members of the team.

There is nothing more dispiriting in television than making a programme that no one seems to have watched. *Question Time* was not like that. It was constantly quoted in the press, and strangers would accost me in the street to comment on the previous night's show. Particularly gratifying were younger viewers (and we had more of them than any other political programme) who said they had only become interested in politics because of watching *Question Time*. From 2009 it trended each week on Twitter. We even had our own fan club, which met for a time in a room above a cinema in Hackney. There, devotees of the programme would meet to watch it. They would take bets on what tie I would wear and perform vigorous Dimbledances to the iconic opening tune. If certain phrases were used by a panellist everyone in the room would have to drink. I am not sure what words qualified for a drink but I suspect it was clichés like 'As I have made clear' or 'As I have already said'. A parody Twitter account run by a robotic replica of me named the Dimblebot live tweeted the show each week to thousands of followers.

During the twenty-five years I was chairing *Question Time*, many other ways of pitting politicians against the public were devised. Radio talk-ins proliferated as did irascible arguments on Twitter. But *Question Time* remained the leader of the pack. Happily, that meant it was always a programme that young researchers and producers were keen to work on. Chairing it was exciting, but, as I used to say to the team, it was like having one's head put on a battering ram and then being charged against the doors of a castle. My job was to lead the charge, but, without the battering ram in the form of the rest of the team, I would be ineffective. In particular, the editors who led these teams were key for the programme's success. I trusted my editors. They became my friends. Had it been otherwise the programme would not have worked. I was the public face of what we did, but they took responsibility for everything: choice of panels, choice of subjects, balance of audiences, complaints from political parties and complaints to the BBC.

It did not mean I was their puppet. Once I was on air, what I said and did was up to me, as was who I called on to speak and how long I allowed a discussion to last. From the production truck the editor could make suggestions, which I could accept or ignore. These could be useful. 'You haven't asked x or y to speak yet,' or, 'It's time to move on.' But it was advice I ignored when I chose, because I had to judge the mood in the studio. This was the theatre where real people were inter-acting, and where I could watch the audience's faces to see whether they were engaged or not, something much harder to discern through a camera in the gallery.

I enjoyed ignoring advice. I enjoyed keeping order over an unruly mob. I enjoyed on one occasion telling a particularly obnoxious audience member to leave the studio. I liked being in charge, and that weekly surge of adrenaline is what I most missed when I decided that twenty-five years of presenting the same programme was enough, observing the old and wise adage: go before you are pushed.

The BBC had tried to push me once. Several years before I left, I was taken out to lunch at a suspiciously expensive London restaurant by my immediate boss. Straight to the point, he told me that my time was up. But it was, he said, seeking to reassure me, not the end of my broadcasting career. There would be a place for me on radio. I wasn't entirely happy about this. By chance a few weeks later I was guest of honour at the Media Society, an organisation of people inter-ested in all aspects of the ways we receive information, from newspapers to television, radio and social media. I was presented with a handsome silver plate, and the incoming Director General of the BBC, Mark Thompson, made a speech. As we were milling about afterwards, I thanked him for his flattering remarks, but added, 'That's all very well but that man over there,' pointing to my erstwhile lunchtime host, 'has just sacked me.' 'Come and have lunch and we'll talk about it' said Mark. At another lunch a few weeks later he rescinded the decision and said, 'You can go on doing *Question Time* for as long as you like', a reprieve that gave me another twelve years of active life. My old boss, who I still count as a friend, has always been embarrassed by his attempt to expel me from the chair and years later explained that it was not his decision, but he had been acting on orders from above in the BBC hierarchy. It had apparently been decided that BBC One should take steps to appeal to a younger audience, and having younger presenters was one way of doing this. The fact that we had more young viewers than any other political programme on television seemed to have eluded them.

When I look through the list of panellists who appeared, over the 914 *Question Times* I chaired in the quarter of a century from 1994 to 2018 (missing only one edition because I had been concussed by a bullock), it is like seeing a kaleidoscope of British politics. The same issues, coming round over and over again with the patterns just slightly and then suddenly shifting. Each edition brings back reminders of what mattered to our audiences, week by week, many of them still centre stage: jobs, the economy, public services, the NHS, schools, drugs, public transport, immigration and Europe. The issues remain much the same but the cast list of politicians changes. I admire them for coming on to face the music – discordant music sometimes – and submit themselves to cross-examination. And I admire the tenacity of the audiences, asking questions that matter and not accepting bluster as an answer.

Some editions stick in my memory. Tony Blair making a solo appearance as Prime Minister in Brighton, having a missile hurled at him by a furious audience member from the back of the hall, a harmless ham sandwich as it turned out, which separated in mid-air, the bread landing on the audience, the ham ending at our feet. Jacob Rees-Mogg in Slough in 2015 answering a question about a third runway at Heathrow and whether the increased noise level would mean it could never be built. 'I used to live not a million miles from Slough with the aeroplanes going over and I must confess they didn't prove too bothersome then,' he said. 'Eton, is that?' I asked mockingly, thinking I had nailed him. Loud laughter. 'That's absolutely right,' he said, 'I was at school with your son.' *Touché*. Louder laughter. Chairman grins ruefully.

There were dramatic editions too, none more so than the special programme we broadcast two days after the massacre of 9/11. Asked to mount a special edition of the programme, we put out a general call for an audience but did not have enough time to carry out our usual vetting procedures. As a result it was unbalanced. Most of the questions submitted were anti-American. Unlike the usual editions this was also transmitted live. On the panel was the recently retired American Ambassador to the UK, Philip Lader. There was an outpouring of horror at what had happened and a discussion about how America should respond. Then a member of the audience said in effect that America had it coming to them because of their own actions in the Middle East, a harsh intervention given that only two days earlier nearly three thousand innocent people had died in the Twin Towers. Press reports the following day said that Lader had been reduced to tears by the intervention. I have watched it back and do not think that was so. Three days later at the memorial service for 9/11 in St Paul's Cathedral I asked Lader whether he had been upset by the programme and he denied it. The BBC, however, was faced with a storm of criticism. It at first defended the programme, saying it regretted any offence caused and conceding that in the immediate aftermath of the event it was hard to stomach some of the strong opinions expressed. Two days later the Director General, Greg Dyke, said that while much of it was an entirely appropriate debate, it should have been recorded and edited before transmission, presumably cutting out some of the more offensive expressions of hostility towards the United States. With hindsight he was right.

Occasionally, when we were in funds, we would take *Question Time* abroad. When we went to the United States, people would invariably say, 'Why don't we have this format here?' Two of our most exciting forays were to countries where democratic debate was not the norm. When we proposed a programme from Russia in 2005, President Putin's advisers at first refused to believe that such a programme existed, with the public free to attack politicians. Putin's spokesman, then as now Dmitry Peskov, asked to see a video of the programme and, persuaded it was genuine, agreed to our transmitting an edition from Moscow. He even agreed to Garry Kasparov, the chess master and one of Putin's most outspoken opponents, being on the panel. Those, you could say, were the days. China agreed to our recording a programme in Shanghai because it was preparing its bid for the Olympic Games and one requirement of the Olympic Committee was that foreign press should be allowed into the country and given free access everywhere. We made *Question Time* a test case. It was an extraordinary programme: the first television broadcast allowing free speech since the revolution sixty years before.

We thought none of our audience would speak out against the government, but one woman did, saying that her father had been threatened with arrest after trying to stage a protest. Afterwards she said she wondered whether she had been wise to speak out and refused to give the journalists who had been watching the programme her name.

For over forty years, *Question Time* has been at the heart of the BBC's commitment to engage the public in the politics and the political process of our democracy. This commitment takes many forms. Its backbone is the objective reporting of politics itself, not just what is said in the House of Commons, but the implications of policies, and their implementation. The voters – members of the public – came late to the party and they are not always adequately represented. The creation of *Question Time* back in 1979 under Robin Day, albeit on the back of an envelope, was the first serious attempt to meet this requirement: with a weekly display of public opinion, and a weekly opportunity for voters to have direct and public access to politicians. At its best it continues to serve a number of purposes. Along with the opinion polls and focus groups used by all political parties it gives politicians a taste of public opinion in the raw – confrontational and full of zest. But more important than that, it can excite the audience watching at home in the process of politics and its complexity. We are living in an age where opinion risks becoming no longer a matter for debate but for assertion. Where my truth is the truth, and your truth must be discounted. This failure to listen to what those who disagree with us are saying is dangerous to democracy. Compromise and mutual respect are sacrificed to the assertions of what any one group simply knows to be right. One hour of television debate each week cannot on its own rectify that, but it can perhaps show that there is another way and a better way of handling the inevitable disagreements of a complex and divided society. Vivat *Question Time*.

A White Man in Africa

Foreign reporting spoils foreign holidays. When I hear
tourists being encouraged to enjoy South Africa's mountain ranges and vast plains teeming with game, or its golden
beaches and sunshine, I see only a country drenched in blood.
I have set foot there for work many times. I could never set
foot there for pleasure.

The prospect of going to South Africa came at a good
moment. For several years I had been presenting *Panorama*,
covering elections in Britain and abroad, travelling the world

to interview heads of state, and sitting through annual party conferences at home. It was enjoyable, exciting, stimulating work, and very varied, but it was its variety that was making me restless.

In one three-week period in 1976 I flew to Geneva to interview Robert Mugabe, the future President of Zimbabwe, who had just been temporarily released from a tin hut in the Rhodesian bush; flew to Chicago to interview the economist Milton Friedman about the theory of monetarism (this three years before the election victory of his admirer Margaret Thatcher); flew to Teheran to interview the Shah; presented the annual Budget programme; and prepared a New Year special looking back at the Queen's Coronation.

Those three weeks were typical of much of my work at the time: exhilarating, demanding, but lacking a theme. A series of programmes that had only my presenting them in common. So when I was asked whether I would be interested in a long-term project filming in South Africa I was intrigued and pleased that I could break away for a time from the role of front man, the jack of all trades.

By the 1970s, most other countries in Africa had seen colonisation give way, under pressure, to independence. Britain, France, Belgium and Portugal had with varying degrees of grace abandoned most of their colonies as no longer practically or morally tenable. But in South Africa, despite increasing pressure from the majority black population, and increasing disapproval from abroad, the whites seemed determined to stay put. The proposed films would explore the character of Afrikanerdom – the attitudes of the white population in South Africa who were stubbornly clinging to power. We wanted to understand the history and culture of these people treated by most of the world as pariahs: the architects and practitioners of the institutionalised racial segregation, harsh laws, petty regulations and inadequate educational provision that ensured the social, economic and political domination of the white population, known as apartheid.

I did not know it then but this would be the start of nearly four decades of reporting on South Africa, from the attempts to suppress black opposition to white rule in the 1970s and 1980s, through mounting turmoil and the violence of the collapse of apartheid in the late 1980s and early 1990s, to the election of Nelson Mandela as President in 1994 and finally his death in 2013. During that time I interviewed three Nationalist prime ministers; followed Nelson Mandela from the day of his release after his twenty-seven-year jail term in 1990 to his inauguration as President to his funeral; and talked to countless people trying to live their lives in this extraordinary country. When I first arrived, apartheid seemed firmly in place. Outside South Africa, condemnation was restricted to political pressure groups. Governments still traded with South Africa and her cricket and rugby teams still toured the world. Looking back it seems impossible that a system of government so obviously in defiance of every tenet of human decency survived for so long.

What drew me to South Africa was 'who?' and 'why?' Who were these people, in this country at the foot of the continent, who resisted change? And why did they believe in what they were doing, when what they were doing depended on the acquiescence or suppression of the five out of six people in the country who were not white? What kept me going back was 'what?' and 'how?' What would happen next? How would the populations of South Africa find a way to live together? I wanted to keep following the story as year by year the pressure on the white population became more intense and it seemed apartheid would be crushed by outside pressure and increasingly violent resistance within.

The Afrikaners, whose Nationalist Party had been ruling South Africa since 1948, are the descendants of the Dutch who first set up a staging point at the Cape in the seventeenth century. They had suffered a series of humiliations at the hands of the British. When Britain established its own colony at the Cape in the late eighteenth and early nineteenth centuries, many Afrikaners left, and trekked east in their wagons across the mountains to live free from British rule. A century later the British reimposed their authority over Afrikaner-administered territories to the north in the Boer Wars. Boer farms were destroyed; the women and children imprisoned in camps, where malnutrition and disease had led to over twenty thousand deaths. Their hatred of the British was inflamed by their treatment once the wars were over. Their language and culture were openly despised by the English-speakers who governed them. They were forced to speak English in school and as adults found themselves excluded from many jobs that were reserved for English-speakers, a form of employment apartheid imposed not by white people on black people but by white people on white people. Over three centuries they had lost any connection with the Netherlands, and had come to see themselves not as colonists but as indigenous.

Given this history, we knew it would be difficult to win the confidence of Afrikaners: to persuade them to talk about their beliefs and their justification for a system of government almost universally condemned. They were hostile to foreign media: we were all, in their eyes, liberal interlopers who did not try to understand Afrikaner culture or the reasoning behind apartheid. Their hostility to the English-speaking BBC was particularly strong. 'Smeer BBC' ('smeer' in Afrikaans means the same as 'smear' in English) was the cheerful epithet we heard whenever we explained who we worked for and what we were about.

However, I had the ideal producer for this venture. While television presenters earn the most money and win the fame, producers do most of the hard work, preparing the ground, contacting potential interviewees, arranging accommodation, taking charge of the budget, choosing camera crew and editors, and incidentally keeping their presenters happy. My producer David Harrison had been to the country often. He was married to a white South African, and his mother-in-law lived in the suburbs of Johannesburg. He had seen at first hand the impact of apartheid and the suffering it caused and was keen to discover not only how the Afrikaners could think that it was a practical solution to the problems of a multi-racial society, but, stranger still, how they could believe it was morally right. More to the point, he is the most stubborn and the most polite producer I have ever worked with. These two qualities made him the perfect person to woo the suspicious Afrikaners.

We arrived in South Africa, David Harrison and me, in the country's early summer – mid-November – to research our project. Our idea was to spend time before we started filming, travelling around the country and meeting a wide range of people – not just Afrikaners – to try to discover the nature of this strange society. It began badly. We took a taxi in from the airport and having briefly told our white driver why we had come were subject to a torrent of racist invective. Using words so vile they are not fit to print, our driver explained his solution to the 'race problem', which seemed to consist mainly of shooting any black African who crossed his path. Racism was not confined to Afrikaners. He was, he said, part Welsh and part Irish. He dropped us off at our hotel with a cheerful, 'Goodbye sir. It's done me good talking to you.'

It was rare to hear overt racism expressed in such violent language. But racism in South Africa took many forms. It was more common to hear that black people were 'not ready' to share power. We were to listen to many explanations from white politicians and religious leaders about how South Africa might resolve its difficulties and live in peace, but they all assumed that white people would remain in control, with everyone else given token influence rather than real power.

Before we set off on our travels around the country we met an Afrikaner icon, Dawie de Villiers. He was a rugby hero, captain of the team that had toured Britain seven years earlier, playing on pitches that Peter Hain – then a young member of the anti-apartheid movement, and by this time a rising British politician, and later a Labour Cabinet Minister – had picketed, in a vain attempt to stop the tour. De Villiers was thirty-seven and still fit, telling me with a sportsman's precision, and vanity, that he ran ten kilometres each morning in '45 to 47' minutes. He explained what he saw as the white dilemma succinctly. In his view, there was no question of one man, one vote. That was impossible. It was what the West wanted, but it would lead to a black dictatorship and a one-party state. What he and members of the so-called enlightened wing of the Nationalist Party were considering were gestures that they hoped might appease international opinion by softening some of the edges of apartheid without dismantling it. For example, he suggested maybe 'we could create a new mixed race class' allowing whites, Indians and coloureds (the word then used by white South Africans to describe people of mixed race), but not blacks, to marry across race lines – 'not,' he added, 'that many would'. As for taking part in government: there was no question of votes for blacks. Coloureds and Indians had 'a long way to go until they will be ready to run their own affairs'. It was a position I was to hear over and over again in the days ahead.

For the next four weeks David and I travelled across South Africa, gradually piecing together a portrait of the Afrikaners. Initially many, like de Villiers, were willing to talk to us, often suggesting ways of making apartheid more palatable, while retaining white power and Afrikaner domination. We had agreed that whoever we met and whatever they said we should not challenge them at this stage, however abhorrent we found what they were saying. We should simply listen. It was by breaking this rule that our project was nearly aborted before it had even begun.

We had been invited to dinner by a former head of the South African Broadcasting Company (SABC), a powerful man in a key position. SABC then, as now, was run directly by the government. Today the ruling African National Congress

(ANC) decides its policy. Then the broadcaster was a propaganda vehicle for the Nationalists and apartheid. Its broadcasters operated under strict rules. black men could not be called 'Mister'. A 'Bantu man' was the correct form. An announcer who worked for them remembers being hauled over the coals for saying that a black man was 'a human being like the rest of us'. Control of broadcasting was in the hands of the Broederbond, or Band of Brothers, a secret society, established in the 1920s by disaffected Afrikaners, to which Afrikaners of good standing in their communities were elected. In a small town it would typically include schoolteachers, bank managers, members of the Dutch Reformed Church and prominent farmers and businessmen. Only men. They would meet in private houses where the wife would provide tea and melktert, the traditional dessert of pastry and custard, and supposedly avert her eyes from those who came through the door to protect their anonymity. The men would discuss any issues that affected the standing of Afrikaners in the area and pass their views upwards through the organisation, whose structure was a cell system similar to that successfully employed by communist parties. The Broederbond had begun as a conspiracy to promote the interests of Afrikaners during British rule of South Africa, which ended with the election of the Nationalist Government in 1948. It had been so successful that by the time we arrived there it controlled every aspect of public life: a secret hand that influenced policy, and helped to implement it. Between 1948 and 1994 all government leaders were members of the Broederbond. We should have realised that they would be scrutinising us and deciding whether to participate in our films.

Our host, Douglas Fuchs, lived on a private game park. Acres of bush were fenced off to protect the wild animals that lived within. He was a genial host. We swam in his pool, and he told us proudly about a baby giraffe that had been born that morning, as he opened the first of many bottles of hock from the Cape. 'It's been lying here six years waiting for this moment.' I think it was the hock that was my undoing. Fuchs was given to orotund pronouncements in a mellifluous baritone. He spoke at length, cherishing his every word. And he was unstoppable. The world, he said, had a neurotic obsession with human rights, but curiously had come to accept violence as an instrument for liberation. Outsiders saw the Afrikaner as huddled in his laager, fearful for his future, but this was not true. 'We know we are under the searchlight. We are aware of – I don't want to call them injustices – let's say certain irregularities in our social set-up. But we know if we do what the outside world wants we are committing hari-kari.' 'Of course,' he continued, 'we are afraid of being overrun by blacks if things do not change. But we cannot share power with them, as Europe wants. We would be wiped off the face of the earth. So to secure white power and at the same time ensure black happiness we must remove injustices by giving blacks the vote, not in the government of the country as a whole, but only in their own areas.'

It was an analysis, impervious to the cruelties, inhumanities and daily humiliations of apartheid, that was to become very familiar. By now more bottles of wine had been opened. Mrs Fuchs, who had made several attempts to interrupt, finally produced the food from the barbeque, which had first been overcooked and had then gone cold. It was one o'clock in the morning when I finally found a moment to stem the torrent. I asked why, if the policies were right, they had not been carried out in the thirty years the Nationalists had been in power. Fuchs agreed. 'We have not done too well, but you'll see, after the election there will be changes.' I suggested that when the Dutch first arrived they had intermarried with the black inhabitants of the Cape and had lived in harmony. Why couldn't they have carried on like that? A multi-racial society. Not true, he said. That had not really happened. The Afrikaners' religion forbade miscegenation, and however tempting it might have been, there was no way they would have given in to lust.

It struck me that this was an argument I was not going to win, but it was worse than that. I had crossed a line. Our plan was to listen, not to judge. My comments were clearly a judgement and we would pay for them. Fuchs was a senior and respected figure in Afrikanerdom and a Broederbond member. We realised too late that the invitation to meet him, which had come out of the blue, was not to make us feel welcome, but to sound us out to see if we could be trusted to tell the story the Afrikaners wanted the world to hear. We had failed the test. Bush telegraph is perhaps an accurate description of how the Broederbond works, and it got to work. Doors started shutting in our faces.

It was surprising that we had been allowed to come into the country at all. Our permits had been issued by the Minister of Information and our first meeting with the minister seemed to have gone well. Instead of the usual litany of complaints about how the outside world misunderstood South Africa he said frankly that South Africa's 'difficulties were almost insurmountable'. The 'steamroller of history' was more powerful than any individual and could not be resisted. His solution was one to which many so-called 'enlightened' Afrikaners now subscribed in an attempt to remain in power while assuaging international condemnation. It was a fantasy world they proposed, in which all black people would be made citizens of countries or states established in their tribal areas. These so-called homelands would be given their own parliaments and in theory be self-governing. Once they were established, black people would become foreigners in white South Africa. 'Hey Presto!' our minister exclaimed. 'We have accepted the steamroller of history.' There were so many flaws in the idea that everyone except the deluded Nationalist Party saw through it. The homelands were impoverished and sometimes split into more than one geographical area. And the wealth of South Africa – most of the gold and diamonds and platinum – would remain in white hands. Black people would come to work as foreigners, immigrants. It was risible.

Word of our evening with Douglas Fuchs spread. The Broederbond had done its work well. The Minister of Information called us back in for another meeting. It had been decided, he said, that we could continue filming, but only on condition that the BBC would agree to show a separate film after ours, made by the South African government, to explain their case. If the BBC refused to accept this, we would be expelled.

We had already told the BBC that we were not getting the access we needed and maybe we should abandon the project. 'No. Keep going,' our own Head of Current Affairs had said, overriding our faint hearts and apparently happy to risk the expense of a fruitless enterprise. Faced with the threat to expel us, the BBC Director General replied to the South African Information Minister that it was out of the question for the BBC to agree to the proposal. We waited for another summons to the Ministry, to be told that our visas had been withdrawn. Nothing happened. Days passed. Silence. No summons. So we carried on, trying to be more careful and polite than ever.

Out of the blue, one Afrikaner came to our rescue. He spoke to us not only on our first visit, but time and time again down the years. He became our litmus test for the state of Afrikanerdom as, over the next decade, apartheid crumbled. He was neither rich nor powerful. He was a farmer with two and a half thousand acres of poor land in Natal, home of the Zulus. There he farmed cattle and arable, employing twelve black workers who lived in a collection of shacks on his land with their parents, wives and children: 150 people in all, he reckoned. So far, so typical of thousands of white South African farmers. What distinguished him was his willingness to talk to us year after year as he saw his fantasy of a peaceful and prosperous country fade. Riaan Kriel was tall, good look-ing, snub nosed, with slightly protruding ears and piercing blue eyes. He had a passing resemblance to the American actor Steve McQueen, a comparison he enjoyed.

We met him because of his involvement in the annual commemoration of the Battle of Blood River, the victory in 1838 of the Boers over the Zulus. At the time the Boer settlers and the Zulus had been in constant conflict with disputes over land and stolen cattle. The Boer leader attempted to

make peace and an agreement was reached. He and his negotiating team went to celebrate with the Zulus, leaving their
weapons behind them as a gesture of goodwill. They were
massacred. The Boers sought retribution. A few days later at
dusk they made a circle of their wagons, over sixty in all, in a
bend in a river. They tied branches of thorns between the
wagons to make a stockade. Armed with muskets and cannon
against Zulu spears they waited for dawn and the expected
attack. By dusk on the following day, 16 December, three
Boers had been injured and three thousand Zulus killed. The
river, stained red with Zulu blood, was renamed Blood River
by the Boers, who swore to keep the day sacred for ever.
Riaan Kriel lived near Blood River and was in charge of the
annual ceremonial, which we planned to film. 'BBC? Bloody
British Communists' was Kriel's genial welcome when we
sought his permission to film, and then he launched into an
explanation of the significance of the day. 'God sent us here
and led us into battle against the Zulus, the fiercest African
tribe, to give us a chance to convert them.' It was a remarka-
ble claim to be making in the 1970s, but then he was, it turned
out, an elder of the Dutch Reformed Church, which continued to use the Bible as justification for racial segregation until
well into the 1980s. Kriel solemnly told me that the book of
Joshua revealed that some people were destined to be 'hewers
of wood and drawers of water'. He believed that black Africans
should be in effect told what was what. 'They should be separate, and that's that.'

Back at his simple stone farmhouse with its corrugated-
iron roof he patted the walls. 'It could come to war, but the
terrorists won't be able to shoot through that easily.' He did

not trust the Prime Minister, John Vorster, who had moved 'too far to the left' from the original concept of apartheid developed by Hendrik Verwoerd. We were in luck. Here was a political hardliner who for some reason had taken to us and could lead us through the labyrinth of Afrikaner political thinking. He was opposed to every attempt to mollify black African opinion, despised those who wanted to give black people self-government in their homelands, and believed it was deceitful to make promises that could not be kept: to offer hope one day and dash it the next. 'We are straight-forward and say what we mean.' His logic was brutal, but consistent with the notion of white rule as a God-given plan for South Africa. I sat with him one evening on a hilltop over-looking his farm talking about the violence that was engulfing the country in protest against the apartheid laws and asking him what he made of it. I mentioned the death in detention of the black leader, Steve Biko, who had been arrested for trav-elling to Cape Town and thereby breaking a banning order the government had placed on him. I asked how he could possibly accept that. 'He who abides by the law has nothing to fear from the law,' he said. 'Except if the law itself is unjust?' I offered. He paused for a moment and then said, 'But the law protects me.' He couldn't have been clearer. The oppressive laws of apartheid were justified as long as they protected him.

The Kriels, like many Afrikaners, distrusted English-speaking white South Africans, feeling that they did not have the stomach for the fight. 'They can always leave, go home to their mother country. We don't have another country to go to. This is our mother country.' His wife was unhappy that they

had left the Orange Free State, where everyone spoke
Afrikaans, to buy their farm in Natal, an English-speaking
part of the country. In the Free State, Riaan explained, 'there
was no divorce, no meddling with other wives, everyone was
married, behaved well, did the right things'. His brother had
sent his children to university and they came back speaking
English. 'Did it shock you?' I asked. 'Yes, it did, really.' Then,
he embarked on a long condemnation of mixed marriages,
speaking, he said, as an elder of the church. They caused all
kinds of difficulty so that after a year or two people wondered
whether it was worthwhile. They fought over which church to
attend and which school to send their children to. He was not
talking about mixed marriage between white and black, but
between English- and Afrikaans-speakers.

In January 1979, after months of filming, we were finally
ready to transmit our reports. We used as our title the words
the Afrikaners used about themselves: *The White Tribe of
Africa*. We were nervous about how the four weekly programmes
might be received, concerned they might be seen as an apolo-
gia for apartheid. It was the Afrikaners themselves we wanted
to explain – their history and traditions. The first film told the
story of the cruelty the Afrikaners had suffered at the hands of
the British, their humiliation at the end of the Boer War, and
the horrors of the concentration camps. We waited to see the
critical reaction. To our relief it was approval from critics of
both right and left. And so it continued as we analysed the
creation of the Broederbond, the invention of the independent
homeland theory and finally the suppression of black
opposition.

As year by year the rickety political, economic and social

structures of South Africa tottered towards collapse, Kriel became increasingly disillusioned with the politicians who led him. When each successive Prime Minister – John Vorster until 1978, P. W. Botha from 1978 to 1984, and finally F. W. de Klerk – tried to persuade the electorate that they had a solution to South Africa's predicament, Kriel despaired. When de Klerk freed Nelson Mandela from his twenty-seven years in jail and negotiated a constitution that would give everyone the vote, Kriel decided the threat to his way of life was now too much to bear. He sold his farm and emigrated to Canada.

I never knew whether successive Afrikaner governments really believed that independent homelands for the black population were feasible or whether they were just putting up the proposal in the absence of any other ideas. On the face of it, it was preposterous. There were 22 million black people living in South Africa, five for every white person, but the land would have remained shared out unequally, with six acres of land out of every seven in white hands. For hour after hour university professors and politicians would explain the homeland proposal to us. 'Would they really be independent?' I asked the minister in charge. 'Each with its own army and navy? Eight armies, eight navies?' 'I don't see why not,' he said.

Early in our first visit we went to one of the first Independence Day celebrations of a homeland. It was called Bophuthatswana, and was supposed to be an independent homeland for Tswana-speaking people. Independence Day was celebrated at a specially built stadium with all the ceremonial that the British deployed when Ghana or Kenya became independent. There were speeches and bands. The South

African flag was lowered, and an independence flame was lit at midnight. The only drawback was that no international guests came to the party. Not one foreign country was willing to recognise the independence of Bophuthatswana. It was still deemed to be entirely under the control of the South African government, and it was not even a geographical entity, but six and later seven patches of land scattered across northern South Africa. 'We are no longer helplessly at the mercy of the arbitrary arrogance of those who until this hour trampled our human dignity into the dust,' its first President boldly declared, but no one believed him. As I stood in the hot sun I noticed crates of champagne stacked behind one of the stands. I had a vision of them exploding in the heat and the audience thinking they were under terrorist attack and scattering. When I left after midnight they were still there in their crates.

Two prime ministers, John Vorster and P. W. Botha, stubbornly pursued the independent homelands policy. I interviewed both. John Vorster was contemptuous of my questions. He sat with his arm hooked over the back of his chair reminding me that he had always hated the British, from the moment he had been forced to speak English in school. In his class of Afrikaners there had been one English-speaker and because of her the whole class had to be taught in English. This explained, he said, why he had argued against South Africa joining Britain in the Second World War. As for detention without trial, a constant source of anger among young black people, he said Britain had no right to lecture him because we were doing exactly that to members of the IRA in Northern Ireland.

P. W. Botha was equally blunt. He was determined that the

homeland policy would work. 'We are not trying to consider the West. We are trying to do the best for South Africa.' And 'Our policies will not necessarily be accepted by the rest of the world, but if we can establish security and progress then public opinion will have to accept it.'

And so for a fruitless decade South Africa pursued the crazy policy of 'independent' homelands hoping to defuse the international opprobrium apartheid had aroused. It was in vain. But it was not international sanctions that brought the experiment to an end so much as the internal turmoil caused both by apartheid and by opposition to it. The economy was stagnant, and industrial disruption backed by the trade unions was preventing growth. A new generation of young radical black people, willing to risk imprisonment and death to speak out, was agitating, boycotting the schools and demonstrating against the inequities of apartheid. Earlier generations had protested and had been willing to use violence to further their cause, but their failure to deliver and the arrest and incarceration of their leaders seemed to have energised the generation that followed.

By now I was hooked on the South African story and keen to go back to record what was happening. In the face of mounting pressure from inside and outside South Africa, the next Nationalist leader, F. W. de Klerk, changed tack. To the astonishment of the outside world and the horror of many white people inside the country, he announced that he was going to lift the ban on the various political groups that were opposing apartheid; free Nelson Mandela from captivity; and negotiate a new settlement with racial groups in South Africa. I was there the day Mandela was released in February 1990.

We hastily arranged a live *Question Time*-style debate in Johannesburg for the following day, titled 'Mandela is Free'. It was a thrilling moment. For the first time anti-apartheid activists and former prisoners from Robben Island, people whose voices successive governments had suppressed, were able to speak without fear of arrest. They were optimistic as they talked about their hopes for a new South Africa, little thinking that the next four years would see some of the worst violence the country had ever known, and a near descent into anarchy and civil war.

The following day I drove into Soweto with David, who had somehow managed to set up a meeting for me with Nelson Mandela. After his release, Mandela had returned to his home, a modest house but well built and comfortable by comparison with most of the shacks that pass for home in this black township outside Johannesburg.

The moment I met Mandela, in the yard outside his house, was unforgettable, but for the wrong reason. I was of course in awe of the man who had survived twenty-seven years in jail, had been forgotten for a time, and had then become the icon of the anti-apartheid movement. 'Free Nelson Mandela' was a cry heard around the world. He emerged from his house and came over to me smiling broadly, this tall handsome hero, shook my hand, and said words I will never forget: 'Ah, the famous Mr Dimbleby.' No greeting could have been more absurd. Here was I, being greeted by the world's most famous man as though he was Stanley and I was 'Dr Livingstone, I presume.' I was nonplussed and embarrassed. Also confused: when would he have seen me on TV? I decided he might have heard my brother Jonathan broadcasting on the radio through the BBC World Service. Over the years that followed, when I met him many times, I realised that flattery was his preferred greeting for everyone, maybe to staunch the adulation that must have become irksome to him. It was a clever device.

The euphoria that greeted Mandela's release did not last. De Klerk proposed a convention of all parties to decide a new constitution for South Africa. Apart from the white and coloured communities, black people were divided against each other. The two major tribal groupings, the Zulus loyal to their Chief Buthelezi and the Xhosas loyal to Mandela, were soon at war, sometimes verbally but often physically. We were soon back to the grisly business of reporting on the violence. We made three more films in 1990 tracking the course of events. Their titles give a clue to the way things were going. *Facing the Unthinkable*, *Drowning in Blood*, and *No Way Back*. Supporters on both sides were hacked to death and their houses burnt. I have a grisly souvenir of the violence, a machete I recovered from a shack burnt to the ground in a revenge killing. When Mandela came to Durban to urge young ANC members to lay down their arms and throw their weapons into the sea, he was met with wolf whistles and boos from a crowd of thousands of his own supporters. Many Zulus worked far from home in Soweto, where they lived without their families in bleak hostels. There were pitched battles between them and local ANC supporters. An attempt at reconciliation in a Soweto football stadium ended with the Zulus armed with knobkerries and shields uttering bloodcurdling war chants until the ANC fled in terror.

Some of the violence was unexplained. It led to accusations that a third force, including disaffected members of the security services, were making trouble because they opposed F. W. de Klerk and his reforms, and wanted to cause chaos. This force was said to be responsible for attacks on the trains that took workers from Soweto into Johannesburg on their daily commute. We got to know one of these commuters well. His name was Solly Madlala and we had first met him back in the 1970s. He lived with his wife and children in a one-roomed house in the poorer part of Soweto. They had no sanitation and no electricity, just a cold tap outside. We talked to Solly again now, by the light of a single candle. He told us about his job, cycling around Johannesburg carrying diamonds in a bag between dealers and stone polishers. His eldest son had been murdered, he did not know by whom, and he had been stabbed, losing the sight in one eye. Now he faced the daily danger of his journey to work. People – nobody knew who they were, he said – were getting on the trains and shooting at random. In all, nearly six hundred people were shot dead on trains during the three years between Mandela's release and the agreement on a new constitution. Thousands more went to work and travelled home each day in fear for their lives.

During this time there were constant outbreaks of violence designed to destabilise the country. Much of it was instigated by white subversives on the far right who hoped that they could inspire an uprising against de Klerk and his plan to abolish apartheid. I remember vividly a call we had early one morning from a contact in Soweto saying that there had been a shooting overnight. We drove into another poor part of

Soweto were taken to a house where a woman sat cradling her dead husband. 'There was a knock at the door in the night,' she said. 'He went out and they shot him.'

'Who?' I asked.

'I don't know. They came from over there,' pointing to waste ground nearby. 'They could have been police. I don't know.' In a nearby house we were shown three more bodies lying in pools of blood. A relation came in, saw them, screamed, and started hurling the furniture around in his rage and grief. Two hours later uniformed police arrived in an armoured truck to collect the bodies as the law said they must. They were surrounded by an angry mob throwing stones and petrol bombs. The police fired live rounds and tear gas and withdrew at speed. Day after day incidents like this happened until the whole country was living in fear. It was during this time that I had an interview with de Klerk to ask him about progress in the negotiations with Mandela, which seemed to be in danger of breaking down. I asked about the activities, which were by then being widely reported, of this 'so-called third force'. De Klerk's reply was that these allegations would be investigated. No evidence was found. It only emerged later that although de Klerk had received reports of a concerted attempt led by some of his senior army officers to subvert his negotiations, there had been no serious investigation. When the evidence was properly investigated, it was revealed that there had indeed been a third force doing exactly what had been suspected.

The great privilege of being a reporter is to be able to see a country for yourself through the eyes of the people who live there, not, dare I say, through the edited versions of people's lives that come through television or newspapers. Of course I cut and edit and shape interviews and observations like everyone else in this trade in the hope that it will give a true picture of the places I have been to and the people I have met. But it is impossible to convey the full complexity of anyone's life in a few minutes of television. It is the time with people and their families outside the formality of an interview that is often more revealing. Talking to Solly Madlala by candlelight in his one-roomed Sowetan house I could for a moment picture how the world seemed to him. I could imagine the hopelessness and despair and rage of a man just relieved to get back home at night alive.

We were regular callers, too, on Dr Nthato Motlana a mile away in his surgery. I remember the scorn he heaped on the idea that he, as a Tswana speaker, should suddenly become a citizen not of South Africa but of Bophuthatswana: 'a place I do not know, have never been to and do not want to go to'. The government's homeland policy, destroyed in a sentence.

I would sometimes go from a day's filming in the poverty of Soweto or another black township to the luxury of a large house on a hill set in its own parkland. Brenthurst belonged to Harry Oppenheimer as, it seemed, did most of the diamond mines and much of the gold in South Africa. He was the Chairman of Anglo-American and De Beers, at that time two of the most powerful corporations in South Africa. Harry had befriended me when I first arrived in South Africa and offered me a lodge in his grounds to live in. I stayed there for a short time but decided the opulence of Brenthurst life was too great a contrast with the squalor I was reporting on each day and fled to a cheap one-room apartment in

Hillbrow, a notoriously insalubrious district of Johannesburg. Harry was always cheerful, always exuding what I thought of as a dangerously misplaced optimism about the future of his country. Beaming with pleasure, he would tip his cherubic face to one side and say, 'Don't you think there may be a chance of this all working out alright in the end?' He was liberal by instinct and for several years a Member of Parliament for the Progressive Party, staunch opponents of the Nationalists. He loathed the oppression of apartheid but I never discovered whether he believed in a universal suffrage. I suspect gradualism was what he would have preferred, believing in the innate good nature of people and their natural tendency to get along with each other, a tendency, as he saw it, frustrated by the narrow self-interest of the national party. I once went to a dinner party at his house. With the table lavishly furnished with crystal glasses and candelabra, and liveried servants pouring the best champagne, it was a plutocratic setting for what could have been a rather dull and conventional evening. Not with Oppenheimer. Guests at the table included not only Dr Motlana from Soweto, explaining the dire effects of apartheid on the lives of his patients, but Dr Viljoen, the magisterial head of the Broederbond, the secret organisation that was still fighting for the interests of the Afrikaner in the Nationalist Party and in every corner of public life. It was an extraordinary gathering of people from all sides of the political divide and illustrated a curious feature of South African politics: that after Mandela's release and with negotiations in full swing many South Africans both black and white wished each other well. They saw themselves as South Africans first and the rest of the world as outsiders, unable to understand the country whose future they and they alone could decide.

I was not in South Africa for the four days of voting in South Africa's first democratic elections in April 1994 but I watched on television, thrilled by the pictures of long queues of people patiently waiting to cast the first vote of their lives. The ANC won a sweeping victory with 62 per cent of the vote, and the first act of the newly elected National Assembly was to elect Mandela as the country's first black President. His inauguration was a flamboyant introduction to what was now being called the New South Africa. I went out as the BBC's commentator for this spectacle, which for so long during the troubles had seemed out of reach. At last, out of the horror, a new way forward had been found and this day, which at times I had thought I would never see, marked the beginning of a new era.

The BBC had rented a top-floor flat overlooking the grand semi-circular sandstone sweep of Union Buildings in Pretoria, the official seat of the South African government. It gave us a perfect view of the crowds below and the dignitaries from 150 countries, from Fidel Castro to the Duke of Edinburgh. On the terraces Nelson Mandela and the outgoing President, F. W. de Klerk, were centre stage inside a bulletproof-glass podium. There were, as is the South African way, interminable speeches, preceded by a praise singer in traditional dress extolling Mandela's virtues. The oath of office was taken, flags were hoisted, and a fly past first of helicopters then of jet fighters streaked across the sky. It was a joyful celebration, though I did wonder what Riaan Kriel was making of it. I imagined him crouched behind his sofa on his new farm in Canada, watching through his fingers. For us in the BBC studio it was one of those spectacular programmes that everyone involved with it remembers: a moment of relief when the turmoil of the past four years could be, at least temporarily, forgotten, and the troubles that might lie ahead ignored.

After our first encounter in Soweto I interviewed Nelson Mandela several times, both during the wrangling over the constitution in the years between his release in 1990 and the 1994 election, and after he became President. Later, when he had retired from the presidency, he was lent a game lodge by a rich supporter, to use as a quiet place to write his memoirs. In 2002 I went to interview him again. There were tortuous negotiations with his lawyers over copyright, equally difficult discussions about how much of his time we could take up, and finally arrangements over whether we should use his study to talk in or the vast sitting room decorated with the heads of wild game shot on the reserve. The six hours of interviews were edited down and broadcast under the title *Mandela: The Living Legend,* as a definitive account of Mandela's life, from his rural childhood through his years as a playboy in Johannesburg, to his becoming a prominent member of the ANC and then, of course, the twenty-seven years in prison and their aftermath: assuming the presidency. In preparation for the interview I had talked to many of Mandela's friends and had read his earlier autobiography *A Long Walk to Freedom,* much of which he had written secretly while in prison on Robben Island. I wanted these interviews to tell his story but also to reveal something of his own reactions to the hardships he had suffered.

It was difficult to persuade him to talk about his personal experiences. He described his time in jail through well-rehearsed anecdotes: how he had threatened a lawsuit if a prison officer struck him; how he had persuaded his fellow prisoners to walk at a snail's pace to the quarry and once there to raise their picks and shovels 'so slowly they might seem to be in a catatonic state'. These anecdotes were repeated during the course of our four interviews. He was eloquent about the politics of the ANC: how he had been drawn into political action as a young lawyer and how he had become a leading light in the movement. Here too though he would revert to a well-worn explanation of leadership, how he had always 'respected the structures of the ANC'. He may have believed this but it always felt to me like a formula to disarm suggestions of arrogance from his critics. None of it, he seemed to be suggesting, was his doing. It was all agreed by committee, by the 'structures'. It was an inadequate explanation for the pivotal role he had taken in pressuring the ANC to resort to violence, abandoning a long history of peaceful protest in favour of bombs and guns and young activists being sent abroad to train as guerrilla fighters.

It also belied the role he had played in negotiating the terms of his release. He had already secured freedom for some of the older members of the ANC from P. W. Botha on condition they did not resort to violence. His own release by de Klerk was quite different. Alone in the warder's house he occupied for the final years of his detention, with its television set, its swimming pool and his own cook, he realised that he held the key that could unlock the peace talks the Nationalists needed with the ANC. He was the ANC's figurehead, its great leader, his name and face now known around the world. Demonstrators, students, sportsmen, pop stars, politicians, all incanting 'Free Nelson Mandela'. The government realised they needed to free him not just to quell the angry voice of protest, the constant wearying condemnation of South Africa, but to have someone to deal with who could deliver. Mandela had reversed the old rule of apartheid. He might still be imprisoned, but he had the upper hand. The negotiations leading up to his release were all on his terms and in secret, so much so that when an ANC delegation visited him in detention they feared he was selling out. His TV set and swimming pool did nothing to dissuade them. As Mandela himself explained to me, the negotiations were testing. He was alone against four or five government officials, and there was no question now of respecting the structures of the ANC or holding committee meetings to agree the policy in line with the rules set down by those structures. The conditions for his release, negotiated by Nelson Mandela personally and alone, were that there would be no conditions. He would only walk out if he walked out a free man. In keeping with his determination to be seen as a loyal member of the ANC, once his negotiations with the government were concluded, he delayed his release, insisting on remaining in jail until an ANC delegation had visited him to agree the text of the speech he should deliver on the day of his freedom from the steps of the Town Hall in Cape Town. A dull speech it turned out to be, written by committee and read in a monotone.

Mandela was happy to describe the detail of the negotiations over his release. He was happy too to lead me through the discussions on Robben Island in the 1970s that had led to his being restored to prominence. Mandela had been sent to prison in 1963. In 1976, the new young leaders of the ANC were arrested after the Soweto uprising, in which hundreds of black students had been killed or injured. They were sent to join Mandela and the old guard in detention. Mandela had become an almost forgotten figure in the outside world. His name was barely uttered in South Africa and it was an offence to publish the word 'Mandela' in newspapers, magazines or books. Impressed by his resolve when they joined him in jail, the new young leaders now chose him as their leader, putting the spotlight back on the man who had by then already spent twelve years behind bars.

He would willingly explain at length the ANC's role in the overturning of apartheid, how he had outmanoeuvred the white government, and how he felt no bitterness towards Afrikaners – even his warders on Robben Island, three of whom he had invited to his presidential inauguration. He talked about the misery of being separated from his wife Winnie Mandela, and how he forgave her for being unfaithful in his absence. He talked about finding love again with Graça Machel, the widow of Samora Machel, the former president of Mozambique. 'Two people who had been very hurt by life', their connection sparked by the 'sense of being lonely and trying to find answers for a very deep sense of pain'.

But the nature of that pain was something he would not reveal. I wanted more from the interviews than a description of key events and the political thinking behind them. I wanted to discover his own response to the indignities and cruelties he had suffered – some insights into how he had coped, stayed sane, and emerged after twenty-seven years seeking reconciliation not retribution. I failed. Mandela avoided introspection. In all his years in jail I assumed there must have been hours of self-doubt, of fear, of hatred and of frustration. But the public Mandela never wavered from what he believed was politically effective. Never betray fear. Never show hatred towards your oppressor. Only sound angry when it suits the cause. The only emotion he ever showed was to say he loved his wife and his children. His closest friends and allies all told me that he was difficult to get close to. His personal assistant, Zelda la Grange, a young Afrikaner woman who organised every detail of his busy life, told me that he was 'not a very emotional person. It sometimes seems that he has a barrier built around him that you can't break into.'

I have read the transcripts and notice that as I try to lead or nudge or coax Mandela into personal revelations he becomes more reserved, more formulaic in his answers. He did describe something of his daily life, of working in the quarry, defying the bullying of the warders, and finding solace in planting vegetables in the prison garden. But as for the emotional effect of those twenty-seven years, the most he would say was, 'before I went to jail I was very arrogant but when I was in jail I had the ability to sit down and just think'. A chance, as he put it, to review his past life and the future role he had to play.

I had hoped to discover how Mandela changed from a genial playboy in Johannesburg, taking his pleasures where he found them, to this heroic figure, an icon to millions, a man of steely determination under a carapace of humour and charm. It remains a mystery.

At Nelson Mandela's funeral in December 2013 there were lengthy speeches extolling his virtues and achievements. They went on long after the time we had been assured his body would have to be buried. According to local religious belief if it was not done by sunset his soul would not rest easy. But everyone had to have their say: priests, political leaders and foreign heads of state. It was not until long after darkness had fallen that I was able to end our live broadcast.

It is always difficult to close a funeral broadcast. I can't just say, 'That ends our coverage of today's events.' If I try something more significant I risk sounding mawkish. What business is it of mine as a commentator to try to summarise the nature of the event and the emotions of the mourners? Still more perilous is to try to find words to encapsulate the character of the deceased. But I was so moved by Mandela's funeral, the commemoration of a man I, like millions of others, had come to know and admire over the years, that I could not just say 'Good night from South Africa.' Instead I said that everyone from statesmen to the crowds watching had been trying to find the words to describe their feelings for him. 'Their affection for his warmth and sparkle, their admiration for his stoicism, their pride in his courage and steadfastness and their determination not to let his vision die. His is a story that will take its place among the great legends of our time. A story so extraordinary that in a hundred years and a hundred years more, people will still say "What a man."'

Windows on the World

How do we ever know that we are being told the truth? It is hard to tell. Untruth ranges from the obvious propaganda and lies spread by Presidents Putin and Trump to the sophisticated spin and distortion practised by our own politicians. The problem has been exacerbated by the rise of social media, that jungle of truth and lies entangled, where my truth and your truth carry equal weight, and we each have to decide which truth to believe. Many people now think the claim to objectivity or impartiality is itself phoney, a delusion. If all this is the case – and it is the case, to the extent that perfection is beyond our reach – what purpose is served by the reporter who strives for objectivity and impartiality? The answer is that it is better than the alternative: reporting that is slanted to make a case, that knowingly distorts the truth, that averts its eyes from evidence that does not fit the thesis it propounds.

As reporters, we have to try our best to be objective – to report the truth – even if that best will never be perfect. Similarly, we have to try our imperfect best to prioritise what really matters. Because we cannot possibly show the whole world. And what we choose to show – what we prioritise – is how people end up seeing the world.

Changes to technology like social media raise fresh challenges, and solutions, to these twin problems of how to choose what to report, and how to report it truthfully. Instagram and Facebook and Twitter and iPhone journalism can make us feel like these are new questions. But they are, rather, fundamental, timeless questions. Back in the 1960s and 1970s when I was plying my trade as a foreign reporter they felt just as relevant as they do today. Then, as now, new technologies were allowing us and requiring us to report the world in new ways.

Today, television has instant access to any part of the world. In the 1950s and 60s the technology was cumbersome. There were no satellites, no digital cameras, no smartphones. Everything was done on film. And film still had to be sent back to London to be developed and then edited by literally cutting the film into sections and sticking them together. The sound came separately on tape and had to be aligned with the picture for transmission. I remember when the first cameras that could simultaneously record sound came into use in the

1960s, bringing life to pictures: the magic of simple effects, like hearing a door closing or a car driving through a tunnel, at its most prosaic; or the cries of a person in pain, the sound of a mortar round being fired or a mine exploding, at its most vividly disturbing. 'Television's Window on the World' was *Panorama*'s boast in the early 1960s, and that is how it felt, as week after week viewers were transported to countries they had only previously read about. Simply to see what these places looked like, and to hear the voices of the people who lived there, was a novelty. Foreign reporting was sometimes not much more than turning up somewhere with a camera and saying 'look at this country'. The phrase, 'Window on the World', was apt. Of course a window gives one a better view than a brick wall. Nonetheless, it unavoidably restricts and frames that view.

In 1965 I went on one of these 'look at this country' assignments to Saudi Arabia. It was the first time a television crew had ever been allowed to report on this secret kingdom and the trip had been arranged by curious means. Saudi Arabia had just arranged to buy Lightning fighter planes from Britain, and the man who had helped broker the deal arranged with the new Saudi king, perhaps to make the deal more palatable for the British public, for the BBC to be allowed to film there. It was not for *Panorama*'s 'Window on the World', but for *Enquiry*: a programme for the new BBC Two channel that had just been launched, with a publicity campaign showing BBC Two as a newly born marsupial emerging from the pouch of a kangaroo labelled BBC One.

Saudi Arabia's new king, King Faisal II, had just ousted his brother from the throne and was supposedly planning to liberalise and modernise the country, albeit under the watchful eye of the religious leaders of the Wahabi sect of Islam, renowned for their austere puritanism and adherence to traditional values. In Saudi Arabia women were still being stoned to death in the public square for adultery, thieves would have their right hands cut off and recalcitrant youths were driven by men with long sticks into the mosque for Friday prayers. This medieval society was operating alongside new wealth, in a country whose oil was being pumped from the sand by the giant American company Aramco. In its cities mud palaces were being replaced with modern concrete offices and camels by chrome-burnished American limousines.

It was a complex political and social story we wanted to tell and, this being for television with its fast turnaround, there was little time to tell it. I did the usual rounds, talking to people who knew the country – journalists and diplomats – and speed-reading what I could, from Wilfred Thesiger's romantic accounts of desert life to Aramco's history of the exploitation of oil. When I set off I knew as much about the country as a well-informed tourist might. Expecting the filming to be stressful I took a box of cigars, and, alcohol being banned in Saudi Arabia, a very large bottle of kaolin and morphine. This was an over-the-counter cure for stomach upsets, but more importantly, it was a replacement for a late-night whisky. Left to settle, the kaolin sinks to the bottom of the bottle and the clear dark brown morphine rises to the top, a perfect substitute for my favourite malt.

Travelling through the country was exciting. We went with our driver and interpreter (on the staff of the Ministry of

Information of course) from Jeddah on the Red Sea to Riyadh in the centre and then across to Dhahran, a town quite out of character with the rest of the country, built along the lines of a California suburb to make American oil workers feel at home. On the way we diverted to film Bedouin living in their goat-hair tents in the wilderness of the desert, its sand dunes sculpted into sharp-edged hills, curling like waves about to break. We filmed in an oasis, with its village of mud houses, palm trees and scented flowers probed by iridescent blue butterflies.

I watched the black-and-white film again recently, wondering what a viewer nearly sixty years ago would have learnt from it. We are so bombarded now with news from the Middle East, whether Assad's murderous regime in Syria, the chaos of Iraq after the Bush/Blair war, or the never-to-end Israeli/Palestinian disputes, to say nothing of ISIS, al-Qaeda and al-Shabab, that the 1960s seem relatively staid. Faisal was an autocratic ruler of his desert kingdom, allied closely to a Britain that still had a powerful political and military presence on the fringes of his territory, fearful of Arab nationalism with its socialist agenda seeping into his conservative domain, and supported by an apparently inexhaustible supply of American dollars from the black liquid under the sand. That was the picture I painted and it was a good political travelogue. It dealt with Saudi Arabia's importance in the Middle East and the influence it wielded through its control of the oil market. Its failure was that it did not explore issues of human rights and political freedom, which still dog Saudi Arabia today. They may no longer stone adulterous women to death, but they do carry out torture and kill opponents.

The king was polite, even welcoming. He had given us permission, he said, to film him at Friday prayers inside the mosque. Why had we not come? I explained that our cameraman, who had been following him in, had taken fright at the sight of the royal bodyguard, their swords unsheathed, glaring down his lens. He feared they might not have been told that we were to be allowed in and, discretion being of course the better part of valour, decided to halt. The king smiled wryly, as he did at points throughout the interview when he felt he had given an astute answer to a question, watching my face as I listened to his interpreter's translation, seeming to understand the English perfectly.

I asked the king about his plans to modernise the country and even make it more democratic, and how he would do this without losing the confidence of the religious leaders who had allowed him to seize power. His answers were all about the need to move slowly when making changes. As we know sixty years later, reform moved and still moves at a snail's pace. But there were no questions about torture, or imprisonment without trial, or women's rights. I had no evidence to put. A grave omission and the BBC were right to comment that it was not the penetrating examination of the country they had been hoping for.

The highlight of my visit was an unscheduled expedition to a camp on the new pilgrim road being built from Jeddah to Mecca. I had been invited by the contractor, who had heard that there was a television crew in town. I was flown up into the mountains early one morning in a two-seater plane that landed on the newly built road. Nearby was a large Bedouin tent, more of a marquee than a tent. Around the edges sat

Bedouin tribesmen eating their breakfast of dates and boiled lamb with rice. At one end, on a large cushion, sat my host. To his left was his interpreter, to his right his scribe. He was illiterate, but he was one of the richest entrepreneurs in Saudi Arabia. It was said that he had trimmed a metre off the width of the tarmac specified for the long road he had built across the desert from Jeddah to Riyadh, causing many crashes but enriching him greatly. He offered me dates and coffee and asked if I could help him by taking boxes full of cine film back to London and having it edited as a record of his work. His name, or a shortened version of his full title of fifty names, was Mohammed bin Laden. He was a Yemeni who had won favour with King Faisal and had an exclusive contract to carry out all government building work – roads, palaces and mosques – hence his billionaire status, and hence the fortune later inherited by his son, Osama, one of his fifty-two children by eleven wives. Mohammed bin Laden asked me to meet one of his sons in London to work out the details of the film-editing deal, which I did. After the al-Qaeda attacks on the United States on 9/11, I wondered whether it might have been Osama that I had met, but on checking I discovered he was only eight years old at the time of my breakfast with his father. The Dimbleby/Bin Laden deal, by the way, came to nothing.

Foreign reporting can be an addiction, and it is not hard to see why. Faced with the choice between an early morning train to Wigan for an edition of *Question Time* and a plane rumbling down the runway bound for Washington, Delhi or Cape Town, I suspect most people would choose the latter.

For the last quarter-century of my broadcasting life I chose the Wigan option and enjoyed it. I liked learning about the problems people faced here in Britain, hearing their passion and learning about the nuances and complexity of the issues. But for many years before that I was seduced by the excitement of foreign reporting, with all its uncertainty, its occasional hazards and its constant novelty. On *Enquiry* there were two of us, taking turn and turn about: me and one of the all-time great reporters, James Mossman. Later I worked for CBS in the United States. Every film involved a crash course on a different culture and a different country. In the absence of Wikipedia, not yet created, I would set off armed with a file of press cuttings and, if I was lucky, after conversations with experts on the issues involved. Total immersion describes the process at its best: absorbing every detail, every argument and counterargument, and deciding who had to be interviewed to bring the story alive and make the report, as far as possible, authoritative.

Sometimes, as in Saudi Arabia, the window I created on the world didn't show the full picture. Other films by having a closer focus did better. Two months after I came back from Saudi Arabia, a cyclone struck the Bay of Bengal, destroying thousands of acres of farmland and villages, killing more than ten thousand people in one day, and leaving over a million more homeless and at risk of starvation. Cyclones occur regularly in this part of the world, with winds of 100 miles an hour or more creating tsunamis that sweep across the low-lying land of what is now Bangladesh, but was then East Pakistan. On 11 May 1965 a cyclone of particular fury struck, with winds blowing for an unconscionable five hours. Waves ten to twelve feet high built up and roared thirty-five miles inland, taking all before them. Once the scale of the devastation was understood, appeals for help went out to organisations like Oxfam and the Red Cross. They were by now experienced at dealing with emergencies of this kind, and their relief work after the earthquakes that had struck Skopje in Yugoslavia and Agadir in Morocco in the previous five years had been effective. Not so in the Bay of Bengal. A month after the cyclone, reports from the area suggested that no relief had yet arrived and a million people were still at risk of starvation. I was sent out to discover what had gone wrong. I shall never forget the four days I spent there: only four days, but four days filming a picture of human misery that needed no interpretation. My cameraman and I hitched a lift on a small river boat hired by the Red Cross. Guided by a river pilot, our captain steered the boat along waterways, serene in the aftermath of the storm, though the stark skeletons of wooden houses and the occasional body lying in the muddy banks were reminders of what had happened here, as were the accounts of the families in the village that was our destination. Despite the protestations of the Red Cross that food was getting through, the families we found had had no food for seven days – only a trickle of seed to replant the paddies with rice – and had been drinking salt water, their wells polluted by the sea. One man told us how he had climbed a palm tree and stayed there for ten hours, until the water subsided. 'And your family?' I asked. 'I lost my wife and two children.'

The problem was political inertia. Food had arrived at the main port of Barishal, but had not been delivered. We filmed the cargo boats that could have delivered it still moored alongside the quays. Inertia, and incompetence, and the neglect of East Pakistan by its richer and more powerful other half, West Pakistan, which ruled the East from a thousand miles away on the other side of India. Little wonder that the East decided independence from the West was its best hope and broke away to become Bangladesh. When I came back to London with this film it was thought to be so powerful that it was transmitted simultaneously on BBC One and Two.

The report from Bangladesh was a story that almost told itself. Take a camera, ask a few questions, and the truth comes spilling out. There is no need for a reporter's conclusions. Let people talk, and let the viewer just watch and listen. It was the same when I went to the United States to make a film about the resurgence of the Ku Klux Klan.

In the 1960s, in the southern states of the USA, in response to the Civil Rights movement fighting racial segregation and discrimination, there was a revival of the white supremacist hate group, the Ku Klux Klan. The KKK had a record of bombing and murder. Their targets were usually black people or their property, and they saw white supporters of civil rights as traitors. In early 1965 a white civil rights activist, Viola Liuzzo, who had travelled to Selma, Alabama, in support of a civil rights march, had been shot dead while driving in her car by four known KKK members. One of the four accused killers was an FBI agent planted in the KKK and, to take the heat off him, J. Edgar Hoover's FBI spread rumours that the murdered woman was a drug addict, a member of the Communist Party and had only travelled to the South to have sex with black men.

In May 1965, just two months after Liuzzo's murder, I was

sent to the deep South of the United States to report on the Klan's resurgence. Contact with the Civil Rights movement was easily made. Contacting the Klan was not so easy and involved a little subterfuge. We were given the name of a jeweller in Alabama who we were told was a Klan member and could help us. We persuaded him that we wanted to hear from the mouths of Klansmen themselves, not from reports in the newspapers, about their motives and why they were resurgent. He agreed to pass us onto the so-called Imperial Wizard, the overall leader of the Klan, Robert Shelton.

Shelton, a former car-tyre salesman and printer living in Tuscaloosa, Alabama, agreed to meet us and be interviewed. Nervous of arrest, he made a rendezvous in an area of woodland outside town. He arrived on his own in a heavy bullet-proofed Cadillac, or maybe a Lincoln, equipped with the latest walkie-talkie communications, which so drained his battery that when the interview was done we packed up and left him stranded in the remote wood, unable to start his car. A mildly pleasing sight.

Shelton invited us to film at a secret Klan rally a few days later. We arrived early, by daylight, to give ourselves time to talk to some of the hundred or so Klansmen as they prepared for the night's events. They did not at this point seem particularly intimidating. They were all poor working-class white men with complaints about the economy and the threat that black emancipation posed to their jobs and their 'way of life'. One proudly showed me his uniform: the white cloak and the pointed hood covering the face with two small eye holes cut in it. He explained how his wife ironed it before a rally so that he would look his best. As darkness fell the hooded Klansmen gathered at the foot of a makeshift wooden stage to hear their leader speak. Robert Shelton's diatribe ended by listing the KKK's traditional enemies: black people, Jewish people and communism. His final diatribe seemed a bit confused. Outlining the cause of America's involvement in the Second World War, he shouted, 'Who was it? Who started it? It was the bankers. The Rockefellers and the Rothschilds. And Rothschild means Red Shield – Communism! That's our enemy.'

After this the meeting took a darker turn. Shelton introduced the killers of Viola Liuzzo. They had been acquitted of murder by the State court. They were later to be found guilty by a Federal court and given long prison sentences. On this night they were still free and were hailed as heroes. Looking nervous, they came onto the stage to loud applause. It was time for the closing ceremony. The Klansmen stood in a circle holding lit torches around a burning cross. We could sense the mood becoming more hostile to our presence, so we filmed the circle then hurried to our cars and left before the gathering dispersed. We had planned to stay in a nearby motel in Charleston but I insisted we drive the four hours to Atlanta to put some distance between us and the Klan. It was just as well I did. The Charleston motel called us the next day to say that later that night an armed gang of the Klan had come looking for us.

The mid-1960s was a busy time for me professionally. It could be glamorous: making a film about the work of the British Embassy in Washington with the charismatic ambassador Lord Harlech, I went for the first time to the White House, gaining access, in those more innocent days, without the security clearance now needed. At the gate I was asked for proof of identity and simply showed the guard the inside of my jacket with the tailor's label printed with my name. I had previously flown to Miami, I am not sure why, and spent the evening in a notorious club that had been a favourite haunt of the Kennedy clan. I remember it only for being propositioned by a mother and her daughter – jointly.

Soon afterwards I went to Borneo to report on the Royal Navy's role in protecting Sarawark from incursion by Indonesian forces. The Indonesian President, President Sukarno, objected to the creation of a Malaysian Federation, which included the then-British colonies of North Borneo and Sarawak on its borders. It was being called a confrontation, not a war, though it had all the appearance of war.

We flew to Kuching, the capital of Sarawak, and from there by helicopter to a Royal Naval outpost on a river in deep jungle, close to the Indonesian border. Nanga Gaat was no more than a helicopter landing site surrounded by a wooden stockade on an outcrop of rock above the fast-running river. The naval crews lived in huts and near them was a traditional longhouse, home to an indigenous Iban family, where we stayed. We must have seemed strange visitors but we were made welcome, and food was prepared for us as the children played with our camera gear and microphones, and their grandmothers looked on, quietly smoking six-inch-long white-leafed cigars. The Iban were famous head-hunters. By tradition young males would hunt down and kill a member of a rival tribe and bring the head back to the longhouse to prove their manhood. They were also devoted to the British Royal Family. On one wall of the longhouse were tributes to their culture. Framed portraits of the Queen and Duke of Edinburgh were hung in pride of place, festooned with human skulls hanging down on either side.

At nightfall there was an entertainment for the Royal Navy. A film had been flown out and was shown on a screen erected in the open air inside the stockade. It was *The Trials of Oscar Wilde* with Peter Finch or perhaps *Oscar Wilde* with Robert Morley. Either way it was a mystery to the Ibans. My abiding memory is of Nanga Gaat at night, monkeys chattering in the trees, the strange screeches of the jungle, and a group of bewildered Iban watching Oscar Wilde demand 'more hock in my seltzer dear boy' at the Cadogan Hotel.

Where to go and what to show was as live an issue then as it is now. It was not hard to argue the case for a report on the rise of violent extremism in the United States or British engagement in colonies in the Pacific. But in 1969, *Panorama* sent me out to cover events on the Caribbean island of Anguilla. It seemed a comic incident even at the time.

Anguilla is tiny, only sixteen miles long and three miles wide with a population of a few thousand. In 1969 it took the full might of the British military and police to restore order there. Anguilla was trying to break away from federation with St Kitts and Nevis, into which it had been forced by Britain. It felt the federation treated it with contempt and declared its independence from St Kitts, with the aim of returning to being a British colony. We arrived on the island before the British forces landed to restore order, although the place seemed peaceful enough apart from a brief attempt by a small mob to burn down the residence of the British Commissioner.

Along with scores of members of the British and foreign press, we watched from the beach as 300 paratroopers made their landing from two Royal Navy frigates. It was a full-scale military operation, the paras ready to face armed resistance, although the only weapons the rebels had were shotguns. It was the journalists, not the rebels, who were most at risk, had the popping of our flashlights been mistaken for gunfire. Faced with this superior military might, the rebel leader fled into the hills and went into hiding. The British were at a loss as to how to stamp their authority on the situation and chose as a first step to expel a US citizen who they said had no right to be there, but who fitted a false narrative that the island was being taken over by the American mafia. Dr Spector was a New Yorker, much loved on the island. He was arrested by the British, taken to the airport and put in a tiny single-engined plane to be flown out. As the plane turned at the end of the runway ready for take-off a group of women ran out from the vegetation surrounding the airstrip, seized the wings of the plane to stop it moving, opened the door, dragged Dr Spector out and disappeared with him back into the bush. This incident was the only story of the day and *Panorama* (i.e. my cameraman and I) duly set out to find him. It took us a day or two but after a tip-off we discovered the good doctor in a house in the hills held captive by the formidable women who had seized him and were holding him hostage. They agreed to let us speak to him. Pale and shaking with nerves, he said, 'I just want to go back to New York.'

The paras were accompanied by a detachment of the

Metropolitan Police led by an assistant commissioner who was notoriously bad-tempered with the press, maybe because he had arrived in the sweltering heat of this tropical island in his London uniform of heavy blue serge. Lightweight tropical kit was ordered and brought to the island by helicopter. To the fury of the assistant commissioner and to our undisguised glee, it never arrived, having been accidentally dropped into the sea. The assistant commissioner continued to perspire, more bad-tempered than ever.

Eventually peace was restored. The Anguillans were 'rescued' from their neighbours and restored to the status of a British Overseas Territory, one of the few remaining outposts of the Empire.

The events in Anguilla were I suppose a mini-UDI, a Unilateral Declaration of Independence. Rhodesia went through a maxi UDI: one that lasted fourteen years, and only ended after years of violence. Rhodesia, now Zimbabwe, was the last of the British colonies in Africa to accept black majority rule. From the Gold Coast, now Ghana, to Tanzania, Uganda and Kenya, in colony after colony the white ruling class had bowed to the inevitable and accepted that the days of white rule were over. Except in Rhodesia. The white settlers there thought they were different. For one thing there were proportionally more of them than in the other colonies: not many more, but enough to make them feel they had a right to stay where they were and run the country. There were 220,000 white people to be precise, and four million black people. Not an overwhelming presence but substantial. Ever since Cecil Rhodes had marched north from South Africa to take over the land at the end of the nineteenth century the whites had been in charge.

At the end of the Second World War, ex-servicemen had been offered land that had belonged to black farmers. The black farmers were moved out and the newcomers quickly established a successful tobacco industry, which along with the exploitation of mineral deposits made Rhodesia a thriving economy. When the British Prime Minister, Harold Macmillan, made his famous speech about the days of colonialism being over and 'the winds of change' blowing through Africa in 1960, white Rhodesians refused to believe the winds were blowing across their country. They were offered independence if they would follow the example of the other colonies and accept majority rule, that is, give black Rhodesians the vote. No way. In 1965 the Prime Minister, Ian Smith, declared Rhodesia independent – the first unilateral break from Britain by one of its colonies since America in 1776. He boasted that not in a thousand years would there be black majority rule. Britain, the Commonwealth and the UN all deemed the UDI illegal. But short of invading the country, which was quickly ruled out, there was not much the British government could do, except try to make Smith change his mind. Sanctions were imposed by Britain and the UN, while they tried to persuade Smith at least to accept gradual progress towards giving all black people the vote. By November 1966, the British Prime Minister Harold Wilson had agreed to negotiate personally with Ian Smith. These talks were held neither in London nor in Salisbury but on what was meant to be neutral territory, a British warship at sea off Gibraltar. I went to Rhodesia to report on how this

initiative was being received. It was my first visit. The country's capital, then Salisbury and now Harare, showed no sign
of being affected by sanctions. Rhodesia's neighbour, South
Africa, was providing supplies of oil and one way or another
with South Africa's help all the creature comforts the white
community could want were being provided. The old cliché
of colonial life being a round of bridge parties and golf with
black servants on hand at all times to drive the cars, clean the
houses, and pour gin and tonics, proved true. There were
exceptions. Some liberal-minded whites believed that there
should be gradual progress to black people having the vote,
usually tied in some way to their level of education. Few
believed in immediate majority rule.

The only whites who were suffering were the tobacco farmers. Sanctions had hit them hard. There were no longer any
foreign buyers for their product and prices at the annual
auctions had slumped. I talked to one farmer who had come
to Rhodesia from Britain in the early 1950s and successfully
built up his farm. Now his income had fallen to a bare subsist-
ence level. He had taken his children out of the private school
he could no longer afford, and was reduced, like his farm
workers he said, to making his own beer. One detail stuck in
my mind as he gave me a cup of tea. None of the china on the
table matched. It was all odd cups and saucers. That would
have been unthinkable in the still-prosperous white suburbs
where keeping up appearances was a creed.

The newly impoverished tobacco farmer showed me
around the village where his workers lived. He showed me the
school he had built and talked about what he did to keep his
workers happy. As we were leaving, one of them took me

aside. I wrote down what he said. 'You will go home and tell people in London how happy we are here. God will judge you if you do that. We are not happy. Even their white children are not happy. This is our country. It does not belong to the white man. Time will show. One day something will happen and then you will see. God will judge you if you say we are happy.'

After this first visit I did not go back to Rhodesia for thirty years, by which time it had become Zimbabwe. Wilson's attempts to resolve things with Smith had failed. Rhodesia had staggered on but finally Smith had to concede that he too had failed. Talks in London led to a new constitution, with universal franchise and a black President, Robert Mugabe. I went back to Zimbabwe to tell the story through the memories of those involved. Television is a compelling witness to living history. Everyone was willing to talk to us, from guerrilla leaders to the commander of the Rhodesian army who had nearly mounted a coup against the agreed settlement. They spoke frankly about their parts in these turbulent events, sometimes wryly, sometimes with humour, and curiously rarely with bitterness or anger. Even President Mugabe, with his unexpectedly limp handshake, talked to me with good humour about the part he had played, from his long imprisonment in the 1960s and 1970s to his guerrilla operations against Ian Smith, negotiating independence, and his overwhelming victory in the 1980 general election that followed. At the time of my visit he had been in power for twenty years. He seemed benign, in a mood to reminisce. But he was still the same Mugabe that I had first met in Geneva in 1976. Talks were being held there between Ian Smith, the British government, and various black opposition parties as UDI started to crumble and Smith looked for a negotiated settlement. Mugabe, rightly held to be the most powerful of the black leaders because his guerrilla forces were the most effective, had been adamant in that interview that white farmers' land would be taken without compensation and Ian Smith, as the head of a criminal gang, should be 'brought to book'. His first ambition was being achieved by the simple process of allowing the veterans of the guerrilla war to occupy and take over white farms. Only a few had been compensated. Ian Smith, on the other hand, had been allowed to retire to his cattle farm and live as a private citizen. He too was prepared to reminisce, speaking dispassionately about UDI.

I saw a different side to Mugabe two years later, in 2000, when I went back on the eve of Zimbabwean elections to interview him again. My agenda this time was not to talk history but to discuss his own twenty years as the country's leader. I wanted to ask him about the collapse of the Zimbabwean economy, the violent seizure of white farmers' land, and, above all, the horrendous massacre of his own citizens in southern Zimbabwe. Three years after independence the Fifth Brigade of his army, trained by North Korea, had massacred thousands of his political opponents in Matabeleland. I had been there and recorded stories of men being shot beside graves they had been forced to dig, and their wives being ordered at gunpoint to fill in the graves and dance and sing on top of them: 'Forward with Mugabe. Down with the dissidents.' Murder, torture and rape were the weapons Mugabe had used to suppress the opposition. He, of course, denied everything. There may have been some incidents, he protested, but they were not his responsibility. 'Even to this day,' he said, 'I don't believe it was just the Fifth Brigade which operated and is now being accused of the atrocities. I don't think they are the only ones who stand accused.' He attacked the new Labour government in Britain. They criticised him, he said, without knowing anything about Zimbabwe. They were 'arrogant little fellows' and he understood 'they have gays among them'. Labour's Minister for Africa, Peter Hain, was gay, he insisted, and was the 'wife' of the gay rights campaigner Peter Tatchell, who had attempted to carry out a citizen's arrest on him during his visit to London the previous year. It was because Zimbabwe criticised homosexuality that the Labour government was attacking him. QED.

This interview, and the contrast with our encounter two years previously, is an example of the difficulty presented by interviews with people in power. Whether it is a British prime minister, an American president, a Saudi king, or a Shah of Iran, the pattern is always the same. You work out the topics well in advance, choosing controversial issues to raise, and the questions that have to be asked.

The dilemma is how to conduct the interview itself. It is one thing to know the issues you want to raise. It is another to find a way of enticing your interviewee to engage with the agenda you have chosen. Heavy-handed hostile interviewing can be unproductive. The interviewee responds in kind. Better to try to coax them into speaking more frankly than they may intend. That involves, and this is the difficult part, trying to imagine what the world seems like from their point of view as well as your own. It does not mean empathising with autocrats who are torturing or killing those who oppose them. It does though mean not expressing outrage to salve your own conscience. Best to remain cool and just keep producing the evidence against them from what you have discovered, or from reports by Amnesty International or the United Nations. An honest answer will never be forthcoming but putting the question – and allowing the viewer to make up their own mind as they study the face of the interviewee while they offer their evasive reply – is what matters.

In 1976 I interviewed the Shah of Iran in his palace in Teheran. He sat at a small ornate writing desk in a corner of a vast room carpeted with the finest Persian rugs, quizzing me before we started about the state of the coal industry in Britain and how unrest there and shortages might affect the price of Iranian oil. Next I had to see his dentist's surgery, which adjoined his office, equipped with every dental gadget imaginable. He explained that his dentist was flown in from Geneva when he needed work on his teeth. At last he was ready to sit down for the interview. Unlike on my visit to Saudi Arabia many years before, I was armed this time with allegations from Amnesty International and others about the imprisonment and torture of opponents of his regime by his secret intelligence service Savak: claims that he said, unconvincingly, were exaggerated but that sparked none of the outrage that, had he been innocent, would have been the natural response.

During my years reporting for *Panorama*, despite its claim to be a 'window on the world', there was a bias in favour of English-speaking countries and particularly of the United

States. There were two reasons. One was a natural interest in America, which seemed at the time (I am not sure it is still true) to be culturally closer to Britain than was continental Europe. The other was a purely practical consideration: interviews or discussions in English were more immediately attractive and comprehensible than those in foreign languages, which had to be shown with subtitles or voiceover translations. This imbalance tended to support the assumption, repeated by government after government, that Britain had a 'special relationship' with the United States. I realised when I spent a year in the States making a series of films about Britain and America, *An Ocean Apart*, that this was a simplification, and that the history of the past century showed it was not always so. The series of films had as their overall producer the young filmmaker Adam Curtis, now famous, with a cult following for his work. They examined the often uncomfortable relationship. Where was the United States during the First World War? Sitting on the sidelines, with Woodrow Wilson winning the 1916 presidential election on the slogan 'He Kept Us Out Of War'. The same President who proposed a peace settlement in 1916 and, warned that Britain and her allies might not accept it, is reported to have told his closest confidante: 'If the Allies want war with us we will not shrink from it.'

The United States only entered that war when German U-boats sank American ships with loss of life. The arrival of their troops in Europe won the war, but it was no act of friendship towards Britain. And what of the Second World War? The country was divided, with a powerful lobby, America First, headed by the aviator Charles Lindbergh, urging President Roosevelt to stay out. Meanwhile, in 1940, Britain was on the verge of military collapse. With difficulty Churchill managed to persuade Roosevelt to send us fifty clapped-out destroyers mothballed since the end of the First World War. In return Roosevelt demanded ninety-nine-year leases on eight British territories in the Americas, on which to build American bases.

A year later an American destroyer was sent to Cape Town to collect $50 million-worth of British gold bullion (worth nearly $1 billion today) as payment for armaments desperately needed to defeat Hitler. 'Harsh and painful,' Churchill called it. It was again only after America was attacked, with the Japanese assault on Pearl Harbor, that the USA was brought into the war. None of this was Roosevelt's fault. He would have liked to do more but half his country wanted to keep out.

The United States pursues her own interests when they diverge from Britain's – and Britain occasionally does the same. In 1956 the United States opposed Britain's attempt to recover the Suez Canal by force from Egypt. In the 1960s and 70s Britain refused to send troops to fight in Vietnam. And yet our political instinct and rhetoric continue to focus on being the United States' closest ally. We continue to see them as our natural friend. We cling to the belief that sticking with them gives us greater clout in a dangerous world. In recent years we have joined forces in the fight against terrorism, not least in the ill-fated invasion of Iraq, and the ill-timed retreat from Afghanistan. And while we may no longer believe that we play the role, as the British Prime Minister Harold Macmillan condescendingly put it, of being Greece to

America's Rome – translated crudely, our brains to her brawn – we are still eager to be first to have an audience with a new president, even one as egregious as Donald Trump.

Television's obsession with everything American has distorted our view of the world and led us to ignore other, equally important, and maybe more important, relationships with our neighbours. There have been countless news reports and documentaries about every aspect of American life – her culture, her social problems, or her education system. There is no quirk of American behaviour that has not been pored over by reporters and filmmakers looking for audience ratings. How often are there similar films or discussions or news items about life in Germany or France, Italy or Scandinavia? About the people with whom we live as neighbours, and who might be better placed to explore our common dilemmas?

The parochialism of understanding the world through predominantly English-speaking voices is further exacerbated by a natural tendency to favour domestic stories over foreign. In Britain, and to an even greater extent in the United States, foreign news is squeezed out in favour of the domestic agenda. The Russian invasion of Ukraine has been well covered in 2022 as that tragedy has unfolded. But what about the years that led up to this, the issues that go back to the collapse of the Soviet Union? Under-reported for three decades.

I first reported on the relationship between Britain and the United States in 1966, in a programme proposed by the American CBS network. It came about from a joint BBC/CBS commemoration of the twentieth anniversary of VE day in May 1965. The commemoration was presented for CBS by the most famous of all US newsmen, Walter Cronkite, and for the BBC by my father, Richard Dimbleby. As part of it, I was sent to the scene of one of my father's most horrifying and memorable war despatches, the Belsen concentration camp, to describe the site as it was now, the long grassy mounds that were the graves of the tens of thousands who had died there. After the broadcast the head of CBS invited me to come to work for them. It was an irresistible invitation, a way of escaping from my father's shadow and making a new start for myself in a country where the name Dimbleby was unknown.

My first project was (it should perhaps have been no surprise) a comparison of the culture of the United States and Britain, or rather, since my fellow reporter was a Texan, a comparison of Texas and Britain. It was a curious match. Dan Rather, who was the American reporter, chose to describe Britain through the lens of 'swinging London', then at the peak of its fame. He talked of fashion, miniskirts and pop music. We heard from photographers and designers and of course from David Hockney. It was a portrait of a new youth culture, innovation, a newfound energy.

For my part I spent a fascinating three months in Texas, focusing on its ostentatious wealth and contrasting it with the poverty of its Hispanic population. I met a range of plutocrats, including, memorably, Roy 'Judge' Hofheinz, who had just built the great Houston Astrodome and had it laid with the newly invented Astroturf, simulated grass that allowed sports to be played all the year round. Hofheinz showed me his boardroom with his gilded chair in the style of Louis XV and his lavatory with its gold fur seat. Memorable too was my meeting with the magnate, H. L. Hunt, whose family's extraordinary wealth was founded on owning oil fields, the first bought from his winnings at poker. He was by now an old man but still keen to expound at great length on the threat communism posed to America. My producer and I had to pinch ourselves to keep awake. Finally he said he would like us to hear a summary of his philosophy. He pressed a bell on his desk and a door opened to reveal a perfectly coiffed blonde woman who emerged, as though from a cupboard, and, hands demurely clasped in front of her, delivered a five-minute word-perfect lecture about the American way of life.

We travelled across the state seeing the LBJ ranch, President Johnson's home, and filming Huntsville prison rodeo, an annual event that attracted huge crowds. The prisoners watched from a cage as fellow inmates tried to stay on the backs of bucking horses and bulls, with a commentator announcing what prison term they were serving. Those in for life were the favourites, taking risks no one who expected to be free one day could possibly have countenanced.

With my pot pourri of Texas recorded, Dan Rather and I met up to compare notes, a conversation that revealed the fatuousness of the project. I defended Britain against his attack that 'the rot had set in'. He said that my conclusion that 'the American dream had turned out to be the wrong dream' misunderstood what the American dream was. We ended by agreeing that there was no way in which Britain was going to become the fifty-first state of America. That at least was prescient.

I worked sporadically for CBS for a few years and would like to have stayed in America for longer. I could have carved out my own career there. At my father's death in 1965 he was the most revered broadcaster in Britain, but the Dimbleby name was a burden for me. It would have been different if I had taken my mother's surname, Thomas, but I was a Dimbleby. It came as a relief, checking into a New York hotel, to be asked, 'What the hell's that for a name?' In America I was unknown. CBS seemed keen to keep me on their books but my father's death at fifty-two left the family adrift. There were siblings still in education, my mother and grandmother to be supported, and aunts, cousins and an uncle to think about as well. They were all shareholders in our small newspaper business in Richmond, which was run by its managers but needed one of the family in overall charge. I was the only one available. After a few months I decided that to understand the business I had to come home.

I did not sever all my links with CBS though and they would still ask me to make the occasional film for their long-running sixty-minute news magazine. I spent a week in Venice talking, inevitably, about the prospect of the city disappearing beneath the waves. I investigated one of the first roguish 'pyramid sellers', Bernie Cornfeld, whose fraudulent enterprise had bought him a fine chateau in Savoy. I made a profile of Emilio Pucci, the Italian designer, who sued us for defamation because he claimed the way the film was edited implied he was gay. I spent time in Balham with Rosemary Brown, who believed in spiritualism and proved its truth by notating music for the piano dictated to her by Mozart and Beethoven, Debussy and Liszt. We took the music to André Previn among others, who agreed that her new music sounded like the composers in question, but felt it was nevertheless pastiche. Her ability to reproduce music in the style of these classical composers was itself extraordinary, but I found her description of Mozart standing beside her at the supermarket checkout to make sure she was not overcharged a claim too far.

The most intriguing assignment CBS gave me depended on subterfuge. In the mid-1960s there were two countries that were inaccessible to television – China and Albania, the tiny state wedged between Greece and what was then Yugoslavia on the Adriatic. China was in the grip of Chairman Mao's Cultural Revolution, a social and political upheaval focused on Mao's personality and his little red book of codes of thought and conduct. Albania, with its own dictator, Enver Hoxha, was the last European country still swearing allegiance to Stalin, long abandoned as a hero by Russia. Hoxha's was a repressive regime ostracised by the rest of the communist world. China was its only friend.

China, in the midst of ferocious social upheaval, had surprisingly announced that tourist visas would be made available to those wanting to visit: guided tours only of course, closely monitored. Albania followed suit. There was intense competition by US television stations to be the first to show film from inside these previously forbidden countries. A CBS correspondent, Morley Safer, had managed to film for two weeks in China, by pretending to be an antiquarian interested in Chinese pottery. His ruse was nearly exposed when his Chinese hosts took him to meet a distinguished professor of ceramics who asked him to identify the date of a particular pot that was in dispute. Safer, no expert, examined the pot assiduously and then, forced to make a choice, plumped for a dynasty. He waited, wondering whether this meant the end of his trip, his cover blown, and possible imprisonment or worse as an American spy. After a pause the professor said, to Safer's relief, 'my view precisely'.

CBS asked if I could pull off the same trick in Albania. Not keen to rely on a cover that required any knowledge of fine art, we came up with an alternative. There were three of us: me, my then wife Jossy, and a professional cameraman who used amateur equipment for this trip. We posed as members of a fictitious Hampstead Cine Club. We flew via Rome to the capital, Tirana, to join other tourists with visas on the government-organised coach trip. Not one of them appeared to be a genuine tourist. One said he had come from Chicago because he was interested in making a study of European railways and their different gauges. CIA of course. There were two elegant Italians in linen suits and tasselled moccasins who kept disappearing for a day or two and then re-joining the gang. We decided they were making an illegal deal with the Albanian government to import phosphates to Italy. I am not sure what they made of us except that they were irritated when we kept asking for the coach to stop so that we could capture yet another scene for our fellow cine enthusiasts back in Hampstead.

We maintained our disguise as best we could, using tips picked up from spy films. Before discussing plans for the day's filming in our hotel rooms we would turn on the water or the radio to drown out the sound of our conversation. If we had important messages for each other we would write them on pieces of paper that we tore up and flushed down the lavatory. We devised a code for talking in public. Everywhere we went we were accompanied by our official guide. He was keen to improve his English and as a way of coaxing him into indiscretions about the regime I recorded passages of English literature for him each night to help him perfect his accent.

In her brilliant 2022 book about her childhood in Albania before and after the collapse of its communist regime, *Free: Coming of Age at the End of History*, Lea Ypi describes the harsh regime she was born into, and how members of her family were imprisoned for years under suspicion of bourgeois tendencies or political dissent. We were there a decade before she was born but her portrait, when I read it, confirmed everything we had seen and heard. The elderly were left in peace as long as they did not try to undermine the regime, although the churches and mosques into which they would sneak to pray had been closed. 'Closed by the demand of the people' read a sign on one. The young, as Ypi confirmed, were another matter. They were brought up to play their full part in the revolution, taking part in the orgies of self-criticism and correction of bourgeois tendencies prescribed by Mao. We met a group of very young teenagers, no more than thirteen or fourteen years old, helping to build roads, wielding picks and pushing heavy wooden wheelbarrows. In the evening they came back into town singing popular numbers such as 'Up the Voluntary Workers Association'. They told us it was good to understand what a worker's life was like and to help convert the peasants to the new communist thinking. What the peasants made of it we never discovered, though they did display a lively xenophobia, women spitting on us in the streets and boys turning their backs to us, pulling down their trousers, and farting.

The poverty of the country was evident everywhere we went. There was soggy bread made from potato flour in the bakery, and in the grocers' shops just one luxury: rows and rows of identical pots of cherry jam to be eaten from a spoon with a cup of coffee. Cherry jam aside, luxuries were rare. One or two shops in Tirana sold second-hand cameras, radios and record players. A scent shop sold a tantalising array of colognes, sweet and sticky, one seductively labelled 'Cologne of the Fourth Congress of the Democratic Front'. As for makeup, there was no mascara and no eye makeup, only face powder sold loose and, I remember, an array of particularly vivid lipsticks, pink and scarlet, the height of Tiranese chic.

We went into the Palace of Culture where a group of girls were studying. On the shelves technical journals were on display, offering a glimpse of the outside world. I noted *The American Journal of Surgery*. The librarian assured us that Western literature – she cited Malraux and Shakespeare – was kept locked away in the vaults, but was available on demand. Other glimpses of the West came from Italian television, which could be picked up in Albania. Although it was illegal to watch it, many preferred its soap operas to the five-year plans being discussed on state-run television. Foreign films were available too, albeit in script form. All foreign films were subject to censorship, but if they were rejected the scripts still circulated illegally. Antonioni and Fellini were ardently discussed by film buffs who had read all the words but never seen a single shot.

Most intriguing were the wall posters that our guide, some-what gleefully I thought, translated for us. The posters were called flete-rufe and the rules of the flete-rufe were that anyone could post protests on them, but if you were attacked you had to reply. Within a few weeks a new edict decreed that protests were not to be personal or trivial but were to be directed against 'the evils of bureaucracy and all forms of opposition to progress'.

There were solemn flete-rufes praising workers or factories who had exceeded their quotas and condemning those who had fallen behind. There were proclamations by workers' groups about their discussions on improving output and furthering the revolution. Elsewhere, a woman in the Ministry of Education was criticised for her high-handedness in failing to place a child in the primary school she had promised and for not replying to the flete-rufe against her. The reply, reluctantly dragged out of her, was that she was not high-handed and the child must wait its turn – a fine example of any bureaucracy's answer to its critics. Another was a complaint that the writer and his family had not been given a place at a state-run holiday resort. The blunt answer: 'Those places are for the best workers only, which you are not.'

Flete-rufe could become personal. For instance, we saw an accusation by a collective that one of their members had left his wife and illegally married another woman, who was known to be of bad character. Reply by the husband: 'I have not married her, we just live together. Anyway, she is a good woman, it is my wife who is bad.' The wife's collective join in next to say that the husband has falsely accused his wife, who is both virtuous and hard-working. Round three to the wife. In round four the collective of the woman who the husband ran off with disregards collective solidarity and says, 'Yes.

The wife's collective was quite right. The woman he ran off with is of bad character and extremely lazy.'

The day came to leave. We were congratulating ourselves on having survived with our cover unbroken. We had packed all our exposed film in brand new containers, which we carefully sealed, putting unused film into the old boxes, hoping that if they seized our film they would take what looked like used film leaving us with our precious footage. Our coach was about to set off when a woman ran down the stairs from the lobby shouting, 'The coach must not leave. Please wait.' We feared the worst. Our ruse had been discovered. 'A coat hanger is missing from Room 30,' she said. 'The coach cannot leave until we find it. Please unload all the luggage.' Room 30 was our room. Two thoughts passed through my mind. 'We are going to jail. Thank goodness I took the precaution of putting on stout walking shoes this morning' and 'What an extraordinary country. This is how obsessive state control works. They actually count the coat hangers.' We were about to open our cases for inspection when another voice said, 'It's alright. We have found the hanger behind the door. The coach may leave.' Mission accomplished. A twenty-minute travelogue of this unknown country, complete with the sign-off CBS requires for all its shows: 'David Dimbleby, CBS News, Tirana, Albania', furtively filmed by the cameraman and me, having insisted the bus stop once more, this time for us to have a pee. We dashed out of sight into a field and came back with the words in the can, doubly relieved you could say.

I spent some time in two other communist countries. China (where astonishingly we were able in 2005 to present an edition of *Question Time* complete with opponents of the regime), and Russia.

I first visited Russia in the 1980s when it was still the Soviet Union. I went there with my daughter who was a fluent Russian speaker and acted as my interpreter. It was mid-winter and we went equipped with goatskin fur hats and leather boots bought from an army surplus store in Wandsworth. The boots were clumsy and difficult to lace up, but at least protected us from the snow. The fur hats, to our consternation, made us an object of ridicule among the babushkas of St Petersburg. We stood at a bus stop on Nevsky Prospect and heard women giggling. It may have been that the design was out of fashion, but I suspect the issue was the pungent smell of goat that they gave off. Proper Russian fur hats, I later realised, can be made of various animal skins: rabbit, muskrat, beaver, coyote, sheepskin, mink or raccoon. But never, ever goat.

In 1991 and 1992 I went back to Moscow, to report on the first free elections in Russia since the revolution, and then to interview Boris Yeltsin, the winner of those elections who had taken over the country's leadership from Mikhail Gorbachev. It was a chaotic time. The Berlin Wall had fallen in 1989 and, with its former states declaring their independence, the Soviet Union was collapsing. Russia was on the eve of its rush to embrace full-blooded capitalism, a transformation that occurred at such speed that it created utter mayhem, impoverishing millions of her citizens, while massively enriching hundreds of others – the new oligarchs.

I returned in 2006 for our *Question Time* from Moscow. It was a time when Russia, holding the chairmanship of the G8, still seemed, despite many setbacks, to be reconciling herself with her old opponents in the West. But by the time of my last visit, to make a film about the popularity of Vladimir Putin, everything had changed once again. It was 2018 and Putin, who had been in power for eighteen years, was facing a general election. All the elements that are now being identified as the reasons for his 2022 invasion of Ukraine were present then. He was popular at home, not because Russia under his autocratic leadership was a prosperous place, but because he had restored order after the chaos that followed the collapse of the Soviet Union. His narrative that Russia was being humiliated by the West and wrongly prevented from restoring the boundary of the old Russia was effective and appealing propaganda. It had already led to the annexation of parts of Eastern Ukraine and of course of Crimea. I met the mother of a large family living in a high-rise flat in the suburbs of Moscow. She admired Putin, proudly displaying the medals she had been awarded by the state for the size of her family. And Crimea? It was a great achievement, she said. Justice done. Russia's territory restored. And what was more she had been offered two weeks' free holiday there to mark the triumph.

Outside Moscow in a rich suburb we visited an estate of flamboyant houses complete with portentous classical porticos. The estate agent in charge of selling one of them explained that its owners had fled abroad. It had all the necessities of an oligarch's life: a spa, a subterranean swimming pool, a grand piano, an air-conditioned room solely to store fur coats in, and another of similar size with racks full of champagne and expensive French wine. Before the invasion of Crimea and subsequent sanctions, its owner had turned down an offer for this palace at $80 million. Now it was on the market for $20 million, and not selling.

The independent opinion pollster, Levada, revealed that Putin's popularity was undamaged by the sanctions that had been imposed on it by the US, the EU, Japan and others. And Putin went on to win the predicted 75 per cent of the vote. How? Put simply, Russia thinks differently. In the United States and Britain the conventional explanation of voting behaviour is 'It's the economy, stupid.' Not so, it would seem, in Russia. Pride in Russia and distrust of the West took precedence over his broken promises about the standard of living. Resentment that Russia was not treated with the respect she deserved, and deep distrust of the motives of the West, were bolstered by remorseless state propaganda, attacks on independent journalists, the closing down of dissenting newspapers and broadcasters, and the unswerving support of the Russian Orthodox Church, which is part of the state. I met the Church's Head of Foreign Affairs, who endorsed Putin's policy. One of Putin's former speechwriters told me that the secret of his success was 'his basic understanding of Russia'. The brave voices of dissent, those who pointed out corruption and its debilitating effect on the economy, or who publicly protested against the loss of liberty, seemed to make no headway against Putin's pursuit of his and, as he would see it, Russia's power. The two in his mind were indistinguishable.

In a former military camp outside St Petersburg I saw a vision of the future, as Putin would want it to be. A group of teenagers and children, the youngest aged seven, were learning how to assemble Kalashnikov rifles, and the older children how to fire them. On the walls of the firing range were propaganda posters exhorting them to be ready to defend the motherland. These young Russians had known no other leader than Putin. They had heard from their parents of the poverty that followed the collapse of communism in the 1990s and saw him as their protector from that kind of chaos. No doubt many of them have ended up fighting in the Donbas. I ended the film by saying that instead of becoming a more prosperous and open society, Russia was moving in the opposite direction. 'With Putin increasingly using hostility to the West as a way of bolstering his support, these are dangerous times for Russia. And dangerous times for Russia are dangerous times for us.' So it has proved.

The coverage of foreign affairs has a long and illustrious history at the BBC. It began in the 1950s with *Panorama*'s proud boast to be a 'Window on the World'. Back then filming abroad was a laborious affair involving reels of film and splicing tape, with the commentary added at the last minute. I remember once sitting in a recording booth and laying down the second half of one of my reports while the first half was already being transmitted. In the nick of time it was finished and rushed to the gallery just in time for a seamless transition. Today, with technology offering copious ways of reporting, from live broadcasts by satellite, to video recording and increasingly sophisticated mobile phones, the means of transmission no longer pose a problem.

What has not changed is the nature of this window on the world. A window is a way to see the world outside without being part of it. The frame defines what we can see. It offers a particular view. And so it is with television reporting. The viewer is at the mercy of the reporter's judgement, their sense of what is important, their interpretation of events. It helps if the reporter is a familiar face whose words we have come to trust, or whose occasional flights of fancy we can discount. But is the reporter parachuted in to cover a foreign story equipped to tell things as they are? Can they know enough about a country that is not their own to paint a sufficiently nuanced picture? Partly to address these concerns and partly to cut costs, increasing use is being made of local reporters, who live in the country on which they are reporting, speak the language, and have experienced the problems at first hand. The instinct is good but this is not ideal either. A local reporter can be vulnerable to all sorts of pressure that a foreign reporter can avoid: unwanted attention, threats or violence directed at them or their families by the hostile and sometimes tyrannous regimes whose stories they are trying to tell. That kind of pressure can tempt a reporter to err on the side of caution. The other source of information we all now have at our fingertips is the whole range of social media, often half-truths and propaganda or outright lies, but sometimes enabling new forms of brilliant crowd-sourced investigative reporting. We are becoming more adept at navigating all of this. We cannot, however, avoid seeing the world through a window. And as the courageous coverage of the war in Ukraine has shown, we still rely on voices we know and trust to help us understand it.

Broadcasting being welcomed by the Muses

IO

An Uncertain Future

Beware of politicians who say they love the BBC and would die in a ditch to defend it. It is usually the preface to an attempt to emasculate an independent organisation whose power and influence they fear.

It must be galling to be a minister, trying to make sense of policies in which you may not believe but which you are condemned, by your Prime Minister or your party manifesto, to implement. Galling to find yourself under constant scrutiny by an organisation whose constitution and funding you yourself have helped determine. *By what right*, you must think, as you traipse from the *Today* programme to the morning television studios to *The World at One, by what right do these popinjays quiz me about my plans as though I were the popinjay? What do they know about the arguments I have had with my Cabinet colleagues and my civil servants, with pressure groups and backbenchers? How can they possibly understand? Armed with a briefing document prepared by their researchers and probably scanned at the last minute as they come into the studio, they behave as though they were my equal. And worse still I have to treat them as though they were, or be criticised for condescension.* It must be a horrible experience and the urge to get your own back, to find some way of cutting them down to size, irresistible. But here the trouble starts. The press can be squared. Or at least, you know where you stand with them. They are either for you or against you. If they are against you there is not much to be done. If they are for you, a scattering of knighthoods and peerages will help keep them sweet. But the BBC is different. It cannot be squared. It cannot be kept sweet. Nor can it be ignored. The polls show that the public trust the BBC way above politicians or the written press. Galling. And hence, as they seek to emasculate the organisation, the mantra: 'I love the BBC' or maybe, through gritted teeth, I am 'one of the BBC's strongest supporters'.

There are plenty of other reasons that politicians, or people in public life, or just people in general, might have to dislike and distrust the BBC. It occupies an extraordinarily privileged position in British life – an institution seen as a priesthood, self-appointed and self-promoting, historically recruited from a middle-class elite, and until recently mainly men, and educated at Oxford or Cambridge. The class and gender imbalance, to say nothing of colour, are distortions that the corporation has in recent years been trying to redress, a bold attempt to defrock its priests.

Once inside, promotion comes from understanding its power structure and its arcane rituals, brilliantly and, sad to say, accurately captured by the television series *W1A*. It is an organisation where advancement comes from second-guessing what the layer of management above you wants to hear, an organisation with layer upon layer of decision-making that can stultify originality and risk-taking. All good people, committed to the BBC, but seen from the outside as defending a fortress, impenetrable and incomprehensible.

And then there is the BBC licence fee, an income stream provided by the public who are forced, at risk of prosecution, to pay for a service they may not even use, just by virtue of owning a television set. One hundred years ago when the BBC provided one radio channel and no television at all, its funding came, albeit briefly, from voluntary contributions. The Post Office, whose job it was to collect the cash, rejected the idea of a compulsory charge, on the grounds that you could never know who had a radio set. Dogs walked the streets, they commented, so their licences could be subject to spot checks, but radios could be hidden in the attic. Despite today's televisions being almost as hard to hide as dogs, few people now defend the licence fee as an equitable tax. But no one has yet found an acceptable substitute. In any case, for enemies of the BBC it is not the manner of its funding that is the issue but the fact that it is publicly funded at all in a world where everyone else has to pay their way.

Conservative animosity towards the BBC in recent years could be attributed to a genuine belief that in the new era of massive expansion of commercially funded television, radio and social media, the imposition of the licence fee is an anachronism and fundamentally unfair.

Their reluctance to allow the BBC's income to keep pace with inflation and the mounting costs of broadcasting may also be a reflection of a belief, I think unfounded, that the BBC has a liberal bias, is instinctively anti-Tory.

There is another, more sinister explanation: that every attempt to diminish the scale of output and influence of the BBC is designed to please powerful supporters in the press. The *Daily Mail*, the *Daily Telegraph*, the *Sun* and even perhaps *The Times*. Murdoch, the Rothermeres, and the Barclay brothers. Ever since the BBC first employed its own news reporters in the 1930s it has been seen as an unwelcome rival by the press, but the scale of its activity in recent years has taken that rivalry to new heights. The successful expansion of the BBC's news online, now the main source of information for many people in Britain and increasingly worldwide, has put it in direct competition with newspapers, their websites, podcasts and even radio and TV stations. Politicians need the press, who unlike the BBC can flaunt their views, on their side, as Tony Blair's schmoozing of Rupert Murdoch in the run-up to New Labour's victory in the 1990s demonstrated. In this media jungle, to be seen to be in favour of a so-called free press rather than an independent BBC makes good sense.

Pleas of poverty by the BBC tend understandably to fall on deaf ears. An organisation that has an annual income of over

£5 billion a year and that employs more than twenty-thousand people is not, on the face of it, in a strong position to argue for more money from the public purse, but a closer look at the ways in which successive governments have already damaged the BBC's output is revealing.

No government has yet had the gall overtly to cut the licence fee, but it has been continually reduced by stealth. There are two ways of achieving this. One is simply not to increase it, while inflation erodes its value. The current deal imposed on the BBC is a three-year freeze. It stays at £159. The effect is to force the BBC to make cuts in its staffing and spend less on its programmes. The other financial weapon politicians have used to damage the BBC is to place extra unfunded obligations on it. In recent years the BBC has been cajoled, persuaded or forced to fully fund new national language channels in Wales and Scotland for the minorities who speak Welsh and Gaelic; to fund more of the BBC World Service, which was once the responsibility of the Foreign Office (never incidentally a particularly healthy arrangement); and, most recently, to absolve those over seventy-five years old from paying their dues.

The BBC World Service is widely respected abroad, and listened to and relied on in countries where the only other sources of information are provided by government-controlled broadcasters, and where newspapers are censored. Travel anywhere in Africa or South America, in Eastern Europe or India, or in the Middle and Far East, and the voice of the BBC is admired for its accuracy and independence. Even in the United States its website is the second most popular source of news. This used to be called soft power, the odd post-colonial concept of Britain 'punching above its weight'. That is a pretentious way of justifying a much simpler idea: that in a world where lies and half-truths and propaganda are the stuff of so much information, truth-telling is a virtue in itself, and one to be cherished. By transferring the cost of this public service to the BBC and therefore to the licence-fee payer, without transferring the full funding, the government has eroded the funds available for domestic broadcasting. The licence-fee payer in a poor family is now paying for what the government used to fund.

Free licences for the over-seventy-fives were introduced in 2000 by Blair's Labour government, to help those thought to be in need of a subsidy, their family budgets strained by the costs of ageing. In 2015, suddenly, at the stroke of a pen, George Osborne, the Conservative Chancellor of the Exchequer, decided the BBC, not the government, should fund the subsidy, a further strain on its resources, for five years. Now, under this weird agreement, the BBC has decided it can no longer afford it, except for the poorest households. So, what began as a populist decision has become a further burden on the BBC, which then suffered the opprobrium of abandoning it.

The negotiations that lead to these licence-fee outcomes are talked of in hushed tones at the BBC. It is a time not to put a foot wrong, not to do anything too challenging. And they are not properly conducted. They allow a Chancellor of the Exchequer to bully the BBC into accepting the deal on offer, knowing that the BBC has no power to reject it, and barely any power to negotiate. All the BBC can do is appeal for support from its audiences. In this age of rising inflation affecting every household, and with the massive expansion of other means of communication, it is an appeal that risks falling on deaf ears. On a late-night train journey back from a *Question Time* in Leeds I shared a carriage with George Osborne. We talked about his decision to transfer the cost of free licences for the over-seventy-fives from government to the BBC. 'I never expected the BBC to accept it,' he said, smiling smugly, and maybe not quite telling the truth.

For as long as the licence fee remains the least bad way of securing the BBC's existence, a better system for negotiating it has to be found. At the very least a committee charged with arranging public hearings and a public examination of the BBC's aims, ambitions and efficiency would help to bring a chancellor's negotiations into the open, throwing some light on a process that is at present shrouded in darkness. Who would sit on this committee and what influence it would have is a moot point, particularly since the politicisation of public bodies now seems to be becoming the hallmark of government appointments. Even so, any public discussion and scrutiny of the level of the licence fee would be better than deals done under pressure and behind closed doors.

A further weapon all governments use against the BBC is the appointment of partisans to the succession of bodies who wield the final authority over the BBC, whether the governors, or the Trustees, or – the latest attempt to manage the organisation effectively and police its public obligations – the BBC Board. The temptation is hard to resist. And politics in Britain has become more partisan. Fifty years ago we lived in a Tweedledum Tweedledee world, where changes of government did not herald radical changes to the great public bodies, the universities, the museums, or the BBC. Margaret Thatcher's election changed that. She loved challenging orthodoxy. Established institutions were not to be taken for granted but rather should be asked to justify themselves. It was not, her former Press Secretary Bernard Ingham told me, done with malice, but with the intention of forcing those who ran public bodies to examine their aims and ways of working. But she was not averse to appointing people to positions of power who she thought would do her bidding, hence Marmaduke Hussey's surprise emergence as Chairman of the BBC. The trend started by Thatcher was being taken to extremes by the Johnson government. No area of public life is safe from political interference, from the boards of national museums to the control of broadcasting. It was Johnson who wanted Paul Dacre, former editor of the *Daily Mail*, to run Ofcom, the ultimate authority over broadcasting – a role finally allotted to Michael Grade, himself now a Tory crony, and a wily operator with a clear preference, like Johnson, for commercially funded broadcasting. It was Johnson who wanted Charles Moore, whose admiration for the BBC seems confined to liking some of Radio 3 and 4, and who otherwise habitually refers to the BBC with contempt, to chair the current Board. And it was Johnson who appointed his ardent follower, Nadine Dorries, as Secretary of State for Digital, Culture, Media and Sport. Her first public contribution to the debate over the future of the BBC was to say, without proposing an alternative, that the licence fee would come to an end in 2027. Her second, by contrast, was a tearful acknowledgement in the House of Commons of the courage and tenacity of the BBC's reporters covering the war in Ukraine.

Sometimes though it is not hostile politicians or commentators who are the BBC's most dangerous enemies, but the BBC itself. The way in which the BBC has responded to the dramatic crises that regularly erupt has often been as damaging as the scandal itself.

I explored earlier the BBC's disastrous handling of Andrew Gilligan's 2003 report on the dossier issued by the Blair government to convince parliament that war on Iraq was justified. If Gilligan had not said that the government published one claim from their intelligence sources knowing it to be untrue, then he and the BBC would both have come out of the controversy not just unscathed but covered in glory for revealing what many suspected but no one had yet asserted: that the dossier was indeed 'sexed up' to make a convincing case for war.

It was not the first time the BBC's instinctively defensive stance made it seem foolish and self-serving. It took twenty-five years and another judge's report for the truth, or at least some of the truth, to come out about Martin Bashir's notorious 1995 interview with Princess Diana. Diana was estranged from her husband, Prince Charles, who had given an interview to my brother, Jonathan, in which he admitted adultery during his marriage to Diana with Camilla Parker-Bowles. It can only be conjecture but Diana seemed to feel abandoned, not just by her husband and his public acknowledgement of his infidelity, but by the collapse of the dream world she must have thought she was entering when she married him. She had not fitted in well, finding court life stuffy, and her husband's coolness depressing. There was constant public speculation about what the future held for her and about her own romantic relationships. She had decided that she must tell her side of the story – if any story can be said to have only two sides.

When Martin Bashir, a young and inexperienced reporter, came to *Panorama* with the news that Diana had agreed to give him an interview, the editor Steve Hewlett was ecstatic. If Bashir could bring it off, it would be the interview of the decade, the interview everyone wanted, a scoop, an exclusive, an award-winner, which would make *Panorama*'s rivals furiously jealous. It seems that no one asked how Bashir had managed to persuade Princess Diana to talk to him. The interview was duly transmitted and over 20 million people watched in astonishment as Diana explained that there were three in her marriage, which was 'a bit crowded', and described her post-natal depression, her bulimia, her own adulterous affair, her doubt about whether Charles would ever become king, and her belief that the monarchy should 'walk hand in hand' with the public, rather than be so distant. She was articulate, moving, thoughtful. Friends of Charles inevitably rounded on her saying that she was unstable, an attention-seeker trying to manipulate public opinion.

How Bashir secured the interview remains a mystery. All we know from Lord Dyson's 2021 investigation, instigated by the BBC, is that the BBC's attempts to discover what had happened were 'woefully inadequate'. We know Bashir had fake bank statements printed purporting to show that an employee of Earl Spencer, Diana's brother, was taking money from the press to pass on insider gossip from the Spencer family. We also know that Bashir produced further fake bank statements showing payments into the accounts of both

Princess Diana's and Prince Charles's private secretaries. Quite what these fake statements were meant to achieve has never been explained. Spencer believes it was to win his confidence and induce him to introduce Bashir to Diana. Bashir says he already knew Diana and had her trust. That Bashir lied to various people at the BBC back in 1995 when they quizzed him about the forged bank statements is beyond doubt. Dyson concluded that the BBC at every level had failed to properly investigate what Bashir had been up to.

Worse still he said that even though the BBC was investigating Bashir's actions they failed to answer legitimate questions being raised in the Press about the issue and failed even to refer to the controversy and their response to it, by then a matter of public concern, in its news bulletins or in its coverage of reports about it in the Press. Dyson says there was a BBC decision not to cover the story and that if it had been left to individual editors it would have been extraordinary if none of them thought it 'not newsworthy'. By failing to do so the BBC he found 'fell short of the high standards of integrity and transparency which are its hallmark.'

When Dyson's report was published Tony Hall, who had been Director of News in 1995, resigned from his most recent office as the Chair of Trustees at the National Gallery. In the intervening years he had left the BBC to restore calm to a troubled Royal Opera House and had returned to the BBC as Director General from 2013 until 2020. Like all those within the BBC involved in this drama Hall refuses to talk publicly about what happened. Mysteries remain even after all these years. Earl Spencer told Lord Dyson that

Bashir's flashing bank statements purporting to show payments to the private secretaries to Prince Charles and Princess Diana, Commanders Aylard and Jephson was 'the absolute clincher' in persuading him to introduce Bashir to his sister. But it seems that no-one told Aylard and Jephson, two men in positions that rely on absolute loyalty and discretion, about Bashir's attempt to undermine their position. Spencer seems to have accepted it at face value as "the absolute clincher". Equally mysterious is how Bashir could conceivably have been appointed in 2016 over twenty years later as of all things the BBC's Religion Editor. The BBC can certainly move in a mysterious way in its wonder to perform.

The damaging conclusions of the Dyson Report were seized on gleefully by the BBC's enemies in parliament and the press. Unlike with the Hutton Report nearly twenty years earlier, this time there was no groundswell of public support for the BBC. On the contrary, the institution was seen to have endorsed, at the very least by default, Bashir's deceitful method of obtaining his interview. The new Director General, Tim Davie, faced with the challenging task of shoring up the BBC's reputation against a hostile government, made profuse apologies both to Spencer and to Diana's children, Princes William and Harry.

And then there was Jimmy Savile. No crisis has done more to betray the BBC's trusted position than the crimes of Jimmy Savile. The crisis revealed widespread sexual abuse at the very heart of our culture, facilitated by our most respected public institutions, perpetrated by one of our most celebrated BBC stars. But it was not just the historic crimes that shook the nation. The BBC's failure to support an exposé of Savile led to an almighty uproar, the near-total collapse of the internal hierarchy, and left an irrevocable stain on the corporation's reputation. In 2012, the BBC announced two enquiries into Savile's relationship with the BBC. One was conducted by former High Court Judge Dame Janet Smith and looked at the culture inside the BBC during the years that Savile's predatory behaviour took place in BBC studios or on location where BBC programmes were being made. The second was carried out by an experienced television executive from outside the BBC, the former head of Sky News Nick Pollard, and asked why the BBC had not pursued a film investigation of Savile after his death. The latter, the Pollard Review, is a fascinating exposé of the way BBC management works and the ambiguity that seems to be the hallmark of any BBC attempt to explain its behaviour.

With hindsight Savile seems an unlikely superstar. Knowing what we know now, his long white hair, white shellsuit, dark glasses and extravagantly long cigars seem sinister. In his heyday he just seemed absurd, a self-parodying egomaniac who spoke in his own meaningless private language. But a star he was. At his death thousands of people flocked to pass by his coffin lying in state in Leeds and tributes were paid to his work for charity. And yet, during his life there had been rumours about his sexual proclivities, suggestions that he had sex with corpses in Leeds infirmary, abused patients at Stoke Mandeville hospital for spinal injuries, and had sex with underage girls and occasionally boys in the mobile home he often stayed in on location. It seems extraordinary now that none of this led to criminal prosecutions. Today we are alert to sexual impropriety in a way that we were not in the years following the sexual revolution or liberation that began in the 1960s.

On stage at the BBC, Savile would surround himself with young fans. One girl, standing next to him, felt him groping her inside her pants during a rehearsal. When she complained to one of the camera crew she was told not to be so silly and was escorted out of the studio. Just one of the victims of Savile's abuse whose complaint went unheard.

The judge's report on Savile's activities acknowledges that many people working in the BBC knew about what Savile was up to, but that this information never apparently reached the higher levels of BBC management and so the BBC as 'a body corporate' was not aware and therefore not guilty of ignoring what was happening. To the layman it seemed a curious conclusion. But as Dame Janet Smith explained to me, the legal definition of corporate responsibility is when those at the top of any organisation are aware of improper or illegal behaviour and do not act to prevent it. She found no evidence that those in ultimate charge of the BBC knew anything about the rumours and allegations around Savile. Unacceptable behaviour is only, it seems, culpable if it reaches the ears of the bosses.

Just as disturbing was the BBC's failure to come clean about Savile when it had the chance. Shortly after his death in October 2011 a *Newsnight* reporter, Liz MacKean, and producer, Meirion Jones, who had suspicions about his behaviour at a girls' remand school recorded an interview on camera with a woman who said she had been abused by him and who said others would come forward to corroborate her claim. What happened next was the subject of nearly two hundred pages of analysis by Nick Pollard in his review into why the film was never made. The principal allegation had been that the BBC, about to pay a fulsome tribute to Savile, was unwilling to destroy the reputation of its superstar. The report, though it found that the BBC had proved itself 'incapable and chaotic' when it came to dealing with the scandal, said that that principal allegation was untrue. But what it failed to discover was why *Newsnight* had not pursued the story, leaving it to ITV to reveal all a few months later.

I have watched the filmed interview that *Newsnight*'s reporter conducted, watched one woman making her accusation, nervously but convincingly. Even as he brought the interview back to his editor, asking to carry on with his investigation, the reporter knew of other women who claimed similar abuse but were not yet willing to speak. For reasons that no one has been able to explain, the editor of *Newsnight*, Peter Rippon, said the investigation should not proceed, a decision he took, on his own admission, without even watching the interview itself. A strange judgement. As strange as *Newsnight* a few weeks later and no longer under Rippon's control allowing Lord McAlpine, a former Tory treasurer, to be wrongly identified as the paedophile in a *Newsnight* report on a Welsh care home. The BBC apologised and paid hefty damages. All *Newsnight* investigations were halted and the Director General George Entwistle was forced to resign.

Conspiracy theories about the failure of the BBC to expose

the behaviour of Savile proliferated, including the allegation that it had been done to protect his reputation, but no one really knows what happened or why. Corporate memories are often conveniently short, confused and contradictory, and none of those involved are willing to say more.

As always in these investigations into its own behaviour, whether over Gilligan and the forty-five-minutes claim, or Diana and Bashir, or Savile, the subsequent enquiries reveal a corporation of sclerotic complexity, where everyone seems to be busy covering their own back, where key documents go missing, and key conversations are not remembered. It may be behaviour common in many large organisations, but when the BBC, which supposedly belongs to us all and aspires to transparency in all its dealings, fails in this way it is particularly damaging.

Every scandal – whether about standards of journalism or about criminal behaviour by BBC employees – chips away at the BBC's claim to be the arbiter of impartial truth. A different charge, but equally damaging, is that the BBC is out of touch with too many of the people it is meant to serve, all of whom are forced to pay for it. What the statistics show is that the BBC's most ardent users can be defined as white, middle-class, southerners. Across the borders into Wales or Scotland or travelling up through the Midlands to the north of England, support falters. It falters too among black and ethnic minority communities and among the young. Critics of the BBC say its failure to reach all parts of Britain and all classes and races springs from its own innate elitism. It is an argument in a way similar to that put by Mary Whitehouse in her assaults on the BBC in the 1960s for promoting the permissive society. There was, she said, a small group of people who expressed themselves out of proportion to their size and at the same time silenced, ignored or ridiculed other voices in the country that could have at least put their views into proportion.

Allegations of metropolitan bias proliferated during the campaign leading up to the 2016 referendum vote on whether Britain should leave the EU. Ardent Brexiteers complained that the BBC had been consistently in favour of Remain and that it showed. I am sure they were right to say that those working at the BBC were in general Remainers. Given that according to every opinion poll, young, university-educated voters were predominantly Remainers, it is unlikely that they would not have predominated in an organisation of young, university-educated people like the BBC. That does not mean though that they allowed their opinions to sway their coverage of the campaign or the events leading up to it. Long before the referendum was called we were debating the issue on *Question Time*, often with Nigel Farage on the panel who would always complain that the audience was biased against him, but then he would, wouldn't he?

A crucial part of the argument for Brexit was that the whole discredited British establishment wanted to remain. Attacking the BBC as part of that establishment was a way of making the point. That does not mean though that the BBC's coverage was biased, just that it was a useful whipping boy, as were the CBI, the banks, the TUC, the judiciary: any institution that could be used to suggest a conspiracy against the will of the people. After the vote so virulent were some of these attacks that an outsider hearing them might have been tempted to think that Remain had won. No doubt somewhere deep in the bowels of one of those universities that specialises in analysing minute-by-minute and speaker-by-speaker, a thesis is already being written about the BBC's coverage. For my part I remember countless editions of *Question Time* where both sides had a fair hearing, followed by debates during the campaign and finally a mammoth eve-of-poll event at Wembley stadium in front of an audience several thousand-strong, where each side put up three speakers to argue the case, Boris Johnson incidentally among them.

Come the night of the referendum we mounted a results programme of some complexity. Unlike in a general election there was no template against which to measure the impact of the first results. The vote to stay in the Common Market over forty years earlier could barely count. The arguments were different then and views had changed. Using a complex calculation of the likely disposition of different parts of the country, John Curtice, Britain's expert in voter behaviour, created a way of measuring the voting trends, showing the way each part of the country was likely to go and what to deduce from variations from these predictions. Early in the evening it became clear that the Leave vote was proving larger than the Remain, but this being the BBC, a stickler for fact over prediction, I was not allowed to give the result until enough votes had been counted for the outcome to be certain. So, it was not until twenty to five in the morning that I was allowed to annouce the result. I set the result in the context of the 1975 referendum to stay in the Common Market, and emphasised that now after months of argument the decision was clear: 'The British people have spoken and the answer is: we're out.'

Polemicists for the Brexit cause say I looked shocked. I have watched it again several times. I am not sure what they wanted from me. Triumphalism perhaps? But stony-faced indifference to election results is the discipline of anchoring programmes like this. The only expression I can find is exhaustion, which, at 4.40 in the morning, may be forgivable.

When I started broadcasting, the BBC was run by white men, most of them university graduates, and mostly from Oxford or Cambridge. It was rare to find a woman who had risen to the top and the calibre of those who did was a rebuke to a culture that kept others back. It was rare to see a black face, except among those who cleaned the studios or served in the canteen. This culture was not exclusive to the BBC in the 1960s. It was common throughout the establishment in all its forms from business to parliament.

The BBC of today is responding to the criticism that it is unrepresentative and out of touch in two ways. To counter the argument that its attitudes are defined by a metropolitan elite, out of touch with the lives of too many people, it is continually moving productions out of London, and recruiting more of its staff from the places where it sets up shop. At the same time it is trying to widen the recruitment of broadcasters, producers, researchers and its administrative staff to make them more representative of the social makeup of the country as a whole. People criticise quotas as a measure of the success of the policy. I believe in them. I cannot think of any other way of achieving a necessary change.

But none of this will on its own deliver what the BBC wants to achieve – to be a broadcaster with universal appeal. In its 100 years it has come a long way from having its radio newsreaders, unseen to the listener, being required to wear dinner jackets. Or from one of Lord Reith's early instructions that working-class voices should be revoiced in Received English so that they could be understood – an instruction that was followed so closely that Received English is now sometimes known as 'BBC English'.

Creating a different culture inside the BBC is a necessary start, but it is no guarantee of success. It will be a different elite, but still an elite, trying to work out how to both encapsulate and reflect the national mood; and deliver something for everyone in an increasingly competitive market, where more and more people will choose to watch other channels or use streaming services like Netflix, Disney or Amazon for their entertainment.

The search is on for a fairer way of funding the BBC. The danger is that what is really being sought is a way of weakening it under cover of looking for this fairer system of funding. Margaret Thatcher's complaint to me that 'every time I try to do anything about the BBC people come out of the woodwork to defend it' (and she meant not a liberal elite but her own advisers in Downing Street and, more importantly, Tory voters she could not afford to upset) may no longer be true. But I believe it would damage us as a country to lose a voice whose only ambition is, as far as is possible, to reflect reality and speak the truth. 'Nation shall speak peace unto Nation' was the motto the BBC adopted for its coat of arms in the 1920s, a noble aspiration sadly unfulfilled. Maybe a new motto should be adopted. 'Speak truth', or in Latin for the coat of arms, *'Veritas Loquenda'*. On second thoughts, putting it in Latin might seem too elitist. In the end the future of the BBC will be decided by the people who pay for it – not the government, but the audience. Do they want to keep listening? Do they want to keep watching?

You may think, reading this, 'He would say that wouldn't he? For seventy years he has taken their shilling. He's hardly going to turn his back on them now.' But if you do think that, you have missed the point. I took their shilling because I believed in what we were trying to do, and I still believe in it. As Lord Reith put it back in 1926, 'to inform, educate and entertain'. To which I would only add, 100 years later, these three, but the greatest of these is to inform.

There is much talk of the British believing in the doctrine of exceptionalism: that we are set apart from other nations, innately superior in the way we handle our affairs. Apart from the obvious point that all nations believe themselves to be unique and set apart, the nature of our exceptionalism is hard to define. It is not the monarchy. Six other countries in Europe have monarchies. It is not the empire. True, we had a great empire founded on exploitation and slavery, now much reviled. So did others. It is not the war. True, we were not invaded and conquered in the Second World War. But we did not win the war alone. It is certainly not George Orwell's picture of old ladies cycling to church, misquoted by John Major extolling those glories of Britain that would last a hundred years. (More today a picture of pedestrians leaping out of the way of demon cyclists.) We are a different country now, fast-changing and facing a dangerous and uncertain world. A middle-ranking country fraught with social and economic problems and with a future, after leaving the EU, as yet uncharted. In the chaos and confusion in which we live I would offer one example of our exceptionalism, and that is the BBC. Exceptional because it is unique. No other country in the world has anything like it.

As the Capitol riots of January 2021 in Washington DC made plain, once a society stops believing in a common set of facts, democracy itself can be at risk. In the midst of the cacophony of voices and opinions, of lies and distortions, of fake news and prejudice, the BBC, with all its flaws, is unique as a bastion of objectivity and impartiality whose only ambition is to serve its audience. It anguishes constantly over how to do it; and is trusted by half a billion people worldwide. That's exceptionalism and a cause worth fighting for.

Acknowledgements

Broadcasting is always a cooperative effort, involving producers, editors, researchers, and camera and technical crew. I am used to working as part of these teams. I thought writing a book would be different. I imagined sitting down on my own to write straight through from the opening line to the last. How wrong I was. So there are many people to whom I am grateful and without whose support this would never have seen the light of day.

Foremost among them, my wife Belinda Giles, to whom this book is dedicated. When I first mentioned the book she was encouraging. When I faltered she urged me on. When finally and somewhat nervously I showed her what I had written she gave me the thumbs-up. Without her support I could not have written it. For that matter I could not have pursued a broadcasting career with all its trials and tribulations without her understanding in difficult times, her comfort at moments when I was downcast, and her shared enthusiasm and excitement when my work was going well.

Until I started working with Deborah Crewe I did not understand what an editor did. Now I do. Every word I wrote passed beneath her beady eye always watchful for mistakes of grammar, lack of clarity, repetition and all the other pitfalls to which I was subject. But more than that she helped me shape the book and frame the arguments coherently. On a more practical level she also made sure that I kept to the tight time-table the publishers required. She is a superb editor and I was very fortunate that she was willing to help me.

Of Lizzie Catt's contribution as my researcher I can only say that I was in awe of her energy, her industry and her judgement. Were you to see the list of abstruse questions I asked her, were you to see the boxes and boxes of old scripts and letters that are piled up in my office, and were you then to see the impeccably prepared answers to my questions, you too would share my admiration.

Sam Stonard, who has been my assistant for many years, kept order from the chaos of my research notes, chapter drafts, and ideas scattered at random around my office. I wrote most of this by hand and she patiently input it for me with only an occasional query about an indecipherable word. That apart, she and I sat for hours working through my engagement diaries from the 1960s to the present day. We could manage two diaries a day until the tedium forced us to stop. The entries reminded me of the work I had done and the places I had been to, interspersed with vivid reminders of times past.

I am also grateful to Hannah Ratford, Archive Collections Manager at BBC Written Archives, for all her help, particularly in preparing the *Yesterday's Men* and Nixon files; and to the quite amazing Miriam Walsh, who has a profound understanding of the BBC and the way it has changed over the years.

The words 'my agent' have always seemed to me a crude way of describing the part my friend Rosemary Scoular (of United Agents) plays in my life. She does, it is true, negotiate my fees. But her real support over many years has been in

understanding the kind of work I have wanted to do and what
I would not touch with a bargepole. If you work in broadcasting you are asked to take on all kinds of ancillary
engagements chairing debates or speaking at public events or
playing bit parts in a variety of programmes. She would pass
on every invitation, often with a note attached: 'not for you I
assume'. She was usually right, though I think we may have
disagreed about *Strictly*. As for this book, she kept quietly
encouraging me, saying, 'Of course you can do it, and you
should.'

I cannot count the number of meetings I have had over the
years with Rupert Lancaster of Hodder & Stoughton. His
acute intelligence and dry wit always made our encounters
stimulating and we discussed various projects that never saw
the light of day. I had thought he might have long given up
hope of my ever putting pen to paper. I was amazed when he
agreed to take on this book and I suspect he was just as
amazed that I actually did it. The team at Hodder have been
superb. Ciara Mongey as Editorial Assistant, Al Oliver and
Kate Brunt who designed and delivered the cover, and Louise
Court responsible for publicity, or making sure *Keep Talking*
sells.

So much for the book. It is about broadcasting, and broadcasting, as I said above, is always a cooperative effort. Over
the years I have been fortunate to work with countless editors
and producers and researchers who have been stimulating
and supportive companions on a long road. I cannot possibly
name them all here, but among those with whom I discussed
this book and talked about the BBC some names stand out.

For some reason Paul Fox championed my work through

thick and thin from my earliest callow days. His robust no-nonsense views about what made good television were a constant encouragement and his occasional rebukes always justified. When he left the BBC to work at Yorkshire Television he was much missed and his brief return to the BBC was widely welcomed.

Alexandra Henderson plumped for me in the audition for the chair of *Question Time* and started me on the most enjoyable twenty-five years of my broadcasting life. It is not possible to do a weekly programme if you do not get on with your editor, and my editors have remained friends. Those I have spoken to for this book include Nick Pisani, Ed Havard, Gill Penlington and Nicolai Gentchev: all astute editors with an instinctive understanding of the public mood. They were stout defenders of the programme, both against the criticisms of political parties and from time to time from the BBC itself. They always fought our corner. As did my great friend Charlie Courtauld, who sadly died at the peak of his powers: clever, funny, quick witted, impatient, a lovely man to work for.

In truth all these editors had a far greater grasp of politics than me and gave me the confidence to appear better informed than I deserved.

There are many others who worked on *Question Time* in their youth as researchers or junior producers. Most have gone on to greater heights. I talked to James Stephenson, Richard Garvin and Brendan Miller about broadcasting, and their opinions were all helpful.

I also pumped Sam Woodhouse for memories of the many election programmes we had done together. He is the master of these complex and stressful events. The general election is the most arduous. But he was also my editor for countless by-elections, local elections, European elections, American elections, budgets and Autumn Statements. Working with him as my producer on a host of these outings was Peter Barnes, who has dug me out of many a hole.

When I first met Adam Curtis he was not the superstar he is today. To tell the truth he did not much like having me imposed on him for our long TV series about the USA, *An Ocean Apart*. I thought he was outrageous and rude. From these mutual irritations we somehow forged a real friendship that lasts to this day. He was full of advice about what I should say about the BBC and broadcasting, some of it even useful.

No list of acknowledgements would be complete without a mention of Basil Comely. He inspired four series of programmes that I made about Britain for which he was executive producer. If you want trenchant views about the BBC talk to Basil. And if you are lucky enough to have Andrea Carnevali as your film editor, as I did for more than twenty films – clever, witty and indefatigable – you are in film-making heaven.

I have never made many friends on the BBC's sixth floor, the place where the gods of television used to sit in the Television Centre at White City. I would rather do my job and go home. But Tony Hall is the exception. I first worked with him when he was the Chief Executive of BBC News and responsible for election coverage, then again when he came back to the BBC as Director General. His enthusiasm for the BBC, indeed his love of it, has always been an inspiration.

While I was writing this book I was also making a series of three films about the BBC to coincide with its centenary. In the course of making these films I talked to Richard Ayre, Weyman Bennett, Anita Boateng, Roger Bolton, Mark Byford, Alastair Campbell, Barnie Choudhury, Mark Damazer, Greg Dyke, Robbie Gibb, Miles Goslett, Michael Grade, Roy Greenslade, Bonnie Greer, Peter Horrocks, Bernard Ingham, Meirion Jones, Tom Kelly, Tony Laryea, Rod Liddle, Kelvin MacKenzie, Kevin Marsh, Seamus Milne, Chris Patten, Mike Phillips, Ros Sloboda, Janet Smith, Peter Snow, Charles Spencer, Rosamund Urwin, John Whittingdale, Will Wyatt and Alan Yentob. I am grateful to them all for their time.

As I am to John Bridcut, who I worked with first on elections and then in Zimbabwe making the series *From Rhodes to Mugabe*. He was making a television series about the BBC at the same time as me. For some reason we were told not to talk to each other about what we were doing, advice we blithely ignored.

Lastly, I must thank all my family. Broadcasting is not a nine-to-five business, always home at weekends and never missing a birthday or sports day or school play. It is the opposite. The tolerance of those I love has been far beyond what I have been entitled to expect and I am forever grateful for their support and understanding. I just hope that in reading this book, if they do, they will understand and excuse the price they paid for my obsession.

Index

Keep Talking

Picture Acknowledgements

Munchausen's Horn © Duncan1890/Getty Images

Young David Dimbleby © William Vanderson/Getty Images

'The Dimbleby Circus' Cartoon © News UK / News
   Licensing

'And Let Me Put This to You Mr Blair . . .' Cartoon
   © Martin Rowson

BBC Election Studio, 274321 © BBC Photos

Royal Wedding Cartoon © News UK / News Licensing

'I Wish You Wouldn't Watch *Question Time*' Cartoon
   © Grizelda/CartoonStock

Mandela Inauguration 7288719b © David Brauchli/AP/
   Shutterstock

David Dimbleby with Ku Klux Klan © BBC Motion
   Gallery / Getty Images

The Muses Welcome Broadcasting Sketch / Author
   Collection